ENCYCLOPEDIA OF MYTHOLOGY

A Collection of Greek and Roman Heroes, Gods, and Monsters with Collectible Ephemera

E. M. BERENS

chartwell books

This edition published in 2025 by Chartwell Books,
an imprint of The Quarto Group
142 West 36th Street, 4th Floor
New York, NY 10018 USA
T (212) 779-4972
www.Quarto.com

First published as *Mythology* in 2015 by Wellfleet Press,
an imprint of The Quarto Group
142 West 36th Street, 4th Floor
New York, NY 10018 USA

Text adapted, edited, and updated from A Hand Book of Mythology: *The Myths and Legends of Ancient Greece and Rome* by E.M. Berens, published in 1894 by Mayard, Merrill, & Co., New York

10 9 8 7 6 5 4 3 2 1

Chartwell titles are also available at discount for retail, wholesale, promotional, and bulk purchase. For details, contact the Special Sales Manager by email at specialsales@quarto.com or by mail at The Quarto Group, Attn: Special Sales Manager, 100 Cummings Center Suite 265D, Beverly, MA 01915, USA.

Grateful acknowledgment is made to the Open Access/Open Content programs that made the distribution of the artwork found herein possible: The Getty Museum, Los Angeles County Museum, Yale University Art Gallery, National Gallery of Art (US), Library of Congress, The British Library Catalogue of Illuminated Manuscripts, and the National Gallery of Denmark. A full listing of image credits can be found on page 278.

Title page: Detail from Le Recoeil des Histoires de Troyes, attributed to the Master of the White Inscriptions, c. 1475–1483. Heracles slays a Nemean lion as part of his labors. Contents page: Venus and a Sleeping Cupid, Jean-Baptiste Mallet, c. 1810. Venus (Aphrodite), the most beautiful of the goddesses, has always been a favorite subject of artists.

ISBN: 978-0-7858-4734-2

Cover Design: Alana Ward

Printed in China

CONTENTS

INTRODUCTION

Before beginning the many wonderous myths of the ancient Greeks, and the extraordinary number of gods they worshipped, we must first discuss what kind of beings these divinities were.

In appearance, the gods were supposed to resemble mortals, whom, however, they far surpassed in beauty, grandeur, and strength, and stature. They resembled human beings in their feelings and habits, intermarrying and having children, and requiring daily nourishment to replenish their strength and refreshing sleep to restore their energies. Their blood, a bright ethereal fluid called ichor, never engendered disease, and, when shed, had the power of producing new life.

The Greeks believed that the mental qualifications of their gods were of a much higher order than those of men, but nevertheless, as we shall see, they were not considered to be exempt from human passions, and we frequently behold them actuated by revenge, deceit, and jealousy. They, however, always punish the evil-doer, and visit with dire calamities any impious mortal who dares to neglect their worship or despise their rites. We often hear of them having visited mankind and partaking of their hospitality, and not infrequently both gods and goddesses become attached to mortals, with whom they unite themselves, the offspring of these unions being called heroes, who were usually renowned for their great strength and courage. But although there were so many points of resemblance between gods and men, there remained the one great distinction: the gods enjoyed immortality. Still, they were not invulnerable, and we often hear of them having been wounded, and suffering in consequence such exquisite torture that they have earnestly prayed to be deprived of their privilege of immortality.

OPPOSITE: *Mars and Venus Surprised by Vulcan*, Joachim Anthonisz. Wtewael, c. 1606–1610. The gods and goddesses often struggled with infidelity. Here, Eros and Apollo uncover Ares (Mars) and Aphrodite (Venus) in bed, to the anger of Aphrodite's aged husband Hephæstus (Vulcan).

The gods knew no limitation of time or space, being able to transport themselves to incredible distances with the speed of thought. They possessed the power of rendering themselves invisible at will, and could assume the forms of men or animals as it suited their convenience. They could also transform human beings into trees, stones, animals, and other objects, either as a punishment for their misdeeds or as a means of protecting the individual, thus transformed, from impending danger. Their robes were like those worn by mortals, but were perfect in form and much finer in texture. Their weapons also resembled those used by mankind; we hear of spears, shields, helmets, and bows and arrows being employed by the gods. Each deity possessed a beautiful chariot, which, drawn by horses or other animals of celestial breed, conveyed them rapidly over land and sea according to their pleasure. Most of these divinities lived on the summit of Mount Olympus, each possessing his or her individual habitation, and all meeting together on festive occasions in the council-chamber of the gods, where their banquets were enlivened by the sweet strains of Apollo's lyre, whilst the beautiful voices of the Muses poured forth their rich melodies to his harmonious accompaniment. Magnificent temples were erected to their honor, where they were worshipped with the greatest solemnity; rich gifts were presented to them, and animals, and sometimes even sacrifices on their altars.

In the study of Grecian mythology we find the answers to daily recurring phenomena, including those that to us in modern times are known to be the result of certain well-ascertained laws of nature, but to the early Greeks were matters of grave speculation. For instance, when they heard the awful roar of thunder, and saw vivid flashes of lightning, accompanied by black clouds and torrents of rain, they believed that the great God of Heaven was angry, and they trembled at his wrath. If the calm and tranquil sea became suddenly agitated, and the crested billows rose to the height of mountains, dashing furiously against the rocks, and threatening destruction to all within their reach, the Sea God was supposed to be in a furious rage. When they beheld the sky glowing with the hues of coming day they thought that the Goddess of the Dawn, with rosy fingers, was drawing aside the dark veil of night, to allow her brother, the Sun God, to enter upon his brilliant career. Thus personifying all the powers of nature, this very imaginative and highly poetical nation beheld a divinity in every tree that grew, in every stream that flowed, in the bright beams of the glorious sun, and the clear, cold rays of the silvery

Archaistic relief showing five divinities, c.25 CE–14 BCE. This ancient artifact shows the Olympian gods Zeus, Hera, Athene, Aphrodite, and Apollo.

moon; for them the whole universe lived and breathed, peopled by a thousand forms of grace and beauty.

The most important of these divinities may have been something more than the mere creations of an active and poetical imagination. They were possibly human beings who had so distinguished themselves in life by their preeminence over their fellow mortals that after death they were deified by the people among whom they lived, and the poets touched with their magic wands the details of lives, which, in more prosaic times, would simply have been recorded as illustrious.

It is highly probable that the reputed actions of these deified beings were commemorated by bards, who, travelling from one state to another, celebrated their praise in song; it therefore becomes exceedingly difficult, nay almost impossible, to separate bare facts from the exaggerations that never fail to accompany oral traditions.

In order to exemplify this, let us suppose that Orpheus, the son of Apollo, so renowned for his extraordinary musical powers, had existed at the present day. We should no doubt have ranked him among the greatest of our musicians, and honored him as such; but the Greeks, with their vivid imagination and poetic license, exaggerated his remarkable gifts, and attributed to his music supernatural influence over animate and inanimate nature. Thus we hear of wild beasts tamed, of mighty rivers arrested in their course, and of mountains being moved by the sweet tones of his voice. The theory here advanced may possibly prove useful in the future, in suggesting to the reader the probable basis of many of the extraordinary accounts we meet with in the study of classical mythology.

And now a few words will be necessary concerning the religious beliefs of the Romans. When the Greeks first settled in Italy, they found in the country they colonized a mythology already belonging to its inhabitants the Celts, which, according to the Greek custom of paying reverence to all gods, known or unknown, they readily adopted, selecting and appropriating those divinities which had the greatest affinity to their own, and thus they formed a religious belief that naturally bore the impress of its ancient Greek source. As the primitive Celts, however, were a less civilized people than the Greeks, their mythology was of a more barbarous character, and this circumstance, combined with the fact that the Romans were not gifted with the vivid imagination of their Greek neighbors, leaves its mark on the Roman mythology, which is far less fertile in fanciful conceits, and deficient in all those fairy-like stories and wonderfully poetic ideas which so strongly characterize that of the Greeks.

—E.M. Berens

Chapter One

MAJOR DIVINITIES

OPPOSITE: ***Phaeton Driving the Chariot of Apollo*****, Jean Jouvenet, c. 1680. Many myths change depending on who is telling them. Here, Phaethon's pride leads him to foolishy ask to drive the Sun God's chariot, which in some myths is not Helios, but Apollo (Helios's successor).**

URANUS AND GÆA § CŒLUS AND TERRA

The ancient Greeks had several different theories with regard to the origin of the world, but the generally accepted notion was that before this world came into existence, there was in its place a confused mass of shapeless elements called Chaos. These elements becoming at length consolidated (some say by Uranus himself), resolved themselves into two widely different substances, the lighter portion of which, soaring on high, formed the sky or firmament, and constituted itself into a vast, overarching vault, which protected the firm and solid mass beneath.

Thus came into being the two first great primeval deities of the Greeks, Uranus and Gæa (or Ge). Uranus, the more refined deity, represented the light and air of heaven, possessing the distinguishing qualities of light, heat, purity, and omnipresence, whilst Gæa, the firm, flat,[1] life-sustaining earth, was worshipped as the great all-nourishing mother. Her many titles refer to her more or less in this character, and she appears to have been universally revered among the Greeks, there being scarcely a city in Greece which did not contain a temple erected in her honor; indeed Gæa was held in such veneration that her name was always invoked whenever the gods took a solemn oath, made an emphatic declaration, or implored assistance.

OPPOSITE: *Victory, Janus, Chronos and Gaea* by Giulio Romano, c. 1532–1534. Earth mother Gaea clutches a snake as she crouches by Cronus's feet. Nike (Victory) flies overhead and Janus, the God of Gates, sits nearby.

THE MARRIAGE of URANUS AND GÆA

Uranus, the heaven, was believed to have united himself in marriage with Gæa, the earth; and a moment's reflection will show what a truly poetical, and also what a logical idea this was; for, taken in a figurative sense, this union actually does exist. The smiles of heaven produce the flowers of earth, whereas his long-continued frowns exercise so depressing an influence upon his loving partner, that she no longer decks herself in bright and festive robes, but responds with ready sympathy to his melancholy mood.

The first-born child of Uranus and Gæa was Oceanus,[2] the ocean stream, that vast expanse of ever-flowing water that encircles the Earth. Here we meet with another logical though fanciful conclusion, which a very slight knowledge of the workings of nature proves to have been just and true. The ocean is formed from the rains which descend from heaven and the streams which flow from earth. Therefore, by making Oceanus the off-

1 The early Greeks supposed the Earth to be a flat circle, in the center of which was Greece. Oceanus, the ocean stream, encircled it; the Mediterranean flowed into this river on the one side, and the Euxine, or Black Sea, on the other.

2 Owing to the vagueness of the various accounts of creation, the origin of the primeval gods is variously accounted for. Thus, for instance, Oceanus, with some, becomes the younger brother of Uranus and Gæa.

spring of Uranus and Gæa, the ancients were merely asserting that the ocean is produced by the combined influence of heaven and earth, whilst at the same time their fervid and poetical imaginations led them to see in this, as in all manifestations of the powers of nature, an actual, tangible divinity.

Uranus, the heaven, the embodiment of light, heat, and the breath of life, produced offspring who were of a much less material nature than his son Oceanus. These other children of his were supposed to occupy the intermediate space that divided him from Gæa.

The Untangling of Chaos, or the Creation of the Four Elements**, Hendrik Goltzius, 1589. This panel from Ovid's *****Metamorphoses***** shows Uranus separating sky and earth.**

Nearest to Uranus, and just beneath him, came Aether (Ether), a bright creation representing that highly rarified atmosphere which immortals alone could breathe. Then followed Aër (Air), which was in close proximity to Gæa, and represented, as its name implies, the grosser atmosphere surrounding the Earth in which mortals could freely breathe, and without which they would perish. Aether and Aër were separated from each other by divinities called Nephelae. These were their restless and wandering sisters, who existed in the form of clouds, ever floating between Aether and Aër. Gæa also produced the mountains, and Pontus (the sea). She united herself with the latter, and their offspring were the sea-deities Nereus, Thaumas, Phorcys, Ceto, and Eurybia.

DARKNESS *and* NIGHT

Co-existent with Uranus and Gæa were two mighty powers who were also the offspring of Chaos. These were Erebus (Darkness) and Nyx (Night), who formed a striking contrast to the cheerful light of heaven and the bright smiles of earth. Erebus, the predecessor of Hades, reigned in that mysterious world below, where no ray of sunshine, no gleam of daylight, nor vestige of health-giving terrestrial life ever appeared. Nyx, the sister of

Erebus, represented Night, and was worshipped by the ancients with the greatest solemnity.

Uranus was also supposed to have been united to Nyx, but only in his capacity as God of Light, he being considered the source and fountain of all light, and their children were Eos (Aurora), the Dawn, and Hemera, the Daylight. Nyx on her side was also doubly united, having been married at some indefinite period to Erebus.

A bronze statuette of a Giant hurling a rock, c. 200–175 BCE. Giants were often portrayed fighting with crude weapons made from the Earth.

THE GIANTS and THE TITANS

In addition to those children of heaven and earth already enumerated, Uranus and Gæa produced two distinctly different races of beings called Giants and Titans. The Giants personified brute strength alone, and could shake the universe to produce earthquakes, but the Titans united their great physical power to intellectual qualifications variously developed. There were three Giants—Briareus, Cottus, and Gyges—who each possessed a hundred hands and fifty heads, and were known collectively by the name of the Hecatoncheires, which signified hundred-handed.

Now Uranus, the chaste light of heaven, the essence of all that is bright and pleasing, held in abhorrence his crude, rough, and turbulent offspring the Giants, and moreover feared that their great power might eventually prove hurtful to himself. He therefore hurled them into Tartarus, that portion of the lower world that served as the subterranean dungeon of the gods.

In order to avenge this oppression of her children, Gæa instigated a conspiracy on the part of the Titans against Uranus, which was carried to a successful issue by her son Cronus. He wounded his father, and from the blood of the wound that fell upon the earth sprang a race of monstrous beings also called Giants. Assisted by his brother-Titans, Cronus succeeded in dethroning his father, who, enraged at his defeat, cursed his rebellious son, and foretold to him a similar fate. Cronus now became invested with supreme power, and assigned to his brothers offices of distinction, subordinate only to himself. Subsequently, however, when, secure of his position, he no longer needed their assistance, he basely repaid their former services with treachery, made war upon his brothers and faithful allies, and, assisted by the Giants, completely defeated them, sending those who resisted his all-conquering arm down into the lowest depths of Tartarus.

CRONUS *&* SATURN

Cronus was the God of Time in its sense of eternal duration. He married Rhea, daughter of Uranus and Gæa, a very important divinity, to whom a section will be devoted hereafter.

Cronus is often represented as an old man leaning on a scythe, with an hourglass in his hand. The hourglass symbolizes the fast-fleeting moments as they succeed each other unceasingly; the scythe is emblematical of time, which mows down all before it.

ZEUS *and* THE TITANOMACHIA

OPPOSITE: *Cronus Carrying off Two Infants* by Lazar Widmann, c. 1742. Fearing they would steal his throne, Cronus swallowed all of his children until he had Zeus, who was resuced by his mother, Rhea.

Cronus's and Rhea's children were three sons: Hades, Poseidon, and Zeus; and three daughters: Hestia, Demeter, and Hera. Cronus, having an uneasy conscience, was afraid that his children might one day rise up against his authority, and thus verify the prediction of his father Uranus. In order, therefore, to render the prophecy impossible of fulfillment, Cronus swallowed each child as soon as it was born,[3] greatly to the sorrow and indignation of his wife Rhea. When it came to Zeus, the sixth and last, Rhea resolved to try and save this one child, at least, to love and cherish, and appealed to her parents, Uranus and Gæa, for counsel and assistance. By their advice she wrapped a stone in baby clothes, and Cronus, in eager haste, swallowed it, without noticing the deception. The child thus saved, eventually, as we shall see, dethroned his father Cronus, became supreme god in his stead, and was universally venerated as the great national god of the Greeks.

Anxious to preserve the secret of his existence from Cronus, Rhea sent the infant Zeus secretly to Crete, where he was nourished, protected, and educated. A sacred goat, called Amalthea, supplied the place of his mother, by providing him with milk; nymphs, called Melissae, fed him with honey, and eagles and doves brought him nectar and ambrosia.[4] He was kept concealed in a cave in the heart of Mount Ida, and the Curetes, or priests

3 The myth of Cronus swallowing his children is evidently intended by the poets to express the melancholy truth that time destroys all things.

4 Nectar was the drink, and ambrosia the food of the gods.

of Rhea, by beating their shields together, kept up a constant noise at the entrance, which drowned the cries of the child and frightened away all intruders. Under the watchful care of the nymphs the infant Zeus thrived rapidly, developing great physical powers, combined with extraordinary wisdom and intelligence. Grown to manhood, he determined to compel his father to restore his brothers and sisters to the light of day, and is said to have been assisted in this difficult task by the goddess Metis, who artfully persuaded Cronus to drink a potion, which caused him to give back the children he had swallowed. The stone that had counterfeited Zeus was placed at Delphi, where it was long exhibited as a sacred relic.

Cronus was so enraged at being circumvented that war between the father and son became inevitable. The rival forces ranged themselves on two separate high mountains in Thessaly; Zeus, with his brothers and sisters, took his stand on Mount Olympus, where he was joined by Oceanus, and others of the Titans, who had forsaken Cronus on account of his oppressions. Cronus and his brother-Titans took possession of Mount Othrys, and prepared for battle. The struggle was long and fierce, and at length Zeus, finding that he was no nearer victory than before, bethought of the existence of the imprisoned Giants, and knowing that they would be able to render him most powerful assistance, he hastened to liberate them. He also called to his aid the Cyclops (sons of Poseidon and Amphitrite),[5] who had only one eye each in the

5 The Cyclops are generally mentioned as the sons of Uranus and Gæa, but Homer speaks of Polyphemus, the chief of the Cyclops, as the son of Poseidon, and states the Cyclops to be his brothers.

middle of their foreheads, and were called Brontes (Thunder), Steropes (Lightning), and Pyracmon (Fire-Anvil). They promptly responded to his summons for help, and brought with them tremendous thunderbolts that the Hecatoncheires, with their hundred hands, hurled down upon the enemy, at the same time raising mighty earthquakes, which swallowed up and destroyed all who opposed them. Aided by these new and powerful allies, Zeus now made a furious onslaught on his enemies, and so tremendous was the encounter that all nature is said to have throbbed in accord with this mighty effort of the celestial deities. The sea rose as high as mountains, and its angry billows hissed and foamed; the earth shook to its foundations, the heavens sent forth rolling thunder, and flash after flash of death-bringing lightning, whilst a blinding mist enveloped Cronus and his allies.

And now the fortunes of war began to turn, and victory smiled on Zeus. Cronus and his army were completely overthrown, his brothers dispatched to the gloomy depths of the lower world, and Cronus himself was banished from his kingdom and deprived forever of the supreme power, which now became vested in his son Zeus. This war was called the Titanomachia, and is most graphically described by the old classic poets such as Hesiod.

With the defeat of Cronus and his banishment from his dominions, Cronus's career as a ruling Greek divinity entirely ceased. But being, like all the gods, immortal, he was supposed to be still in existence, though possessing no longer either influence or authority, his place being filled to a certain extent by his descendant and successor, Zeus.

OPPOSITE: ***Saturn*** **by Hendrik Goltzius, 1592. This engraving of the Roman version of Cronus, Saturn, was the first in a series called *The Set of the Antique Gods.***

THE DIVISION *of* THE WORLD

Zeus and his brothers, having gained a complete victory over their enemies, began to consider how the world that they had conquered should be divided amongst them. At last it was settled by lot that Zeus should reign supreme in heaven, whilst Hades governed the lower world, and Poseidon had full command over the sea, but the supremacy of Zeus was recognized in all three kingdoms, in heaven, on earth (in which of course the sea was included), and under the earth. Zeus held his court on the top of Mount Olympus, whose summit was beyond the clouds; the gloomy dominions of the lower world soon took own the name of their ruler, Hades; and Poseidon reigned over the sea. It will be seen that the realm of each of these gods was enveloped in mystery. Olympus was shrouded in mists, the lower world was wrapt in gloomy darkness, and the sea was (and indeed still is) a source of wonder and deep interest. Hence we see that what to other nations were merely strange phenomena, served this poetical and imaginative people as a foundation upon which to build the wonderful stories of their mythology.

The division of the world being now satisfactorily arranged, it would seem that all things ought to have gone on smoothly, but such was not the case. Trouble arose in an unlooked-for quarter. The Giants, those hideous monsters (some with legs formed of serpents) who had sprung from the earth and the blood of Uranus, declared war against the triumphant deities of Olympus, and a struggle ensued that, because of Gæa having made the Giants invincible as long as they kept their feet on the ground, was wearisome and protracted. Gæa's precaution, however, was rendered unavailing by pieces of rock being hurled upon them, which threw them down, and their feet being no longer placed firmly on their mother-earth, they were overcome, and this tedious war (called the Gigantomachia) at last came to an end.

***Alabastron with Typhon*, c. 610–600 BCE. This ancient terracotta vase, called an alabastron, depicts Typhon, who was so terrifying that he chased Zeus's enemies all the way to Eygpt.**

Among the most daring of these earth-born Giants were Enceladus, Rhœtus, and the valiant Mimas, who, with youthful fire and energy, hurled against heaven great masses of rock and burning oak trees, and defied the lightnings of Zeus. One of the most powerful monsters who helped the Giants in this war was called Typhon (Typhœus). He was the youngest son of Tartarus and Gæa, and had a hundred heads, with eyes that struck terror in the beholders, and filled them with awe-inspiring voices frightful to hear. This dreadful monster resolved to conquer both gods and men, but his plans were at length defeated by Zeus, who, after a violent encounter, succeeded in destroying him with a thunderbolt, but not before he had so terrified the gods that they had fled for refuge to Egypt, where they metamorphosed themselves into different animals and thus escaped.

The ROMAN SATURN

The Romans, according to their custom of identifying their deities with those of the Greek gods whose attributes were similar to their own, declared Cronus to be identical with their old agricultural divinity Saturn. They believed that after his defeat in the Titanomachia and his banishment from his dominions by Zeus, he took refuge with Janus, king of Italy, who received the exiled deity with great kindness, and even shared his throne with him. Their united reign became so thoroughly peaceful and happy, and was distinguished by such uninterrupted prosperity, that it was called the Golden Age.

Saturn is usually represented bearing a sickle in the one hand and a wheat-sheaf in the other. A temple was erected to him at the foot of the Capitoline Hill, in which were deposited the public treasury and the laws of the state.

RHEA § OPS

Rhea, the wife of Cronus, and mother of Zeus and the other great gods of Olympus, personified the earth, and was regarded as the Great Mother and unceasing producer of all plantlife. She was also believed to exercise unbounded sway over animal creation, most especially over the lion, the noble king of beasts. Rhea is generally represented wearing a crown of turrets or towers and seated on a throne, with lions crouching at her feet. She is sometimes depicted sitting in a chariot, drawn by lions.

The Elements Paying Tribute to Friendship, **Louis-Simon Boizot, c. 1783. Rhea was often shown with lions at her feet, such as in this marble relief.**

The principal seat of her worship, which was always of a very riotous character, was at Crete. At her festivals, which took place at night, the wildest music of flutes, cymbals, and drums resounded, whilst joyful shouts and cries, accompanied by dancing and loud stamping of feet, filled the air.

The CRETAN CYBELE

Rhea was introduced into Crete by its first colonists from Phrygia, in Asia Minor, and in this country she was worshipped under the name of Cybele. The people of Crete adored her as the Great Mother, more especially in her signification as the sustainer of the vegetable world. Seeing, however, that year by year, as winter appears, all her glory vanished, her flowers faded, and her trees became leafless, they poetically expressed this process of nature under the figure of a lost love. She was said to have been tenderly attached to a youth of remarkable beauty, named Atys, who, to her grief and indignation, proved faithless to her. He was about to unite himself to a nymph named Sagaris, when, in the midst of the wedding feast, the rage of the incensed goddess suddenly burst forth upon all present. A panic seized the assembled guests, and Atys, becoming afflicted with temporary madness, fled to the mountains and destroyed himself. Cybele, moved with sorrow and regret, instituted a yearly mourning for his loss, when her priests, the Corybantes, with their usual noisy accompaniments, marched into the mountains to seek the lost youth. Having discovered him[6] they gave full vent to their ecstatic delight by indulging in the most violent gesticulations, dancing, shouting, and, at the same time, wounding and gashing themselves in a frightful manner.

OPPOSITE: *Cybele before the Council of the Gods*, Pietro de Cortona, 1633. Rhea was known as Cybele when she was first introduced to Crete by colonists from Phyrgia.

The ROMAN OPS

In Rome the Greek Rhea was identified with Ops, the Goddess of Plenty, the wife of Saturn, who had a variety of appellations. She was called Magna-Mater, Mater-Deorum, Berecynthia-Idea, and also Dindymene. This last title she acquired from three high mountains in Phrygia, whence she was brought to Rome as Cybele during the second Punic war, 205 BCE, in obedience to an injunction contained in the Sybilline books. She was represented as a matron crowned with towers, seated in a chariot drawn by lions.

6 Possibly an image of him placed in readiness.

ZEUS § JUPITER

A relief of Zeus, c. 1–150 CE. This piece of silver may have originally been attached to a piece of armor, like a ceremonial shield.

Zeus,[7] the great presiding deity of the universe, the ruler of heaven and earth, was regarded by the Greeks first, as the God of Aerial Phenomena; second, as the personification of the laws of nature; third, as lord of the state; and fourth, as the father of gods and men.

As the God of Aerial Phenomena Zeus could, by shaking his ægis,[8] produce storms, tempests, and intense darkness. At his command the mighty thunder rolled, the lightning flashed, and the clouds opened and poured forth their refreshing streams to nourish the ground below.

As the personification of the operations of nature, Zeus represented those grand laws of unchanging and harmonious order, by which not only the physical but also the moral world is governed. Hence he is the God of Regulated Time as marked by the changing seasons, and by the regular succession of day and night, in contradistinction to his father Cronus, who represented time absolutely (that is, eternity).

As the lord of the state, he was the founder of kingly power, the upholder of all institutions connected with the state, and the special patron of princes, whom he guarded and assisted with his advice and counsel. He protected the assembly of the people, and, in fact, watched over the welfare of the whole community.

As the father of the gods, Zeus saw that each deity performed his or her individual duty, punished their misdeeds, settled their disputes, and acted toward them on all occasions as their all-knowing counselor and mighty friend.

7 From *Diaus*, the sky.

8 A sacred shield made for Zeus by Hephæstus, which derived its name from being covered by the skin of the goat Amalthea, the word Ægis signifying goat's skin.

As the father of men, he took a paternal interest in the actions and well-being of mortals. He watched over them with tender solicitude, rewarding truth, charity, and uprightness, but severely punishing perjury, cruelty, and want of hospitality. Even the poorest and most forlorn wanderer found in him a powerful advocate, for he, by a wise and merciful dispensation, ordained that the mighty ones of the earth should aid their distressed and needy brethren.

As the worship of Zeus formed so important a feature in the religion of the Greeks, his statues were necessarily both numerous and magnificent. He is usually represented as a man of noble and imposing mien, his countenance expressing all the lofty majesty of the omnipotent ruler of the

Photographic print of the Temple of Jupiter Olympus, c. 1850–1880. The ruins of Zeus's temple in Athens, Greece.

ARBORVM GENERA NVMINIBVS SVIS DICATA
PERPETVO SERVANTVR·VT·IOVI ÆSCVLVS,
APOLLINI LAVRVS, MINERVÆ OLEA,
VENERI MIRTVS, HERCVLI POPVLVS.
·PLIN LIB XII·
·1547·
·L·D·

universe, combined with the gracious, yet serious, benignity of the father and friend of mankind. He may be recognized by his rich flowing beard and thick masses of hair, which rise straight from his high and intellectual forehead and fall to his shoulders in clustering locks. His head is frequently encircled with a wreath of oak leaves. His nose is large and finely formed, and his slightly opened lips impart an air of sympathetic kindliness that invites confidence. He generally bears in his uplifted hand a sheaf of thunderbolts, just ready to be hurled, whilst in the other he holds the lightning.

The most celebrated statue of the Olympian Zeus was that by the famous Athenian sculptor Phidias, which was forty feet high, and stood in the temple of Zeus at Olympia. It was formed of ivory and gold, and was such a masterpiece of art that it was reckoned among the Seven Wonders of the World. It represented the god, seated on a throne, holding in his right hand a life-sized image of Nike (the Goddess of Victory), and in his left a royal sceptre, surmounted by an eagle. It is said that the great sculptor had concentrated all the marvelous powers of his genius on this sublime conception, and earnestly entreated Zeus to give him decided proof that his labors were approved. An answer to his prayer came through the open roof of the temple in the shape of a flash of lightning, which Phidias interpreted as a sign that the God of Heaven was pleased with his work.

OPPOSITE: *Jupiter*, Léon Davent, 1547. This French etching shows Zeus surrounded by other Olympian gods.

Zeus is almost always accompanied by an eagle, which either surmounts his sceptre, or sits at his feet. This royal bird was sacred to him, probably from the fact of its being the only creature capable of gazing at the sun without being dazzled, which may have suggested the idea that it was able to contemplate the splendor of divine majesty unshrinkingly.

The oak tree, and also the summits of mountains, were sacred to Zeus. His sacrifices consisted of white bulls, cows, and goats.

THE LOVES *of* ZEUS

Zeus had seven immortal wives—Metis, Themis, Eurynome, Demeter, Mnemosyne, Leto, and Hera. In the stories of Zeus and most of his goddess wives we find that an allegorical meaning is conveyed. His marriage with Metis, who is said to have surpassed both gods and men in knowledge, represents supreme power allied to wisdom and prudence. His union with Themis, the Goddess of Justice, typifies the bond that exists between divine majesty and justice, law, and order. Eurynome, as the mother of the Graces, supplies the refining and harmonizing influences of grace and beauty, whilst the marriage of Zeus with Mnemosyne typifies the union of genius with memory.

In addition having seven immortal wives, Zeus was also allied to a number of mortal maidens whom he visited under various disguises, as it was supposed that if he revealed himself in his true form as king of heaven the splendor of his glory would cause instant destruction to mortals. The mortal consorts of Zeus were a favorite theme of poets, painters, and sculptors. Further tales of their adventures can be found on pages 22–27.

Zeus, 100–200 CE. Zeus was often seen with an eagle, said to be his sacred bird because they are only creatures capable of gazing directly at the sun.

MOUNT OLYMPUS

The Greeks believed that the home of this mighty and all-powerful deity was on the top of Mount Olympus, a high and lofty mountain between Thessaly and Macedon, whose summit, wrapt in clouds and mist, was hidden from mortal view. It was supposed that this mysterious region that even a bird could not reach extended beyond the clouds right into Aether, the realm of the immortal gods. The poets describe this ethereal atmosphere as bright, glistening, and refreshing, exercising a peculiar, gladdening influence over the minds and hearts of those privileged beings permitted to share its delights. Here youth never aged and the passing years left no traces on its favored inhabitants.

On the cloud-capped summit of Olympus was the palace of Zeus and Hera, made of burnished gold, chased silver, and gleaming ivory. Lower down were the homes of the other gods, which, though less commanding in position and size, were similar to that of Zeus in design and workmanship, all being the work of the divine artist Hephæstus. Below these were other palaces of silver, ebony, ivory, or burnished brass, where the Heroes, or Demi-gods, resided.

Cameo of Zeus from the 18th or 19th century. Zeus was often depicted with long hair.

METIS *and the* BIRTH *of* ATHENE

Metis, Zeus's first wife, was one of the Oceanides, or sea-nymphs. She was the personification of prudence and wisdom, a convincing proof of which she displayed in her successful administration of the potion that caused Cronus to yield up his children. She was endowed with the gift of prophecy, and foretold to Zeus that one of their children would gain ascendency over him. But in order to avert the possibility of the prediction being fulfilled, he swallowed her before any children were born to them. Feeling afterwards violent pains in his head, he sent for Hephæstus, and ordered him to open it with an axe. His command was obeyed, and out sprang, with a loud and martial shout, a beautiful being, clad in armor from head to foot. This was Athene, Goddess of Armed Resistance and Wisdom.

THEMIS, ZEUS'S COUNSEL

Themis, Zeus's second wife, was the Goddess of Justice, Law, and Order. The daughter of Cronus and Rhea, she presided over formal assemblies of people and the laws of hospitality. To her was entrusted the office of convoking the assembly of the gods, and she was also mistress of ritual and ceremony. She is usually represented as being in the full maturity of womanhood, of fair aspect, and wearing a flowing garment that drapes her noble, majestic form; in her right hand she holds the sword of justice, and in her left the scales that indicate the impartiality with which every cause is carefully weighed by her, her eyes being bandaged so that the personality of the individual should carry no weight with respect to the verdict. On account of her great wisdom, Zeus himself frequently sought her counsel and acted upon her advice.

Themis was a prophetic divinity, and had an oracle near the river Cephissus in Bœotia. Themis, like so many other Greek divinities, takes the place of a more ancient deity of the same name who was a daughter of Uranus and Gæa. This elder Themis inherited from her mother the gift of prophecy, and when she became merged into her younger representative she transmitted to her this prophetic power.

LETO and PYTHON

Leto (Latona) was the daughter of Cœus and Phœbe, and Zeus's fifth wife after Eurynome and Mnemosyne. She was gifted with great beauty, and was tenderly loved by Zeus, but her lot was far from being a happy one, for Hera, being extremely jealous of her, persecuted her with inveterate cruelty, and sent the dreadful serpent Python[9] to terrify and torment her wherever she went. But Zeus, who had observed with the deepest compassion her weary wanderings and agonized fears, resolved to create for her some place of refuge, however humble, where she might feel herself safe from the venomous attacks of the serpent.

Detail from *L'Épître Othéa*, attributed to the Master of the Cité des Dames and workshop, c. 1410–1414. The panel from this ancient manuscript shows the story of Latona (the Roman version of Leto), who turned peasants into frogs after they wouldn't allow her to drink from a pond.

He therefore brought her to Delos, a floating island in the Ægean Sea that he made stationary by attaching it with chains of adamant[10] to the bottom of the sea. Here she gave birth to her twin children, Apollo and Artemis, two of the most beautiful of the immortals.[11]

---

9 This frightful monster had sprung from the slimy and stagnant waters that had remained on the surface of the Earth after the deluge of Deucalion.

10 A heavy rock.

11 According to some versions of the story of Leto, Zeus transformed her into a quail, in order that she might thus elude the vigilance of Hera, and she is said to have resumed her true form when she arrived at the island of Delos.

ANTIOPE, AMPHION, *and* ZETHUS

Antiope, to whom Zeus appeared under the form of a satyr, was one of Zeus's most famous mortal lovers, but not because of Zeus. Antiope was the daughter of Nicteus, king of Thebes. To escape the anger of her father she fled to Sicyon, where King Epopeus, enraptured with her wonderful beauty, made her his wife without asking her father's consent. This so enraged Nicteus that he declared war against Epopeus, in order to compel him to restore Antiope.

At his death, which took place before he could succeed in his purpose, Nicteus left his kingdom to his brother Lycus, commanding him, at the same time, to carry on the war, and execute his vengeance. Lycus invaded Sicyon, defeated and killed Epopeus, and brought back Antiope as a prisoner.

On the way to Thebes she gave birth to her twin sons, Amphion and Zethus, who, by the orders of Lycus, were at once exposed on Mount Cithaeron, and would have perished but for the kindness of a shepherd who took pity on them and preserved their lives.

***Jupiter and Antiope*, Girolamo Fagiuoli, c. 1565. Here Zeus takes the form of a satyr to woo his mortal love Antiope.**

***Statue of Leda and the Swan*, unknown arist, c. 1–1000 CE. The marble statue shows Zeus taking the form of a swan to avoid the anger of mortal men who may also want to court Leda.**

Antiope was held captive for many years by her uncle Lycus, and compelled to suffer the utmost cruelty at the hands of his wife Dirce. But one day her bonds were miraculously loosened, and she flew for shelter and protection to the humble dwelling of her sons on Mount Cithaeron. During the long period of their mother's captivity the babes had grown into sturdy youths, and, as they listened angrily to the story of her wrongs, they became impatient to avenge them. Setting off at once to Thebes, they succeeded in possessing themselves of the town, and after slaying the cruel Lycus they bound Dirce by the hair to the horns of a wild bull, which dragged her hither and thither until she expired. Her mangled body was cast into the fount near Thebes, and she has been associated with fountains ever after.

Amphion became king of Thebes in his uncle's stead. He was a friend of the Muses, and devoted to music and poetry. His brother, Zethus, was famous for his skill in archery, and was passionately fond of the chase. It is said that when Amphion wished to enclose the town of Thebes with walls and towers, he had but to play a sweet melody on the lyre (given to him by Hermes) and the huge stones began to move, and obediently fitted themselves together.

LEDA, MOTHER *of* CASTOR AND POLLUX

Leda, whose affections Zeus won under the form of a swan, was the daughter of Thestius, king of Ætolia. Her twin sons, Castor and Pollux

(Polydeuces),[12] were renowned for their tender attachment to each other. They were also famous for their physical accomplishments, Castor being the most expert charioteer of his day, and Pollux the first boxer. Their names appear both among the hunters of the Calydonian boar-hunt (as will be recounted beginning on page 84) and the heroes of the Argonautic expedition (as will be recounted beginning on page 208).

The brothers became attached to the daughters of Leucippus, prince of the Messenians, who had been betrothed by their father to Idas and Lynceus, sons of Aphareus. Having persuaded Leucippus to break his promise, the twins carried off the maidens as their brides. Idas and Lynceus, naturally furious at this proceeding, challenged the twins to mortal combat, in which Castor perished by the hand of Idas, and Lynceus by that of Pollux.

Zeus wished to confer the gift of immortality upon Pollux, but he refused to accept it unless allowed to share it with Castor. Zeus gave the desired permission, and the faithful brothers were both allowed to live, but only on alternate days.

Castor and Pollux received divine honors throughout Greece, and were worshipped with special reverence at Sparta.

The Apulian Red-Figure Chous, attributed to Black Fury Group, c. 360 BCE. This terracotta wine jug, or chos, portrays Callisto in the woods on a rock covered in animal skins.

CALLISTO, EUROPA, and ALCMENE

A huntress who was personally trained by Artemis, Callisto, the daughter of King Lycaon of Arcadia, was devoted to the pleasures of the chase and had made a vow never to marry; but Zeus, who had taken the form of Artemis, succeeded in obtaining her affections. Hera, being extremely jealous of Callisto, changed her into a bear, and caused Artemis (who failed to recognize her attendant under this form) to hunt her in the chase, and put an end to her existence. After her

12 Castor and Pollux were known by the name of the Dioscuri, from *dios*, gods, and *kuroi*, youths.

death she was placed by Zeus among the stars as a constellation, under the name of Arctos, or the bear. This constellation would later be known as Ursa Major, or the Big Dipper.

Europa was the beautiful daughter of Agenor, king of Phœnicia. She was one day gathering flowers with her companions in a meadow near the seashore, when Zeus, charmed with her great beauty and wishing to win her love, transformed himself into a beautiful white bull, and trotted quietly up to the princess, so as not to alarm her. Surprised at the gentleness of the animal, and admiring its beauty as it lay placidly on the grass, she caressed it, crowned it with flowers, and, at last, playfully seated herself on its back. Hardly had she done so than the disguised god bounded away with his lovely burden, and swam across the sea with her to the island of Crete.

OPPOSITE: *The Abduction of Europa*, Rembrandt Harmensz. van Rijn, 1632. This famous painting was one of Rembrandt's few that depicted a Greek myth, in this case, Zeus's transformation into a white bull who steals away with beautiful mortal Europa.

Europa was the mother of Minos, Aeacus, and Rhadamanthus. Minos, who became king of Crete, was celebrated for his justice and moderation, and after death he was made one of the judges of the lower world, an office he held in conjunction with his brothers.

Alcmene, the daughter of Electryon, king of Mycenae, was betrothed to her cousin Amphytrion; but, during his absence on a perilous undertaking, Zeus assumed Amphytrion's form, and obtained her affections. Heracles (whose world-renowned exploits are related beginning on page 215) was the son of Alcmene and Zeus.

THE CONSUMPTION *of* SEMELE

Semele, a beautiful princess, the daughter of Cadmus, king of Phœnicia, was greatly beloved by Zeus. Like the unfortunate Callisto, she was hated by Hera with jealous malignity, and the haughty queen of heaven was determined to destroy her. Therefore, she disguised herself as Berœ, Semele's faithful old nurse, and artfully persuaded her to insist upon Zeus visiting her, as he appeared to Hera, in all his power and glory—well knowing that this would cause Semele's instant death. Semele, suspecting no treachery, followed the advice of her supposed nurse, and the next time Zeus came to her, she earnestly entreated him to grant the favor she was about to ask. Zeus swore by the river Styx (which was to the gods an irrevocable oath) to accede to her request whatsoever it might be. Semele, therefore, secure of gaining her petition, begged of Zeus to appear to her in all the glory of his divine power and majesty. As he had sworn to grant whatever she asked of him, he was compelled to comply with her wish; so he revealed himself as the mighty lord of the universe, accompanied by thunder and lightning, and she was instantly consumed in the flames.

Before Semele was consumed she gave birth to Dionysus, the God of Wine, who later descended to the realm of shades in search of his ill-fated mother, whom he conducted to Olympus, where, under the name of Thyone, she was admitted into the assembly of the immortal gods.

IO *and the* GIANT

Io, daughter of Inachus, king of Argos, was a priestess of Hera. She was very beautiful, and Zeus, who was much attached to her, transformed her into a white cow, in order to defeat the jealous intrigues of Hera, who, however, was not to be deceived. Aware of the stratagem, she contrived to obtain the animal from Zeus, and placed her under the watchful care of a Giant named Argus Panoptes, who fastened her to an olive tree in the grove of Hera. He had a hundred eyes, of which, when asleep, he never closed more than two at a time; being thus always on the watch, Hera found him extremely useful in keeping guard over Io.

OPPOSITE: *The Birth of Bacchus*, Giulio Romano and workshop, c. 1530s. Semele gives birth to Bacchus while beholding Zeus in all his glory, which immediately causes her death.

However, Hermes, the messenger of the gods, by the command of Zeus, succeeded in putting all his eyes to sleep with the sound of his magic lyre, and then, taking advantage of his helpless condition, slew him. The story goes that, in commemoration of the services that Argus Panoptes had rendered her, Hera placed his eyes on the tail of a peacock, as a lasting memorial of her gratitude. Ever fertile in resources, Hera now sent a gadfly to worry and torment the unfortunate Io incessantly, and she wandered all over the world in hopes of escaping from her tormentor. At length she reached Egypt, where she found rest and freedom from the persecutions of her enemy. On the banks of the Nile she resumed her original form and gave birth to a son called Epaphus, who afterwards became king of Egypt, and built the famous city of Memphis.

PHILEMON *and* BAUCIS

The Greeks supposed that the divine ruler of the universe occasionally assumed a human form, and descended from his celestial abode, in order to visit mankind and observe their proceedings, his aim being generally either to punish the guilty, or to reward the deserving.

On one occasion Zeus, accompanied by Hermes, made a journey through Phrygia, seeking hospitality and shelter wherever they went. But nowhere did they receive a kindly welcome till they came to the humble cottage of an old man, Philemon, and his wife, called Baucis, who entertained them with the greatest kindness, setting before them what

***Jupiter and Io*, Hendrik Goltzius, 1589. Zeus turned Io into a white cow to escape the jealousy of Hera.**

frugal fare their humble means permitted, and bidding them welcome with unaffected cordiality. Observing in the course of their simple repast that the wine bowl was miraculously replenished, the aged couple became convinced of the divine nature of their guests. The gods now informed them that on account of its wickedness, their village was doomed to destruction, and told them to come with them up the neighboring hill, which overlooked the village where they dwelt. To their dismay they beheld at their feet, in place of the spot where they had passed so many happy years together, nothing but a watery plain. The only house to be seen was their own little cottage, which suddenly changed itself into a temple before their eyes. Zeus now asked the worthy pair to name any wish they particularly desired and it should be granted. They accordingly begged that they might serve the gods in the temple below, and end life together.

Their wish was granted, for, after spending the remainder of their lives in the worship of the gods, they both died at the same instant, and were transformed by Zeus into trees, remaining forever side by side.

KING LYCAON

Upon another occasion Zeus, wishing to ascertain for himself the truth of the reports concerning the atrocious wickedness of mankind, made a journey through Arcadia. Being recognized by the Arcadians as king of heaven, he was received by them with becoming respect and veneration; but Lycaon, their king, who had rendered himself infamous by the gross impiety of himself and his sons, doubted the divinity of Zeus, ridiculed his people for being so easily duped, and, according to his custom of killing all strangers who ventured to trust his hospitality, resolved to murder him. Before executing this wicked design, however, he decided to put Zeus to the test, and having killed a boy for the purpose, placed before him a dish containing human flesh. But Zeus was not to be deceived. He beheld the revolting dish with horror and loathing, and angrily upsetting the table upon which it was placed, turned Lycaon into a wolf, and destroyed all his fifty sons by lightning, except Nyctimus, who was saved by the intervention of Gæa.

***Jupiter*, Giovanni Girolamo Frezza after Francesco Albani, 1704. The Roman Jupiter was different from the Greek Zeus in that he never descended from the heavens.**

The ROMAN JUPITER

The Roman Jupiter, who was so frequently confounded with the Greek Zeus, was identical to him only as being the head of the Olympic gods, and the presiding deity over Life, Light, and Aerial Phenomena. Jupiter was lord of life in its widest and most comprehensive signification, having absolute power over life and death, in which respect he differed from the Greek Zeus, who was to a certain extent controlled by the all-potent sway of the Moiræ or Fates. Zeus, as we have seen, often condescended to visit mankind, either as a mortal, or under various disguises, whereas Jupiter always remained essentially the supreme God of Heaven, and never appeared upon earth.

HERA ∫ JUNO

Juno, Joseph Nollekens, 1776. This statue of Hera from the United Kingdom originally stood alongside statues of Athene, Aphrodite, and Paris, representing the story of the Judgment of Paris.

Hera, the eldest daughter of Cronus and Rhea, was born at Samos, or, according to some accounts, at Argos, and was reared by the sea-divinities Oceanus and Tethys, who were models of conjugal fidelity.[1] She was the principal wife of Zeus, and, as queen of heaven, participated in the honors paid to him, but her dominion only extended over the air (the lower aerial regions).

Hera was the sublime embodiment of strict matronly virtue, and was on that account the protectress of purity and married women. Faultless herself in her fidelity as a wife, she essentially personified the sanctity of the marriage tie, and held in abhorrence any violation of its obligations. So strongly was she imbued with this hatred of any immorality, that, finding herself so often called upon to punish the failings of both gods and men in this respect, she became jealous, harsh, and vindictive. Her exalted position as the wife of the supreme deity, combined with her extreme beauty, caused her to become exceedingly vain, and she consequently resented with great severity any infringement on her rights as queen of heaven, or any apparent slight against her personal appearance.

Hera was the mother of Ares (Mars), Hephæstus, Hebe, and Eileithyia. Ares was the God of War; Hephæstus, of Fire; Hebe, of Youth; and Eileithyia presided over the birth of mortals.

On the first day of every month a ewe-lamb and sow were sacrificed to Hera.

Hera is usually represented seated on a throne, holding a pomegranate in one hand and a sceptre

13 The ancient Greeks attributed much of the subsequent character of an individual to early influences; hence Hera, the future queen and mistress of heaven, is represented as being brought up in a domesticated and orderly household, where home virtues were carefully inculcated.

Venus, Juno, and Minerva, with Cupid, Giovanni Andrea Sirani, c. 1650. Hera is seen at the right, sceptre in hand, with Athene (Minerva) at left and the lovely Aphrodite (Venus) in the middle with Eros (Cupid) on her lap.

surmounted by a cuckoo in the other. The hawk, goose, and more particularly the peacock[14] were sacred to her. Flocks of these beautiful birds generally surround her throne and draw her chariot, whilst Iris, the Rainbow, is seated behind her.

Hera appears as a calm, dignified matron of majestic beauty, robed in a tunic and mantle, her forehead broad and intellectual, her eyes large and fully opened, and her arms dazzlingly white and finely molded. Her attributes are the diadem, veil, sceptre, and peacock. Her favorite flowers were the dittany, poppy, and lily.

14 In the Homeric age peacocks were unknown; it is therefore the later poets who describe Hera surrounded with peacocks, which were brought to Greece from India.

THE WORSHIP of HERA

Roman coin, c. 161–175 CE. Hera and her signature peacock are featured on the back of this silver coin that shows Faustina the Younger (the daughter of emperor Antoninus Pius) on the front.

Hera dearly loved Greece, and indeed always watched over and protected Greek interests, her beloved and favorite cities being Argos, Samos, Sparta, and Mycenæ. Her principal temples were at Argos and Samos. She was also greatly venerated at Olympia, and her temple there, which stood in the altis or sacred grove, was five hundred years older than Zeus's temple on the same spot. Some interesting excavations have brought to light the remains of this ancient edifice, showing that it contains among other treasures of antiquity several beautiful statues, the work of famous sculptors of ancient Greece. At first this temple was built of wood, then of stone, then finally formed of a conglomerate of shells.

In the altis, races were run by young maidens in honor of Hera, and the fleetest of foot received in token of her victory an olive-wreath and a piece of the flesh of the sacrifices. These races, like the Olympic games, were celebrated at intervals of four years, and were called Heræ. A beautiful robe, woven by sixteen women chosen from the sixteen cities of Elis, was always offered to Hera on these occasions, and choral songs and sacred dances formed part of the ceremonies.

THE JUDGMENT of PARIS

The Judgment of Paris, a popular tale in mythology that had lasting ramifications that led to the Trojan War, signally illustrates how ready Hera was to resent any slight offered to her.

At the marriage of the sea-nymph Thetis with a mortal called Peleus, all the gods and goddesses were present, except Eris (the Goddess of Discord). Indignant at not being invited, Eris decided to cause dissension in the assembled party, and for this purpose threw into the midst of the guests a golden apple with the inscription on it "For the Fairest." Now, as all the goddesses were extremely beautiful, each claimed the apple; but at length, the rest having relinquished their pretensions, the number of candidates was reduced to three—Hera, Athene, and Aphrodite—who agreed to appeal to Paris for a settlement of this delicate question, he being noted for the wisdom he had displayed in his judgment upon several occasions. Paris was the son of Priam, king of Troy, who, ignorant of his noble birth, was at this time feeding his flocks on Mount Ida, in Phrygia.

Hermes, as messenger of the gods, conducted the three rival beauties to the young shepherd, and with breathless anxiety they awaited his decision. Each fair candidate

The Judgment of Paris, Marcantonio Raimondi, c. 1480–1534. Paris bestows upon Aphrodite the golden apple, as Hera plans her vengence.

endeavored to secure his favor with the most tempting offer. Hera promised him extensive dominions; Athene, martial fame and glory; and Aphrodite, the loveliest woman in the world. But whether he really considered Aphrodite the fairest of the three, or preferred a beautiful wife to fame and power, we cannot tell; all we know is that to her he awarded the golden apple, and she became ever after universally acknowledged as the Goddess of Beauty.

Hera, having fully expected that Paris would give her preference, was so indignant that she never forgave him, and not only persecuted him, but all the family of Priam, whose dreadful sufferings and misfortunes during the Trojan War were attributed to her influence. In fact, she carried her animosity to such an extent that it was often the cause of domestic disagreements between herself and Zeus, who espoused the cause of the Trojans.

HERA and THE GOLDEN CHAIN

Hollow scarab in swivel ring, c. 400–300 BCE. This gold ring is engraved with the head of Hera Lakinia, a local interpretation of Hera from the Kroton area of ancient Italy.

Among the many stories of Hera's frequent quarrels with Zeus there is one connected with Heracles, the favorite son of Zeus, which is as follows: Hera having raised a storm at sea in order to drive Heracles off his ship's course, Zeus became so angry that he hung her in the clouds by a golden chain, and attached heavy anvils to her feet. Her son Hephæstus tried to release his mother from her humiliating position, for which Zeus threw him out of heaven, and his leg was broken by the fall.

Hera, being deeply offended by Zeus, determined to separate herself from him forever, and she accordingly left him and took up her abode in Eubœa. Surprised and grieved at this unlooked-for desertion, Zeus resolved to leave no means untried to win her back again. In this emergency he consulted Cithaeron, king of Platea, who was famed for his great wisdom and subtlety. Cithaeron advised him to dress up an image in bridal attire and place it in a chariot, announcing that this was Platea, his future wife. The artifice succeeded. Hera, incensed at the idea of a rival, flew to meet the procession in great anger, and seizing the supposed bride, she furiously attacked her and dragged off her nuptial attire. Her delight on discovering the deception was so great that a reconciliation took place, and, committing the image to the flames, with joyful laughter she seated herself in its place and returned to Olympus.

The ROMAN JUNO

Juno, the Roman divinity supposed to be identical with the Greek Hera, differed from her in the most salient points, for whereas Hera invariably appears as the haughty, unbending queen of heaven, Juno, on the other hand, is revered and beloved as the perfect matron and housewife. She was worshipped in Rome under various titles, most of which point to her vocation as the protectress of married women. Juno was believed to watch over and guard the life of every woman from her birth to her death.

On the 1st of March a grand annual festival, called the Matronalia, was celebrated in her honor by all the married women of Rome, and this religious institution was accompanied with much solemnity.

ATHENE § MINERVA

Athene, also called Pallas-Athene or Athena, was the Goddess of Wisdom and Armed Resistance, and was a purely Greek divinity; that is to say, no other nation possessed a corresponding conception.

She was supposed (as related on page 19) to have issued from the head of Zeus himself, clad in armor from head to foot. The miraculous advent of this maiden goddess is beautifully described by Homer in one of his poems: "snow-capped Olympus shook to its foundation; the glad earth re-echoed her martial shout; the billowy sea became agitated; and Helios, the Sun God, arrested his fiery steeds in their headlong course to welcome this wonderful emanation from the godhead." Athene was at once admitted into the assembly of the gods, and henceforth took her place as the most faithful and sagacious of all her father's counselors.

The Hope Athena, c. 100–200 CE. Athene is depicted in her helmet and snake-fringed armor with the Medusa-head breastplate.

Athene is usually represented fully draped; she has a serious and thoughtful aspect, as though replete with earnestness and wisdom; the beautiful oval contour of her face is adorned by the luxuriance of her wealth of hair, which is drawn back from the temples and hangs down in careless grace; she looks like the embodiment of strength, grandeur, and majesty; whilst her broad shoulders and small hips give her a slightly masculine appearance.

Athene was the patroness of learning, science, and art, more particularly where these contributed directly toward the welfare of nations. She presided over all inventions connected with agriculture, invented the plough, and taught mankind how to use oxen for farming purposes. She also instructed man-

kind in the use of numbers, trumpets, and chariots, and presided over the building of the Argo,[15] thereby encouraging the useful art of navigation. She also taught the Greeks how to build the wooden horse by means of which the destruction of Troy was effected.[16]

The safety of cities depended on her care, for which reason her temples were generally built on the citadels, and she was supposed to watch over the defense of the walls, fortifications, harbors, and so forth. A divinity who so faithfully guarded the best interests of the state, by not only protecting it from the attacks of enemies, but also by developing its chief resources of wealth and prosperity, was worthily chosen as the presiding deity of the state, and in this character as an essentially political goddess she was called Athene-Polias.

Athene was universally worshipped throughout Greece, but was regarded with special veneration by the Athenians, she being the guardian deity of Athens. Her most celebrated temple was the Parthenon, which stood on the Acropolis at Athens, and contained her world-renowned statue by Phidias, which ranks second only to that of Zeus by the same great artist. This colossal statue was thirty-nine feet high, and was composed of ivory and gold; its majestic beauty formed the chief attraction of the temple. It represented her standing erect, bearing her spear and shield; in her hand she held an image of Nike, and at her feet there lay a serpent.

The tree sacred to her was the olive, which she herself produced in a contest with Poseidon. The olive tree thus called into existence was preserved in the temple of Erectheus, on the Acropolis, and is said to have possessed such marvelous vitality that when the Persians burned it after sacking the town, it immediately burst forth into new shoots.

The owl, cock, and serpent were the animals sacred to her, and her sacrifices were rams, bulls, and cows.

The principal festival held in honor of Athene was the Panathenæa.

OPPOSITE: ***Project for a Cartouche: An Allegory of Minerva, Fame, History and Faith Overcoming Ignorance and Time,*** **François Boucher, c. 1727. Athene poses above and to the right of where an inscription will later appear in this antique artwork.**

BELOW: Nolan Amphora showing Athena and Hermes, attributed to Berlin Painter, c. 500–475 BCE. When Athene was portrayed holding her helmet rather than wearing it, it was thought to portray peace.

15 The first large ship possessed by the Greeks fit for more than coast navigation, and the vessel that gave the Argonauts their name. See pages 207–208.

16 See page 256.

Plate from *L'Épître Othéa*, attributed to Master of the Cité des Dames, c. 1410–1414. Athene distributes armor to her followers in *The Epistle of Othea* by Christine de Pisan, a woman poet and spiritualist.

ATHENE *the* WARRIOR

The fact of Athene having been born clad in armor, which merely signified that her virtue and purity were unassailable, has given rise to the erroneous supposition that she was the presiding Goddess of War; but a deeper study of her character in all its bearings proves that, in contradistinction to her brother Ares, the God of War, who loved strife for its own sake, she only took up arms to protect the innocent and deserving against tyrannical oppression. It is true that in the *Iliad* we frequently see her on the battlefield fighting valiantly, and protecting her favorite heroes; but this was always at the command of Zeus, who even supplied her with arms for the purpose, as it is supposed that she possessed none of her own. A marked feature in the representations of this deity is the ægis, that wonderful shield given to her by her father as a further means of defense, that, when in danger, she swung so swiftly round and round that it kept at a distance all antagonistic influences;

hence her name Pallas-Athene, from *pallo*, "I swing." In the center of this shield, which was covered with dragon's scales and bordered with serpents, and which she sometimes wore as a breastplate, was the awe-inspiring head of the Gorgon Medusa, which had the effect of turning to stone all its beholders.

Athene was a brave, dauntless goddess, so exactly the essence of all that was noble in the character of Zeus, chaste in word and deed, and kind at heart, without exhibiting any of those failings that somewhat mar the nobler features of Zeus. This direct emanation from Sky God's own self, justly his favorite child, his better and purer counterpart, received from him several important prerogatives: she was permitted to hurl the thunderbolts, to prolong the life of man, and to bestow the gift of prophecy; in fact Athene was the only divinity whose authority was equal to that of Zeus himself, and when he had ceased to visit the Earth in person she was empowered by him to act as his deputy.

It was her special duty to protect the state and all peaceful associations of mankind, which she possessed the power of defending when occasion required. She encouraged the maintenance of law and order, and defended the right on all occasions, for which reason, in the Trojan War she espouses the cause of the Greeks and exerts all her influence on their behalf. The Areopagus, a court of justice where religious causes and murders were tried, was believed to have been instituted by her, and when both sides happened to have an equal number of votes she gave the casting-vote in favor of the accused.

THE GODDESS *of* SPINNING *and* WEAVING

In addition to the many functions that she exercised in connection with the state, Athene presided over two chief departments of feminine industry, spinning and weaving. In the latter art she herself displayed unrivaled ability and exquisite taste. She weaved her own robe and that of Hera, which is said to have been embroidered very richly; she also gave Jason a cloak weaved by herself when he set forth in quest of the Golden Fleece.

Greek Tetradrachm, c. 286–281 BCE. Athene sits peacefully on the back of this coin, issued by King Lysimachos of Thrace (in Northern Greece). A bust of Alexandar the Great is on the front.

Being on one occasion challenged to a contest in weaving by a mortal maiden named Arachne, whom she had instructed in the art, she accepted the challenge and was completely vanquished by her pupil. Angry at her defeat, she struck the unfortunate maiden on the forehead with the shuttle that she held in her hand; and Arachne, being of a sensitive nature, was so hurt by this indignity that she hung herself in despair, and was changed by Athene into a spider.

ATHENE *and the* FLUTE

Athene is said to have invented the flute when Perseus, with the help of Athene, had cut off the head of the hideous Medusa, whose hair was composed of snakes. The Medusa caused a sad dirge-like song to issue from the mouths of the many snakes, whereupon Athene, pleased with the sound, imitated the melody on a reed, and thus invented the flute. Athene played the flute with considerable talent until one day, being laughed at by the assembled gods and goddesses for the contortions that her face assumed during these musical efforts, she hastily ran to a fountain in order to see her reflection and convince herself whether she deserved their ridicule. Finding to her intense disgust that such was indeed the fact, she threw the flute away, and never raised it to her lips again.

***Athena Changing Arachne into a Spider*, Antonio Tempesta and Wilhelm Janson, 1606. After Arachne beats Athene in a weaving contest, the goddess transforms her into a spider.**

The ROMAN MINERVA

The Minerva of the Romans was identified with the Athene of the Greeks. Like Athene, she presided over learning and all useful arts, and was the pa-

Judgment of Jupiter, John Deare, c. 1786–1787. When Athene is portrayed alongside other goddesses, as she is here, clustered with Aphrodite and Hera with her back turned, she is easily recognizable by her armor and less feminine appearance.

troness of the feminine accomplishments of sewing, spinning, and weaving. Schools were under her special care, and schoolchildren, therefore, had holidays during her festivals (the Greater Quinquatria), when they always brought a gift to their master, called the Minerval.

It is worthy of notice that the only three divinities worshipped in the Capitol were Jupiter, Juno, and Minerva, and in their joint honor the Ludi Maximi or Great Games were held.

HESTIA § VESTA

Hestia was the daughter of Cronus and Rhea. She was the Goddess of Fire in its first application to the wants of mankind, hence she was essentially the presiding deity of the domestic hearth and the guardian spirit of man, and it was her pure and benign influence that was supposed to protect the sanctity of domestic life.

In ancient times, the hearth was regarded as the most important and most sacred portion of the dwelling, because the protection of the fire was an important consideration, for if once permitted to become extinct, reignition could be extremely difficult. In fact, the hearth was held so sacred that it constituted the sanctum of the family, for which reason it was always erected in the center of every house. It was a few feet in height and was built of stone; the fire was placed on the top of it, and served the double purpose of preparing the daily meals and consuming the family sacrifices. Around this domestic hearth or altar would gather the various members of the family, the head of the house occupying the place of honor nearest the hearth. Here prayers were said and sacrifices offered, and here also every kind and loving feeling was fostered, which even extended to the hunted and guilty stranger, who, if he once succeeded in touching this sacred altar, was safe from pursuit and punishment, and was henceforth placed under the protection of the family. Any crime committed within the sacred precincts of the domestic hearth was invariably visited by death.

In Grecian cities there was a common hall, called the Prytaneum, in which the members of the government had their meals at the expense of the state, and here too was the Hestia, or public hearth, with its fire, by means of which those meals were prepared. It was customary for emigrants to take with them a portion of this sacred fire, which they jealously guarded and brought with them to their new home, where it served as a connecting link between the young Greek colony and the mother country.

Hestia is generally represented standing, and in accordance with the dignity and sanctity of her character, always appears fully draped. Her countenance is distinguished by a serene gravity of expression.

Temple of Vesta, Rome, **Mrs. Jane St. John, c. 1856–1859. Vesta's temple was one of Rome's finest.**

Vestal Making Sacrifice at Altar, **c. 1870. Those who guarded the fire in Vesta's temple to make sure it never went out were so dedicated that they had to take a vow of chasity. They were known as vestal virgins.**

The ROMAN VESTA

Vesta occupies a distinguished place among the earlier divinities of the Romans. Her temple in Rome, containing as it were the hearthstone of the nation, stood close beside the palace of Numa Pompilius. It was circular in form, and contained the sacred and highly prized Palladium of Troy, which was instrumental in winning the Trojan War.[17]

On her altar burned the never-ceasing fire, which was tended by her priestesses, the vestal virgins.

The great festival in honor of Vesta, called the Vestalia, was celebrated on the 9th of June.

17 See page 255.

DEMETER ∫ CERES

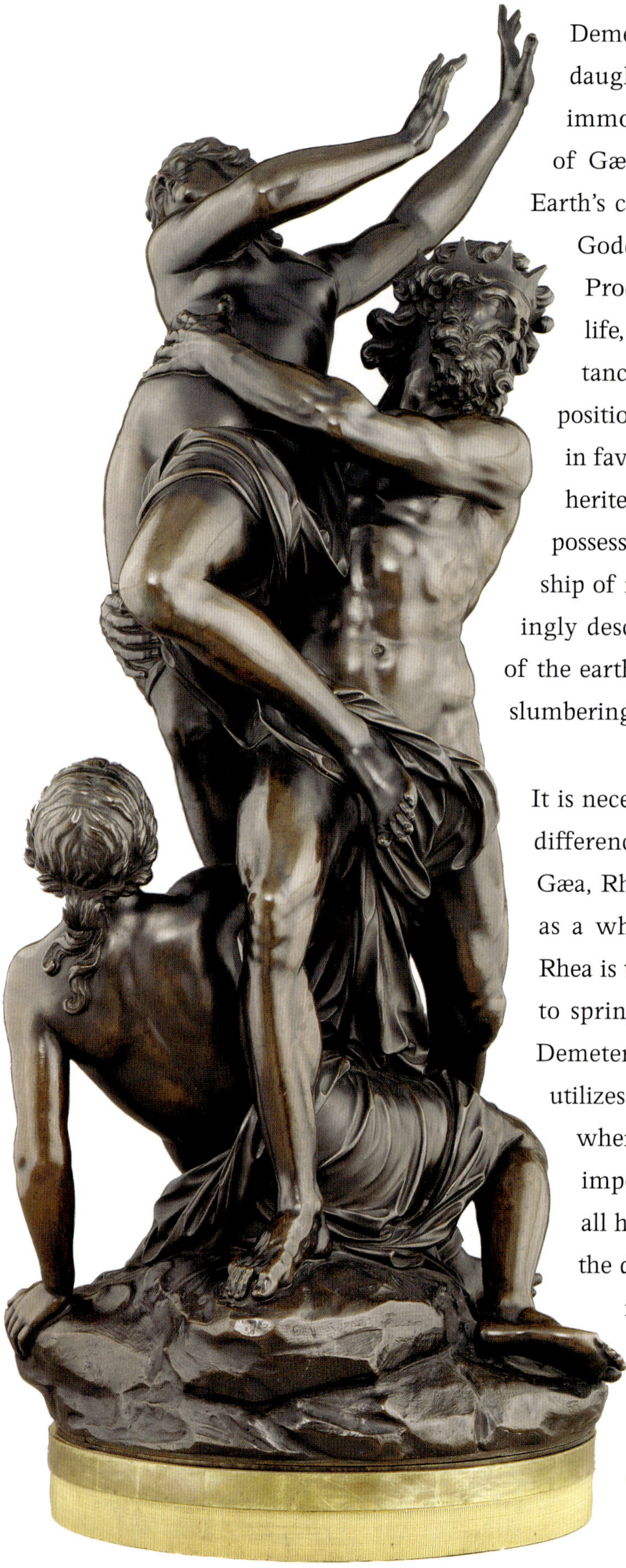

Demeter (from *Ge-meter*, "earth-mother") was the daughter of Cronus and Rhea and one of Zeus's immortal wives.[18] She represented that portion of Gæa (the whole solid earth) that we call the Earth's crust, and which produces all vegetation. As Goddess of Agriculture, Field-Fruits, Plenty, and Productiveness, she was the sustainer of material life, and was therefore a divinity of great importance. When ancient Gæa lost, with Uranus, her position as a ruling divinity, she abdicated her sway in favor of her daughter Rhea, who henceforth inherited the powers that her mother had previously possessed, receiving in her place the honor and worship of mankind. In a very old poem Gæa is accordingly described as retiring to a cavern in the bowels of the earth, where she sits in the lap of her daughter, slumbering, moaning, and nodding forever and ever.

It is necessary to keep clearly in view the distinctive difference between the three great Earth goddesses Gæa, Rhea, and Demeter. Gæa represents the Earth as a whole, with its mighty subterranean forces; Rhea is that productive power that causes vegetation to spring forth, thus sustaining men and animals; Demeter, by presiding over agriculture, directs and utilizes Rhea's productive powers. But in later times, when Rhea, like other ancient divinities, lost her importance as a ruling deity, Demeter assumed all her functions and attributes, and then became the deity of the life-producing and life-maintaining earth-crust. We must bear in mind the fact that man in his primitive state knew neither how to sow nor how to till the

18 Some, with but little reason, make Demeter the daughter of Uranus and Gæa.

ground; when, therefore, he had exhausted the pastures that surrounded him he was compelled to seek others that were as yet unreaped; thus, roaming constantly from one place to another, settled habitations, and consequently civilizing influences, were impossible. Demeter, however, by introducing a knowledge of agriculture, put an end, at once and forever, to that nomadic life that was now no longer necessary.

The favor of Demeter was believed to bring mankind rich harvests and fruitful crops, whereas her displeasure caused blight, drought, and famine. The island of Sicily was supposed to be under her special protection, and there she was regarded with particular veneration, the Sicilians naturally attributing the wonderful fertility of their country to the partiality of the goddess.

Demeter is usually represented as a woman of noble bearing and majestic appearance—tall, matronly, and dignified—with beautiful golden hair that falls in rippling curls over her stately shoulders, the yellow locks being emblematical of the ripened ears of corn. Sometimes she appears seated in a chariot drawn by winged dragons, at others she stands erect, her figure drawn up to its full height, and always fully draped; she bears a sheaf of wheat-ears in one hand and a lighted torch in the other. The wheat-ears are not infrequently replaced by a bunch of poppies, with which her brows are also garlanded, though sometimes she merely wears a simple ribbon in her hair.

OPPOSITE: *Pluto Abducting Proserpine*, François Giradrdon, c. 1693–1710. The story of Persephone was a favorite of poets and artists alike.

Demeter had many children with both gods and mortals. With Zeus, she had the doomed Persephone; with Poseidon, she had Despoena, the Goddess of Mysteries, and Arion, a horse divinely inspired with the gift of speech.

Plutus, the son of Demeter and a mortal called Iasion, was the God of Wealth, and was represented as being lame when he makes his appearance, yet winged when he makes his departure. He was supposed to be both blind and foolish, because he bestows his gifts without discrimination, and frequently upon the most unworthy objects.

The ABDUCTION *of* PERSEPHONE

The favorite child of Demeter was Persephone (Proserpine), to whom she was so tenderly attached that her whole life was bound up in her, and she knew no happiness except in her company. One day, however, whilst Persephone was gathering flowers in a meadow, attended by the ocean-nymphs, she saw to her surprise a beautiful narcissus, from the stem of which sprang forth a hundred blossoms. Drawing near to examine this lovely flower, whose exquisite scent perfumed the air, she stooped down to gather it, suspecting no evil, when a yawning abyss opened at her feet, and Hades, the grim ruler of the lower world, appeared from its depths, seated in his dazzling chariot drawn by four black horses. Regardless of her tears and the shrieks of her female attendants, Hades seized the terrified maiden, and bore her away to the gloomy realms over which he reigned in melancholy grandeur. Helios, the all-seeing Sun God, and Hecate, a mysterious and very ancient divinity, alone heard her cries for aid, but were powerless to help her.

When Demeter became conscious of her loss her grief was intense, and she refused to be comforted. She knew not where to seek for her child, but feeling that repose and inaction were impossible, she set out on her weary search, taking with her two torches that she lighted in the flames of Mount Etna to guide her on her way. For nine long days and nights she wandered on, inquiring of everyone she met for tidings of her child. But all was in vain! Neither gods nor men could give her the comfort that her soul so hungered for.

Head of a Woman or Goddess, perhaps Demeter, c. 98–117 CE. In addition to being the mother of earth, Demeter was sympathetic to all mothers due to her devotion to her daughter Persephone.

At last, on the tenth day, the disconsolate mother met Hecate, who informed her that she had heard her daughter's cries, but knew not who it was who had borne her away. By Hecate's advice Demeter consulted Helios, whose all-seeing eye nothing escaped, and from him she learnt that it was Zeus himself who had permitted Hades to seize Persephone, and transport her to the lower world in order that she might become Hades's wife. Indignant with Zeus for having given his sanction to the abduction of his daughter, and filled with the bitterest sorrow, she abandoned her home in Olympus, and refused all heavenly food. Disguising herself as an old woman, she descended upon Earth, and commenced a weary pilgrimage among mankind.

One evening she arrived at a place called Eleusis, in Attica, and sat down to rest near a well beneath the shade of an olive tree. The youthful daughters of Celeus, the king of the country, came with their pails of brass to draw water from this well, and seeing that the tired wayfarer appeared faint and dispirited, they spoke kindly to her, asking who she was, and whence she came. Demeter replied that she had made her escape from pirates, who had captured her, and added that she would feel grateful for a home with any wor-

***The Abduction of Proserpine*, Alessandro Allori, 1570. Nymphs frolic in the background as Persephone (Proserpine) is carried off by Hades.**

thy family, whom she would be willing to serve in a menial capacity. The princesses, on hearing this, begged Demeter to have a moment's patience while they returned home and consulted their mother, Metaneira. They soon brought the joyful intelligence that she was desirous of securing her services as nurse to her infant son Demophoon (also known as Triptolemus).

When Demeter arrived at the house a radiant light suddenly illumined her, which so overawed Metaneira that she treated the unknown stranger with the greatest respect, and hospitably offered her food and drink. But Demeter, still grief-worn and dejected, refused her friendly offers, and held herself apart from the social board. At length, however, the maid-servant Iambe succeeded, by means of playful jests and merriment, in somewhat dispelling the grief of the sorrowing mother, causing her at times to smile in spite of herself, and even inducing her to partake of a mixture of barley-meal, mint, and water, which was prepared according to the directions of the goddess herself.

Time passed on, and the young child throve amazingly under the care of his kind and judicious nurse, who, however, gave him no food, but anointed him daily with ambrosia, and every night laid him secretly in the fire in order to render him immortal and exempt from old age. But, unfortunately, this benevolent design on the part of Demeter was put to a halt by Metaneira herself, whose curiosity, one night, impelled her to watch the proceedings of the mysterious being who nursed her child. When to her horror she beheld her son placed in the flames, she shrieked aloud. Demeter, incensed at this untimely interruption, instantly withdrew the child, and throwing him on the ground, revealed herself in her true character.

The bent and aged form had vanished, and in its place there stood a bright and beauteous being, whose golden locks streamed over her shoulders in richest luxuriance, her whole aspect bespeaking dignity and majesty. She told the awe-struck Metaneira that she was the goddess Demeter, and had intended to make her son immortal, but that her fatal curiosity had rendered this impossible. Adding, however, that the child, having slept in her

arms and been nursed on her lap, should ever command the respect and esteem of mankind. She then demanded that a temple and altar be erected to her on a neighboring hill by the people of Eleusis, promising that she herself would direct them how to perform the sacred rites and ceremonies that should be observed in her honor. With these words she took her departure never to return.

Obedient to her commands, Celeus called together a meeting of his people, and built the temple on the spot that the goddess had indicated. It was soon completed, and Demeter took up her abode in it, but her heart was still sad for the loss of her daughter, and the whole world felt the influence of her grief and dejection. This was indeed a terrible year for mankind. Demeter no longer smiled on the earth she was wont to bless, and though the husbandman sowed the grain, and the groaning oxen ploughed the fields, no harvest rewarded their labor. All was barren, dreary desolation. The world was threatened with famine, and the gods with the loss of their accustomed honors and sacrifices; it became evident, therefore, to Zeus himself that some measures must be adopted to appease the anger of the goddess. He accordingly despatched Iris and many of the other gods and goddesses to implore Demeter to return to Olympus; but all their prayers were fruitless. The incensed goddess swore that until her daughter was restored to her she would not allow the grain to spring forth from the earth. At length Zeus sent Hermes, his faithful messenger, to the lower world with a petition to Hades, urgently entreating him to restore Persephone to the arms of her disconsolate mother.

Opposite: *Landscape with Ceres (Allegory of Earth)*, Jan Brueghel the Younger and Hendrik van Balen, c. 1630–1639. Demeter is surrounded by woodland creatures, one of whom is holding her characteristic sheaf of wheat.

When he arrived in the gloomy realms of the lower world, Hermes found Hades seated on a throne with the beautiful Persephone beside him, sorrowfully bewailing her unhappy fate. On learning his errand, Hades consented to resign Persephone, who joyfully prepared to follow the messenger of the gods to the abode of life and light. But before taking leave of her husband, he presented to her a few seeds of the pomegranate, which in her excitement she thoughtlessly swallowed, and this simple act, as the sequel will show, materially affected her whole future life.

The meeting between mother and child was one of unmixed rapture, and for the moment all the past was forgotten. The loving mother's happiness would now have been complete had not Hades asserted his rights. These were that if any immortals were to eat food in his realms, they were bound to remain there forever. Of course the ruler of the lower world had to prove this assertion. This, however, he found no difficulty in doing, as Ascalaphus, the son of Acheron and Orphne, was his witness to the fact.[19]

19 Some versions of the tale say that Demeter transformed Ascalaphus into an owl for revealing the secret. Others say she trapped him under a rock.

Zeus, pitying the disappointment of Demeter at finding her hopes thus blighted, succeeded in effecting a compromise by inducing his brother Hades to allow Persephone to spend six months of the year with the gods above, whilst during the other six she was to be the joyless companion of her grim lord below. Accompanied by her daughter, the beautiful Persephone, Demeter now resumed her long-abandoned dwelling in Olympus; the sympathetic earth responded gaily to her bright smiles; the corn at once sprang forth from the ground in fullest plenty; the trees, which as of late were sered and bare, now donned their brightest emerald robes; and the flowers, so long imprisoned in the hard, dry soil, filled the whole air with their fragrant perfume. Thus ends this charming story, which was a favorite theme with all the classic authors.

It is very possible that the poets who first created this graceful myth merely intended it as an allegory to illustrate the change of seasons; in the course of time, however, a literal meaning became attached to this and similar poetical fancies, and thus the people of Greece came to regard it as an article of religious belief what, in the first instance, may have been nothing more than a poetic simile.

The ELEUSINIAN MYSTERIES

OPPOSITE: ***Votive relief to Demeter and Kore*, 400–425 BC. Reliefs like this were placed at altars to the gods. This one features Demeter (sitting), and her daughter Kore, who was an essential deity associated with the Eleusinian Mysteries**

In the temple erected to Demeter at Eleusis, the famous Eleusinian Mysteries were instituted by the goddess herself. It is exceedingly difficult, as in the case of all secret societies, to discover anything with certainty concerning these sacred rites. The most plausible supposition is that the doctrines taught by the priests to the favored few whom they initiated were religious truths that were deemed unfit for the uninstructed mind of the multitudes. For instance, it is supposed that the myth of Demeter and Persephone was explained by the teachers of the Mysteries to signify that temporary loss that mother-earth sustains every year when the icy breath of winter robs her of her flowers and fruits and grain.

It is believed that in later times a still deeper meaning was conveyed by this beautiful myth, that is, the doctrine of the immortality of the soul. The grain, that, as it were, remains dead for a time in the dark earth, only to rise one day dressed in a newer and lovelier garb, was supposed to symbolize the soul, that, after death, frees itself from corruption, to live again under a better and purer form.

When Demeter instituted the Eleusinian Mysteries, Celeus and his family were the first to be initiated, Celeus himself being appointed high-priest. His son Triptolemus and his

daughters, who acted as priestesses, assisted him in the duties of his sacred office. The Mysteries were celebrated by the Athenians every five years, and were, for a long time, their exclusive privilege. They took place by torchlight, and were conducted with the greatest solemnity.

In order to spread abroad the blessings that agriculture confers, Demeter presented Triptolemus with her chariot drawn by winged dragons, and, giving him some grains of corn, desired him to journey through the world, teaching mankind the arts of agriculture and husbandry.

STELLIO *and* ERESICTHON

Demeter exercised great severity towards those who incurred her displeasure. We find examples of this in the stories of Stellio and Eresicthon. Stellio was a youth who ridiculed the goddess for the eagerness in which she was eating a bowl of porridge, when weary and faint in the vain search for her daughter. Resolved that he should never again have an opportunity of thus offending, she angrily threw into his face the remainder of the food, and changed him into a spotted lizard.

Eresicthon, son of Triopas, drew upon himself the anger of Demeter by cutting down her sacred groves, for which she punished him with a constant and insatiable hunger. He sold all his possessions in order to satisfy his cravings, and was forced at last to devour his own limbs. His daughter Metra, who was devotedly attached to him, possessed the power of transforming herself into a variety of different animals. By this means she contrived to support her father, who sold her again and again each time she assumed a different form, and thus he dragged on a pitiful existence.

The ROMAN CERES

The Roman Ceres is actually the Greek Demeter under another name, her attributes, worship, festivals, and so forth being precisely identical. The Romans were indebted to Sicily for this divinity, her worship having been introduced by the Greek colonists who settled there.

The Cerealia, or festivals in honor of Ceres, commenced on the 12th of April, and lasted several days.

Ceres Turning a Boy into a Lizard, Antonio Tempesta, 1606. Demeter transforms Stellio into a lizard to punish him for making fun of her for eating too quickly.

APHRODITE § VENUS

Aphrodite (from *aphros*, "sea-foam," and *dite*, "issued"), was the Goddess of Love and Beauty. As she was the most beautiful of the goddesses, the gods all vied with each other in aspiring to the honor of her lovely hand, but Hephæstus became the envied possessor of her hand in marriage when she was given to him by Zeus, as a gift in thanks for forging his thunderbolts. The marriage brought much unhappiness, owing to the preference Aphrodite showed at various times for some of the other gods and also for mortal men.

Aphrodite was the mother of Eros (Cupid), the God of Love, who she had with Ares (Mars). She was also the mother of Æneas (with the mortal Anchises), the great Trojan hero and the head of the Greek colony that settled in Italy that became the city of Rome. As a mother Aphrodite claims our sympathy for the tenderness she exhibits towards her children. Homer tells us in his *Iliad*, how, when Æneas was wounded in battle, she came to his assistance, regardless of personal danger, and was herself severely wounded in attempting to save his life.

The celebrated *Venus de Milo*, now in the Louvre museum, is an exquisite statue of this divinity. The head is beautifully formed; the rich waves of hair descend on her rather low, but broad forehead and are caught up gracefully in a small knot at the back of her head; the expression on her face is most bewitching, and bespeaks the perfect joyousness of a happy nature combined with the dignity of a goddess; the drapery falls in careless folds from the waist downwards; and her whole attitude is the embodiment of all that is graceful and lovely in womanhood. She is of medium height, and the form is perfect in its symmetry and faultless proportions.

***Aphrodite*, 400–1 BCE. Because of her beauty, Aphrodite has been a favorite subject of artists through the ages, including the unknown sculptor who crafted this statue out of bronze.**

Aphrodite is also frequently represented in the act of confining her dripping locks in a knot, whilst her attendant nymphs envelop her in a gauzy veil. Her usual attendants are the Charites or Graces (Euphrosyne, Aglaia, and Thalia), who are represented undraped and intertwined in a loving embrace.

The animals sacred to her were the dove, swan, swallow, and sparrow. Her favorite plants were the myrtle, apple tree, rose, and poppy.

***Venus Disarming Cupid,* Alessandro Allori, c. 1570. In Roman mythology, Eros (Cupid) was said to be Aphrodite's messenger, and not necessarily her son.**

Aphrodite possessed a magic girdle (the famous cestus) that she frequently lent to unhappy maidens suffering from the pangs of unrequited love, as it was endowed with the power of inspiring affection for the wearer, whom it invested with every attribute of grace, beauty, and fascination.

THE BIRTH *of* APHRODITE

In Hesiod's *Theogony* Aphrodite is supposed to belong to the more ancient divinities, and, whilst those of later date are represented as having descended one from another, and all more or less from Zeus, Aphrodite has a variously accounted for, yet independent origin.

Some myths say she was the daughter of Zeus and a sea-nymph called Dione, who gave birth to her beneath the waves; but the child of the heaven-inhabiting Zeus was forced to ascend from the ocean-depths and mount the snow-capped summits of Olympus in order to breathe that ethereal and most refined atmosphere that pertains to the celestial gods.

The most poetical version of her birth, however, is that when Uranus was wounded by his son Cronus, his blood mingled with the foam of the sea, whereupon the bubbling waters at once assumed a rosy tint, and from their depths arose, in all the surpassing glory of her loveliness, Aphrodite, Goddess of Love and Beauty!

Shaking her long, fair tresses, the water-drops rolled down into the beautiful seashell in which she stood, and became transformed into pure glistening pearls. Wafted by the soft and balmy breezes, she floated on to Cythera, and was thence transported to the island of Cyprus. Lightly she stepped on shore, and under the gentle pressure of her delicate foot the dry and rigid sand became transformed into a verdant meadow, where every varied shade of color and every sweet odor charmed the senses. The whole island of Cyprus became clothed with verdure, and greeted this fairest of all created beings with a glad smile of friendly welcome.

Here she was received by the Horæ (Seasons), who decked her with garments of immortal fabric, encircling her fair brow with a wreath of purest gold, whilst from her ears depended costly rings, and a glittering chain embraced her swan-like throat. And now, arrayed in all the panoply of her irresistible charms, the nymphs escorted her to the dazzling halls of Olympus, where she was received with ecstatic enthusiasm by the admiring gods and goddesses.

***Venus Reclining on a Sea Monster with Cupid and Putto*, John Deare, 1787. Being from the sea herself, Aphrodite often intermingled with sea divinities.**

APHRODITE and ADONIS

Aphrodite was most tenderly attached to a lovely youth, called Adonis, whose exquisite beauty has become proverbial. He was a motherless babe, and Aphrodite, taking pity on him, placed him in a chest and entrusted him to the care of Persephone, who became so fond of the beautiful youth that she refused to part with him. Zeus, being appealed to by the rival foster-mothers, decided that Adonis should spend four months of every year with Persephone, four with Aphrodite, whilst during the remaining four months he should be left to his own devices. He became, however, so attached to Aphrodite that he voluntarily devoted to her the time at his own disposal.

Adonis was killed, during the chase, by a wild boar, to the great grief of Aphrodite, who bemoaned his loss so persistently that Hades, moved with pity, permitted him to pass six months of every year with her, whilst the remaining half of the year was spent by him in the lower world.

Venus and Adonis, **Abraham Bloemaert, 1632. Aphrodite begs Adonis not to go on the boar hunt that will kill him.**

The ROMAN VENUS

The Venus of the Romans was identified with the Aphrodite of the Greeks. The worship of this divinity was only established in Rome in comparatively later times. Annual festivals, called Veneralia, were held in her honor, and the month of April, when flowers and plants spring forth afresh, was sacred to her. She was also worshipped as Venus Cloacina (or the Purifier), and as Venus Myrtea (or the Myrtle Goddess), an epithet derived from the myrtle, the emblem of Love.

HELIOS § SOL

Helios, who was the son of the Titans Hyperion and Theia, was the God of the Sun. He is described as rising every morning in the east, preceded by his sister Eos (the Dawn), driving his flame-darting chariot along the accustomed track. This chariot, which was of burnished gold, was drawn by four fire-breathing steeds, behind which the young god stood erect with flashing eyes, his head surrounded with rays, holding in one hand the reins of those fiery coursers that in all hands save his were unmanageable. When toward evening he descended the curve[20] in order to cool his burning forehead in the waters of the deep sea, he was followed closely by his sister Selene (the Moon), who was then prepared to take charge of the world, and illumine with her silver crescent the dusky night. Helios, meanwhile, rested from his labors, and, reclining softly on the cool fragrant couch prepared for him by the sea-nymphs, recruited himself for another life-giving, joy-inspiring, and beauteous day.

Some poets state that when Helios had finished his course, a winged-boat, or cup, that had been made for him by Hephæstus awaited him there, and conveyed him rapidly, with his glorious equipage, to the east, where he recommenced his bright and glowing career.

The worship of Helios was introduced into Greece from Asia. According to the earliest conceptions of the Greeks, Helios was not only the Sun God, but also the personification of life and all life-giving power, for light is well-known to be an indispensable condition of all healthy terrestrial life.

This divinity was invoked as a witness when a solemn oath was taken, as it was believed that nothing escaped his all-seeing eye, and it was this fact that enabled him to inform Demeter of the fate of her daughter Persephone. He was said to possess flocks of

20 The course that the sun ran was considered by the ancients to be a rising and descending arc, the center of which was supposed to be reached by Helios at mid-day.

SOL

birds and herds of livestock in various localities, which may possibly be intended to represent the days and nights of the year, or the stars of heaven.

Helios married Perse, daughter of Oceanus, and their children were Aëtes, king of Colchis (celebrated as the possessor of the Golden Fleece), and Circe, the renowned sorceress.

CLYTIE *the* FLOWER

Helios was in love with Clytie, another daughter of Oceanus, who ardently returned his affection; but in the course of time the fickle Sun God transferred his devotion to Leucothea, the daughter of Orchamus, king of the eastern countries. This so angered the forsaken Clytie that she informed Orchamus of his daughter's attachment, and he punished Leucothea by inhumanly burying her alive. Helios, overcome with grief, endeavored by every means in his power to recall her to life. At last, finding all his efforts unavailing, he sprinkled her grave with heavenly nectar, and immediately there sprang forth from the spot a shoot of frankincense, which spread around its aromatic perfume.

Sol, Hendrik Goltzius, 1592. In ancient times, Helios's name was often invoked when a solemn oath was taken, as it was believed that he could see all.

The jealous Clytie gained nothing by her cruel conduct, for the Sun God came to her no more. Inconsolable at his loss, she threw herself upon the ground, and refused all sustenance. For nine long days she turned her face towards the glorious God of Day, as he moved along the heavens, till at length her limbs became rooted in the ground, and she was transformed into a flower that ever turns towards the sun.

PHAETHON *and the* CHARIOT *of the* SUN

In addition to his children with Perse, Helios had another son named Phaethon, whose mother was Clymene, one of the Oceanides. The youth was very beautiful, and a great favorite of Aphrodite, who entrusted him with the care of one of her temples. The flattering proof of her regard caused him to become very vain and presumptuous. So his friend Epaphus, son of Zeus and Io, endeavored to check his youthful vanity by pretending to disbelieve his assertion that the Sun God was his father.

Phaethon, full of resentment, and eager to be able to refute the slander, hastened to his mother Clymene, and besought her to tell him whether Helios was really his father. Moved by his entreaties, and at the same time angry at the reproach of Epaphus, Clymene pointed to the glorious sun, then shining down upon them, and assured her son that in that bright orb he beheld the author of his being, adding that if he had still any doubt, he might visit the radiant dwelling of the great God of Light and inquire for himself. Overjoyed at his mother's reassuring words, and following the directions she gave him, Phaethon quickly wended his way to his father's palace.

As he entered the palace of the Sun God, the dazzling rays almost blinded him, and prevented him from approaching the throne on which his father was seated, surrounded by the Hours, Days, Months, Years, and Seasons. Helios, who with his all-seeing eye had watched him from afar, removed his crown of glittering rays, and bade him not to be afraid, but to draw near to his father. Encouraged by this kind reception, Phaethon entreated him to bestow upon him such a proof of his love, that all the world might be convinced that he was indeed his son; whereupon Helios desired him to ask any favor he pleased, and swore by the Styx that it should be granted. The impetuous youth immediately requested permission to drive the chariot of the sun for one whole day.

His father listened horror-struck to this presumptuous demand, and by representing the many dangers that would beset his path, endeavored to dissuade him from so perilous an undertaking; but his son, deaf to all advice, pressed his point with such pertinacity, that Helios was reluctantly compelled to lead him to the chariot.

Phaethon paused for a moment to admire the beauty of the glittering equipage, the gift of the God of Fire, who had formed it of gold, and ornamented it with precious stones that reflected the rays of the sun. And now Helios, seeing his sister, the Dawn, opening her doors in the rosy east, ordered the Hours to yoke the horses. The goddesses speedily obeyed the command, and the father then anointed the face of his son with a sacred balm, to enable him to endure the burning flames that issued from the nostrils of the steeds, and sorrowfully placing his crown of rays upon his head, allowed him to ascend the chariot.

Basalt Relief with the Head of Helios, 300–100 BCE. Helios's hair forms a sun-like crown in this ancient relief.

The eager youth joyfully took his place and grasped the coveted reins, but no sooner did the fiery coursers of the sun feel the inexperienced hand that attempted to guide them, than they became restive and unmanageable. Wildly they rushed out of their accustomed track, now soaring so high as to threaten the heavens with destruction, now descending so low as nearly to set the earth on fire. At last the unfortunate charioteer, blinded with the glare, and terrified at the awful devastation he had caused, dropped the reins from his trembling hands. Mountains and forests were in flames, rivers and streams were dried up, and a general conflagration was imminent.

Jupiter and the Other Gods Asking Helios to Resume Control of the Chariot, **Hendrik Goltzius, 1590. After Helios lets his son Phaethon drive his sun chariot, disaster causes Zeus (Jupiter) and the other gods to beg him to take back the reins.**

The scorched earth now called on Zeus for help, who hurled his thunderbolt at Phaethon, and with a flash of lightning brought the fiery steeds to a standstill. The lifeless body of the youth fell headlong into the river Eridanus,[21] where it was received and buried by the nymphs of the stream. His sisters mourned so long for him that they were transformed by Zeus into poplars, and the tears they shed, falling into the waters, became drops of clear, transparent amber.

Cycnus, the faithful friend of the unhappy Phaethon, felt such overwhelming grief at his terrible fate that he pined and wasted away. The gods, moved with compassion, transformed him into a swan, which forever brooded over the fatal spot where the waters had closed over the head of his unfortunate friend.

The COLOSSUS of RHODES

The chief seat of the worship of Helios was the island of Rhodes, which according to the following myth was his special territory. At the time of the Titanomachia, when the gods

21 Also called the river Po.

were dividing the world by lot, Helios happened to be absent, and consequently received no share. He, therefore, complained to Zeus, who proposed to have a new allotment, but this Helios would not allow, saying that as he pursued his daily journey, his penetrating eye had beheld a lovely, fertile island lying beneath the waves of the ocean, and that if the immortals would swear to give him the undisturbed possession of this spot, he would be content to accept it as his share of the universe. The gods took the oath, whereupon the island of Rhodes immediately raised itself above the surface of the waters.

The famous Colossus of Rhodes, which was one of the Seven Wonders of the World, was erected in honor of Helios. This wonderful statue was 105 feet high, and was formed entirely of brass; it formed the entrance to the harbor at Rhodes, and the largest vessel could easily sail between the legs, which stood on piers on each side of the harbor. Though so gigantic, it was perfectly proportioned in every part. Some idea of its size may be gained from the fact that very few people were able to span the thumb of this statue with their arms. In the interior of the Colossus was a winding staircase leading to the top, from the summit of which, by means of a telescope, the coast of Syria, and also the shores of Egypt, are said to have been visible.[22]

SELENE ∫ LUNA

OPPOSITE: *Selene and Endymion*, Ubaldo Gandolfi, c. 1770. Each night, Selene watched over a young shepherd named Endymion, who was blessed with beauty and eternal youth.

Just as Helios personified the sun, so his sister Selene represented the moon, and was supposed to drive her chariot across the sky whilst her brother was reposing after the toils of the day.

When the shades of evening began to enfold the earth, the two milk-white steeds of Selene rose out of the mysterious depths of Oceanus. Seated in a silvery chariot, and accompanied by her daughter Herse, the Goddess of the Dew, appeared the mild and gentle queen of the night, with a crescent on her fair brow, a gauzy veil flowing behind, and a lighted torch in her hand.

Selene greatly admired a beautiful young shepherd named Endymion, to whom Zeus had accorded the privilege of eternal youth, combined with the faculty of sleeping whenever he desired, and as long as he wished. Seeing this lovely youth fast asleep on Mount Latmus, Selene was so struck with his beauty, that she came down every night from heaven to watch over and protect him.

22 This great work of antiquity was destroyed by an earthquake fifty-six years after its erection, 256 BCE. The fragments remained on the ground for many centuries, until Rhodes was conquered by the Turks, and they were eventually sold by one of the generals of Caliph Othman IV to a merchant of Emesa in 672 BCE.

EOS § AURORA

Eos, the Dawn, like her brother Helios, whose advent she always announced, was also deified by the early Greeks. She too had her own chariot that she drove across the vast horizon both morning and night, before and after the Sun God. Wrapping around herself the rich folds of her violet-tinged mantle, she left her couch before the break of day, and herself yoked her two horses, Lampetus and Phaethon, to her glorious chariot. She then hastened with active cheerfulness to open the gates of heaven, in order to herald the approach of her brother, the God of Day, whilst the tender plants and flowers, revived by the morning dew, lifted their heads to welcome her as she passed.

With her rosy fingers, Eos painted the tips of the mountains, and drew aside that misty veil through which her brother was about to appear. Hence she was not merely the personification of the rosy morn, but also of twilight, for which reason her palace was placed in the west, on the island Ææa.

OPPOSITE: **Eos so loved Tithonus that she obtained for him the gift of eternal life from Zeus. However, she neglected to ask for eternal youth, too, and when Thithonus aged she left him—or by some accounts, turned him into a cricket.**
BELOW: ***Aurora*, Giovanni Girolamo Frezza, 1704. Like most goddesses known for their beauty, Eos is often portrayed partially undraped.**

The abode of Eos was a magnificent structure, surrounded by flowery meads and velvety lawns, where nymphs and other immortal beings wind in and out in the mazy figures of the dance, whilst the music of a sweetly tuned melody accompanied their graceful, gliding movements.

Eos is described by the poets as a beautiful maiden with rosy arms and fingers, and large wings, whose plumage is of an ever-changing hue; she bears a star on her forehead, and a torch in her hand.

***Aurora*, Guido Reni, c. 1845–1855. Eos (far right) precedes her brother Helios, the God of Day, in the sky each morning.**

Eos first married the Titan Astræus,[23] and their children were Heosphorus (Hesperus), the evening star, and the Winds. She afterward became united to Tithonus, son of Laomedon, king of Troy.

EOS and TITHONUS

Tithonus, her true love, won her affection by his unrivaled beauty. Eos, unhappy at the thought of their being ever separated by death, obtained for him from Zeus the gift of immortality, forgetting, however, to add to it that of eternal youth. The consequence was that when, in the course of time, Tithonus grew old and decrepit, and lost all the beauty that had won her admiration, Eos became disgusted with his infirmities, and at last shut him up in a chamber, where soon little else was left of him but his voice, which had now sunk into a weak, feeble quaver. According to some of the later poets, he became so weary of his cheerless and miserable existence that he begged to be allowed to die. This was, however, impossible; but Eos, pitying his unhappy condition, exerted her divine power, and changed him into a grasshopper, that is, as it were, all voice, and whose monotonous, ceaseless chirpings may not inaptly be compared to the meaningless babble of extreme old age.

23 According to some authorities, Strymon.

APOLLO

Apollo, also known as Phœbus-Apollo, was the God of Light, Prophecy, Music, Poetry, and the Arts and Sciences, and is by far the noblest conception within the whole range of Greek mythology. His worship, which not only extended to all the states of Greece, but also to Asia Minor and to every Greek colony throughout the world, stands out among the most ancient and strongly marked features of Grecian history, and exerted a more decided influence over the Greek nation, than that of any other deity, not excepting Zeus himself.

Apollo was the God of Light in a twofold signification: first, as representing the great orb of day that illumines the world; and secondly, as the heavenly light that animates the soul of man. He inherited his function as Sun God from Helios, with whom in later times he was so completely identified that the personality of the one became gradually merged in that of the other. We, accordingly, find Helios frequently confounded with Apollo, myths belonging to the former attributed to the latter; and with some tribes—the Ionic, for instance—so complete is this identification that Apollo is called by them Helios-Apollo.

As the divinity whose power was developed in the broad light of day, Apollo brought joy and delight to nature, and health and prosperity to man. By the influence of his warm and gentle rays, he dispersed the noxious vapors of the night, and assisted the grain to ripen and the flowers to bloom.

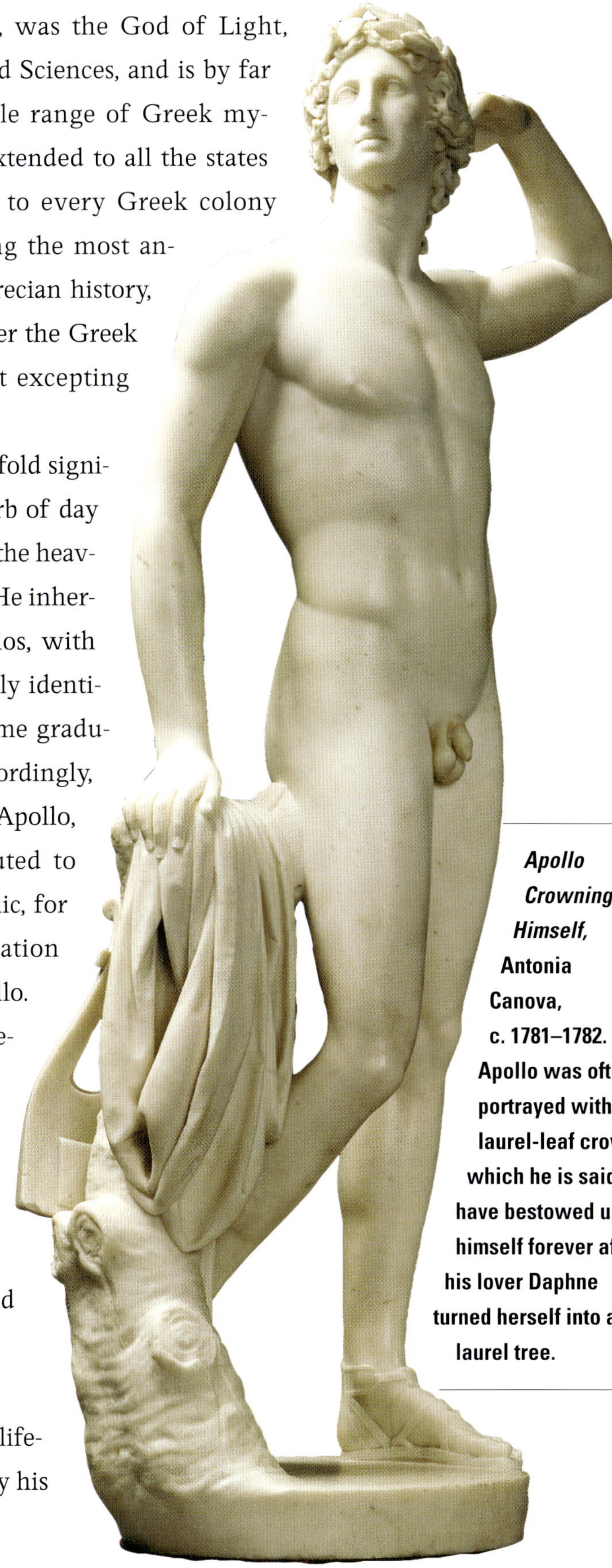

Apollo Crowning Himself, **Antonia Canova, c. 1781–1782. Apollo was often portrayed with a laurel-leaf crown, which he is said to have bestowed upon himself forever after his lover Daphne turned herself into a laurel tree.**

But although as God of the Sun he was a life-giving and life-preserving power, who, by his

Soleil

genial influence, dispelled the cold of winter, he was, at the same time, the god who, by means of his fiercely darting rays, could spread disease and send sudden death to men and animals; and it is to this phase of his character that we must look for the explanation of his being considered, in conjunction with his twin sister, Artemis (as Moon Goddess), a divinity of death. The brother and sister share this function between them, he taking man and she woman as her aim, and those especially who died in the bloom of youth, or at an advanced age, were believed to have been killed by their gentle arrows. But Apollo did not always send an easy death. We see in the *Iliad* how, when angry with the Greeks, the "God of the Silver Bow" strode down from Olympus, with his quiver full of death-bringing darts, and sent a raging pestilence into their camp. For nine days he let fly his fatal arrows, first on animals and then on men, till the air became darkened with the smoke from the funeral pyres.

OPPOSITE: ***Apollo, or the Sun Rising*, Jacque-Fabien Gautier Dagoty, 1743. Apollo inherited his role as Sun God from Helios.**

BELOW: Greek Tetradrachm with Antiochus I, c. 281–261 BCE. Apollo sits upon the *omphalos*, the symbolic center of the Oracle at Delphi, on the back of this coin issued by the Seleucid dynasty.

In his character as God of Light, Apollo is the protecting deity of shepherds, because it is he who warmed the fields and meadows, and gave rich pastures to the flocks, thereby gladdening the hearts of the herdsman.

Wolves and hawks were sacrificed to Apollo, and the birds sacred to him were the hawk, raven, and swan.

Apollo is represented by the poets as being eternally young; his face, glowing with joyous life, is the embodiment of immortal beauty; his eyes are of a deep blue; his forehead low, but broad and intellectual; his hair, which falls over his shoulders in long waving locks, is of a golden, or warm chestnut hue. He is crowned with laurel, and wears a purple robe; in his hand he bears his silver bow, which is unbent when he smiles, but ready for use when he menaces evil-doers.

Sadly, Apollo, the eternally beautiful youth, the perfection of all that is graceful and refined, rarely seemed to have been happy in love; either his advances met with a repulse, or his union with the object of his affection was attended with fatal consequences.

The renowned singer Orpheus was the son of Apollo and Calliope, the muse of epic poetry, and, as might be expected with parents so highly gifted, was endowed with most distinguished intellectual qualifications.

The BIRTH of APOLLO

Apollo was the son of Zeus and Leto, and was born beneath the shade of a palm tree that grew at the foot of Mount Cynthus, on the barren and rocky island of Delos. The poets tell us that the earth smiled when the young god first beheld the light of day, and that Delos became so proud and exultant at the honor thus conferred upon her that she covered herself with golden flowers; swans surrounded the island, and the Delian nymphs celebrated his birth with songs of joy.

The unhappy Leto, driven to Delos by the relentless persecutions of Hera, was not long permitted to enjoy her haven of refuge. Being still tormented by her enemy, the young mother was once more obliged to fly; she therefore resigned the charge of her newborn babe to the goddess Themis, who carefully wrapped the helpless infant in swaddling clothes, and fed him with nectar and ambrosia; but he had no sooner partaken of the heavenly food than, to the amazement of the goddess, he burst asunder the bands that confined his infant limbs, and springing to his feet, appeared before her as a full-grown youth of divine strength and beauty. He now demanded a lyre and a bow, declaring that henceforth he would announce to mankind the will of his father Zeus. "The golden lyre," said he, "shall be my friend, the bent bow my delight, and in oracles will I foretell the dark future." With these words he ascended to Olympus, where he was received with joyful acclamations into the assembly of the celestial gods, who acknowledged him as the most beautiful and glorious of all the sons of Zeus.

OPPOSITE: *Apollo and the Muses on Mount Parnasses*, George Sigmund and Johann Facius, 1794. Apollo was the God of Music and leader of the Muses.

The GOD of MUSIC

Apollo, being the God of Light, was responsible for the first beams of his genial light, which awoke all of nature to renewed life, and the woods echoed with the jubilant sound warbled by thousands of feathered choristers. Hence, by a natural inference, Apollo was also the God of Music as well as the God of Poetry, and acted as the special patron of the arts and sciences.

Apollo was the heavenly musician among the Olympic gods, whose banquets were gladdened by the wondrous strains that he produced from his favorite instrument, the seven-stringed lyre. In the cultus of Apollo, music formed a distinguishing feature. All sacred dances, and even the sacrifices in his honor, were performed to the sound of musical instruments; and it is, in a great measure, owing to the influence that the music in his worship that Apollo came to be regarded as the leader of the nine Muses, the legitimate divinities of poetry and song. In this character he is called Musagetes, and is always rep-

resented robed in a long flowing garment; his lyre, to the tones of which he appears to be singing, is suspended by a band across the chest; his head is encircled by a wreath of laurel; and his long hair, streaming down over his shoulders, gives him a somewhat effeminate appearance.

The ORACLE of DELPHI

All the other functions and attributes of Apollo sink into comparative insignificance before the great power that he exercised as God of Prophecy. It is true that all Greek gods were endowed, to a certain extent, with the faculty of foretelling future events; but Apollo, as Sun God, was the concentration of all prophetic power, as it was supposed that nothing escaped his all-seeing eye that penetrated the most hidden recesses, and laid bare the secrets that lay concealed behind the dark veil of the future.

The chief seat of the worship of Apollo was at Delphi, and here was the most magnificent of all his temples, the foundation of which reached far beyond all historical knowl-

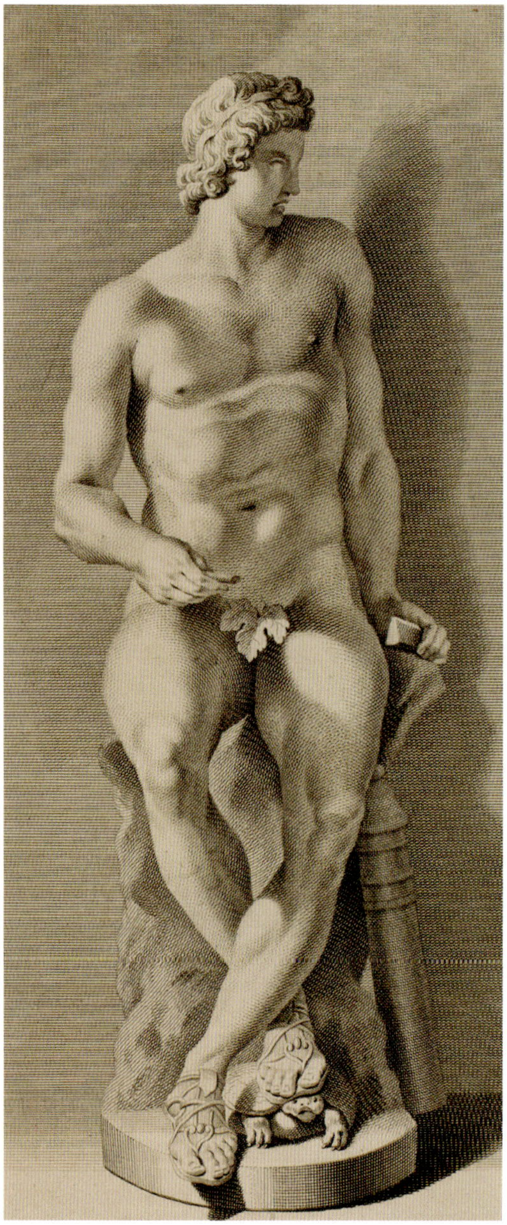

***Apollo*, Johan Martin Preisler, c. 1715–1794. Here Apollo is seen with his foot on a tortoise, perhaps because it was said that the first lyre, Apollo's sacred instrument, was made from a tortoise shell.**

edge, and that contained immense riches: the offerings of kings and private persons who had received favorable replies from the oracle. The Greeks believed Delphi to be the central point of the Earth, because two eagles sent forth by Zeus, one from the east, the other from the west, were said to have arrived there at the same moment.

The Pythian games, celebrated in honor of the victory of Apollo over the Python, took place at Delphi every four years. At the first celebration of these games, gods, goddesses, and heroes contended for the prizes, which were at first of gold or silver, but consisted, in later times, of simple laurel wreaths.

The founding of Apollo's oracle of Delphi has its own legend. Once Apollo assumed his god-like form, he took his place among the immortals; but he had not long enjoyed the rapturous delights of Olympus before he felt within him an ardent desire to fulfil his great mission of interpreting to mankind the will of his mighty father, Zeus. He accordingly descended to Earth, and traveled through many countries, seeking a fitting site upon which to establish an oracle. At length he reached the southern side of the rocky heights of Parnassus, beneath which lay the harbor of Crissa. Here, under the overhanging cliff, he found a secluded spot, where, from the most ancient times, there had existed an oracle, in which Gæa herself had revealed the future to man, and which, in Deucalion's time, she had resigned to Themis. It was guarded by the huge serpent Python, the scourge of the surrounding neighborhood, and the terror alike of men and cattle. The young god, full of confidence in his unerring aim, attacked and slew the monster with his arrows, thus freeing land and people from their mighty enemy.

The grateful inhabitants, anxious to do honor to their deliverer, flocked round Apollo, who proceeded to mark out a plan for a temple, and, with the assistance of numbers of eager volunteers, a suitable edifice was soon erected. It now became necessary to choose ministers, who would offer up sacrifices, interpret his prophecies to the people, and take charge of the temple. Looking round, he saw in the far distance a vessel bound from Crete to the Peloponnesus, and determined to avail himself of her crew for his service.

Assuming the shape of an enormous dolphin, he agitated the waters to such a degree that the ship was tossed violently to and fro, to the great alarm of the mariners; at the same time he raised a mighty wind that drove the ship into the harbor of Crissa, where she ran aground. The terrified sailors dared not set foot on shore; but Apollo, under the form of a vigorous youth, stepped down to the vessel, revealed himself in his true character, and informed them that it was he who had driven them to Crissa, in order that they might become his priests, and serve him in his temple.

Arrived at the sacred fane, he instructed them how to perform the services in his honor, and desired them to worship him under the name of Apollo-Delphinios, because he had first appeared to them under the form of a dolphin. Thus was established the far-famed oracle of Delphi, the only institution of the kind that was not exclusively national, for it was consulted by Lydians, Phrygians, Etruscans, and Romans, and, in fact, was held in the highest repute all over the world. In obedience to its decrees, the laws of Lycurgus were introduced, and the earliest Greek colonies founded. No cities were built without first consulting the Delphic oracle, for it was believed that Apollo took special delight in the founding of cities, the first stone of which he laid in person; nor was any enterprise ever undertaken, without inquiring at this sacred fane as to its probable success.

The Lansdowne Throne of Apollo, c. 50–100 CE. This marble throne is similar to one Apollo may have had at Delphi. Carved into it are Apollo's signature bow and quiver with arrows, along with a snake that may represent Python, the guardian of the Oralce at Delphi.

But that which brought Apollo more closely home to the hearts of the Greeks was the belief, gradually developed alongside their belief in morality, that Apollo was the god who accepted repentance as an atonement for sin, who pardoned the contrite sinner, and who acted as the special protector of those who had committed a crime that required long years of atonement. One such famous tale is that of Orestes, as relayed on pages 262–263.

The LOVES of APOLLO

Apollo's first love was Daphne (daughter of Peneus, the River God), who was so averse to marriage that she entreated her father to allow her to lead a life of celibacy, and devote herself to the hunt, which she loved to the exclusion of all other pursuits.

But one day, soon after his victory over the Python, Apollo happened to see Eros bending his bow, and proud of his own superior strength and skill, he laughed at the efforts of the little archer, saying that such a weapon was more suited to the one who had just killed the terrible serpent. Eros angrily replied that his arrow should pierce the heart of the mocker himself, and flying off to the summit of Mount Parnassus, he drew from his quiver two darts of different workmanship—one of gold, which had the effect of inspiring love; the other of lead, which created aversion. Taking aim at Apollo, he pierced his breast with the golden shaft, whilst the leaden one he discharged into the bosom of the beautiful Daphne.

Detail from *L'Épître Othéa*, attributed to the Master of the Cité des Dames and workshop, c. 1410–1414. Apollo fell in love with the nymph Daphne thanks to Eros's bow, but she turned into a laurel tree as soon as he embraced her.

Apollo instantly felt the most ardent affection for the nymph, who displayed such great dislike towards Apollo that, at his approach, fled from him like a hunted deer. He called upon her in the most endearing accents to stay, but she still sped on, until at length, becoming faint with fatigue, and fearing that she was about to succumb, she called upon the gods to come to her aid.

Hardly had she uttered her prayer before a heavy torpor seized her limbs, and just as Apollo threw out his arms to embrace her, she became transformed into a laurel bush. He sorrowfully crowned his head with its leaves, and declared that in memory of his love it should henceforth remain evergreen, and be held sacred to him.

He next sought the love of Marpessa, the daughter of Evenus; but though her father approved, the maiden preferred a youth named Idas, who contrived to carry her off in a winged chariot that he had procured from Poseidon. Apollo pursued the fugitives, whom he quickly overtook, and forcibly seizing the bride, refused to resign her. Zeus then interfered, and declared that Marpessa herself must decide which of her lovers should claim her as his wife. After due reflection she accepted Idas as her husband, judiciously concluding that although the attractions of the divine Apollo were superior to those of her lover, it would be wiser to unite herself to a mortal, who, growing old with herself, would be less likely to forsake her, when advancing years should rob her of her charms.

Cassandra, daughter of Priam, king of Troy, was another object of the love of Apollo. She pretended to return his affections, and promised to marry him, provided he would confer upon her the gift of prophecy; but having received the boon she desired, the treacherous maiden refused to comply with the conditions upon which it had been granted. Incensed at her breach of faith, Apollo, unable to recall the gift he had bestowed, rendered it useless by causing her predictions to fail in obtaining credence.

Cassandra became famous in history for her prophetic powers, but her prophecies were never believed. For instance, she warned her brother Paris that if he brought back a wife from Greece he would cause the destruction of his father's house and kingdom; she also warned the Trojans not to admit the wooden horse within the walls of the city, and foretold to Agamemnon all the disasters that afterward befell him.

APOLLO *the* SHEPHERD

Apollo eventually married Coronis, a nymph of Larissa, and thought himself happy in the possession of her faithful love; but once more he was doomed to disappointment, for one day his favorite bird, the crow, flew to him with the intelligence that his wife had transferred her affections to a youth of Haemonia. Apollo, burning with rage, instantly destroyed her with one of his death-bringing darts. Too late he repented of his rashness, for she had been tenderly beloved by him, and he would fain have recalled her to life; but, although he exerted all his healing powers, his efforts were in vain. He punished the crow for its garrulity by changing the color of its plumage from pure white to intense black, and forbade it to fly any longer among the other birds.

Coronis left an infant son named Asclepius, who afterwards became God of Medicine. His powers were so extraordinary that he could not only cure the sick, but could even restore the dead to life. At last Hades complained to Zeus that the number of shades conducted to his dominions was daily decreasing, and the great ruler of Olympus, fearing that mankind, thus protected against sickness and death, would be able to defy the gods themselves, killed Asclepius with one of his thunderbolts. The loss of his highly gifted son so exasperated Apollo that, being unable to vent his anger on Zeus, he destroyed the Cyclops, who had forged the fatal thunderbolts. For this offence, Apollo would have been banished by Zeus to Tartarus, but at the earnest intercession of Leto he partially relented, and contented himself with depriving him of all power and dignity, and imposing on him a temporary servitude in the house of Admetus, king of Thessaly.

OPPOSITE: *Coronis and Apollo*, workshop of Adam Elsheimer, c. 1607–8. Apollo murdered his wife Coronis in a jealous rage and forever regretted his rash decision.

Apollo faithfully served his royal master for nine years in the humble capacity of a shepherd, and was treated by him with every kindness and consideration. During the period of his service the king sought the hand of Alcestis, the beautiful daughter of Pelias, son of Poseidon; but her father declared that he would only resign her to the suitor who should succeed in yoking a lion and a wild boar to his chariot. With the aid of his divine shepherd, Admetus accomplished this difficult task, and gained his bride.

This was not the only favor that the king received from the exiled god. Apollo obtained from the Fates the gift of immortality for his benefactor, on the condition that when his last hour approached, some member of his own family must be willing to die in his stead. When the fatal hour arrived, and Admetus felt that he was at the point of death, he implored his aged parents to yield to him their few remaining days. But life is sweet even to old age, and they both refused to make the sacrifice demanded of them.

Alcestis, however, who had secretly devoted herself to death for her husband, was seized with a mortal sickness that kept pace with his rapid recovery. The devoted wife breathed her last in the arms of Admetus, and he had just consigned her to the tomb, when Heracles chanced to come to the palace. Admetus held the rites of hospitality so sacred that he at first kept silence with regard to his great bereavement; but as soon as his friend heard what had occurred, he bravely descended into the tomb, and when death came to claim

his prey, he exerted his marvelous strength, and held him in his arms, until he promised to restore the beautiful and heroic queen to the bosom of her family.

HYACINTHUS and CYPARISSUS

Whilst pursuing the peaceful life of a shepherd, Apollo formed a strong friendship with two youths named Hyacinthus and Cyparissus, but the great favor shown to them by the god did not suffice to shield them from misfortune. The former was one day throwing the discus with Apollo, when, running too eagerly to take up the one thrown by the god, he was struck on the head with it and killed on the spot. Apollo was overcome with grief at the sad end of his young favorite, but being unable to restore him to life, he changed him into the flower called after him the Hyacinth.

Cyparissus, meanwhile, had the misfortune to kill by accident one of Apollo's favorite stags, which so preyed on his mind that he gradually pined away, and died of a broken heart. He was transformed by the god into a cypress tree, which owes its name to this story.

After these sad occurrences Apollo quitted Thessaly and repaired to Phrygia, in Asia Minor, where he met Poseidon, who, like himself, was in exile, and condemned to a temporary servitude on Earth. The two gods now entered the service of Laomedon, king of Troy, Apollo undertaking to tend his flocks, and Poseidon to build the walls of the city. But Apollo also contributed his assistance in the erection of those wonderful walls, and, by the aid of his marvelous musical powers, the labors of his fellow worker, Poseidon, were rendered so light and easy that his otherwise arduous task advanced with astonishing swiftness; for, as the master-hand of the God of Music grasped the cords of his lyre,[24] the huge blocks of stone moved of their own accord, adjusting themselves with the utmost nicety into the places designed for them.

APOLLO'S MUSICAL CONTESTS

But though Apollo was renowned in the art of music, there were two individuals who had the effrontery to consider themselves equal to him in this respect, and, accordingly, each challenged him to compete with him in a musical contest. They were Marsyas and Pan. Marsyas was a satyr, who, having picked up the flute that Athene had thrown away in disgust (as relayed on page 40), discovered, to his great delight and astonishment, that, in consequence of its having touched the lips of a goddess, it played of itself in the most

24 This wonderful lyre, which had been given to Apollo by Hermes (Mercury) in exchange for the Caduceus or rod of wealth, is said to have possessed such extraordinary powers that it caused a stone upon which it was laid to become so melodious that ever afterward, on being touched, it emitted a musical sound that resembled that produced by the lyre itself.

charming manner. Marsyas, who was a great lover of music, and much beloved on this account by all the elf-like denizens of the woods and glens, was so intoxicated with joy at this discovery, that he foolishly challenged Apollo to compete with him in a musical contest.

The challenge being accepted, the Muses were chosen umpires, and it was decided that the unsuccessful candidate should suffer the punishment of being flayed alive. For a long time the merits of both claimants remained so equally balanced that it was impossible to award the palm of victory to either, seeing that Apollo, resolved to conquer, had added the sweet tones of his melodious voice to the strains of his lyre, and this at once turned the scale in his favor. The unhappy Marsyas, being defeated, had to undergo the terrible penalty, and his untimely fate was universally lamented; indeed the satyrs and Dryads, his companions, wept so incessantly at his fate that their tears, uniting together, formed a river in Phrygia that was known by his name.

Detail from *L'Épître Othéa*, attributed to the Master of the Cité des Dames and workshop, c. 1410–1414. King Midas judges a musical contest between Apollo and Pan. Apollo will curse him with the ears of an ass for having the bad taste to choose Pan.

The result of the contest with Pan was by no means of so serious a character. The God of Shepherds having affirmed that he could play more skillfully on his flute of seven reeds (the syrinx or Pan's pipe), than Apollo on his world-renowned lyre, a contest ensued, in which Apollo was pronounced the victor by all the judges appointed to decide between the rival candidates. Midas, king of Phrygia, alone demurred at this decision, having the bad taste to prefer the uncouth tones of the Pan's pipe to the refined melodies of Apollo's lyre. Incensed at the obstinacy and stupidity of the Phrygian king, Apollo punished him by giving him the ears of an ass. Midas, horrified at being thus disfigured, determined to hide his disgrace from his subjects by means of a cap; his barber, however, could not be kept in ignorance of the fact, and was therefore bribed with rich gifts never to reveal it. Finding, however, that he could not keep the secret any longer, he dug a hole in the ground into which he whispered it; then closing up the aperture he returned home, feeling greatly relieved at having thus eased his mind of its burden. But after all, this very humiliating secret was revealed to the world, for some reeds that sprung up from the spot murmured incessantly as they waved to and fro in the wind: "King Midas has the ears of an ass."

THE DEATHS *of* NIOBE

In the sad and beautiful story of Niobe, daughter of Tantalus, and wife of Amphion, king of Thebes, we have another instance of the severe punishments meted out by Apollo to those who in any way incurred his displeasure. Niobe was the proud mother of seven sons and seven daughters, and exulting in the number of her children, she, upon one occasion, ridiculed the worship of Leto, because she had but one son and daughter, and desired the Thebans, for the future, to give to her the honors and sacrifices that they had hitherto offered to the mother of Apollo and Artemis.

OPPOSITE: ***Apollo Punishing Niove by Killing her Children*, Abraham Bloemaert, 1591. Apollo dealt out a harsh punished to Niobe for worshipping another god.**

The sacrilegious words had scarcely passed her lips before Apollo called upon his sister Artemis to assist him in avenging the insult offered to their mother, and soon their invisible arrows sped through the air. Apollo slew all the sons, and Artemis had already slain all the daughters save one, the youngest and best beloved, whom Niobe clasped in her arms, when the agonized mother implored the enraged deities to leave her at least one out of all her beautiful children; but, even as she prayed, the deadly arrow reached the heart of this child also. Meanwhile the unhappy father, unable to bear the loss of his children, had destroyed himself, and his dead body lay beside the lifeless corpse of his favorite son.

Widowed and childless, the heartbroken mother sat among her dead, and the gods, in pity for her unutterable woe, turned her into a stone, which they transferred to Siphylus, her native Phrygian mountain, where it still continues to shed tears.

ARTEMIS ∫ DIANA

Artemis was the daughter of Zeus and Leto, and twin sister of Apollo. She was the Goddess of Hunting and Chastity, and having obtained from her father permission to lead a life of celibacy, she ever remained a maiden divinity. Artemis was the feminine counterpart of her brother, the glorious God of Light, and like him, she dealt out destruction and sudden death to men and animals, but she was also able to alleviate suffering and cure diseases. Like Apollo, she was skilled in the use of the bow, but in a far more eminent degree. For Artemis, who devoted herself to the chase with passionate ardor, this was an all-distinguishing feature. Armed with her bow and quiver, and attended by her train of huntresses, who were nymphs of the woods and springs, she roamed over the mountains in pursuit of her favorite exercise, destroying in her course the wild animals of the forest. When the chase ended, Artemis and her maidens loved to assemble in a shady grove, or on the banks of a favorite stream, where they joined in a merry song or graceful dance and made the hills resound with their joyous shouts.

BELOW: Intaglio of Diana, Nicolo paste, c. 100–200 CE. This intaglio, made by injecting ink into a gem, shows Artemis with her bow and arrow.
OPPOSITE: *Diana*, Jacob Matham, c. 1607–1610. Though she was a fierce huntress, Artemis was also graceful, gathering with her maidens after their hunt to sing and dance.

As the divinity of purity and chastity, Artemis was especially venerated by young maidens, who, before marrying, sacrificed their hair to her. She was also the patroness of those vowed celibacy, and punished severely any infringement of their obligation.

The Huntress Goddess is represented as being a head taller than her attendant nymphs, and always appears as a youthful and slender maiden. Her features are beautiful, but wanting in gentleness of expression; her hair is gathered negligently into a knot at the back of her well-shaped head; and her figure, though somewhat masculine, is most graceful in its attitude and proportions. The short robe she wears leaves her limbs free for the exercise of the chase, her devotion to which is indicated by the quiver that is slung over her shoulder, and the bow that she bears in her hand.

There are many famous statues of this divinity; but the most celebrated is that known as the Diana

Diana.
Inuē.
Matham excu
4

Diana and Actaeon, **Jacopo del Sellaio, c. 1485. Artemis was ruthlessly cruel to anyone who crossed her. When she caught Actaeon spying on her and her maidens bathing, she turned him into a stag, and he was eaten by his dogs immediately.**

of Versailles, which forms a not unworthy companion to the Apollo-Belvedere of the Vatican. In this statue, the goddess appears in the act of rescuing a hunted deer from its pursuers, on whom she is turning with angry mien. One hand is laid protectingly on the head of the stag, whilst with the other she draws an arrow from the quiver that hangs over her shoulder.

Just as her brother Apollo drew into himself by degrees the attributes of that more ancient divinity Helios, the Sun God, so in like manner Artemis came to be identified in later times with Selene, the Moon Goddess. When in character as Selene-Artemis she is always represented as wearing on her forehead a glittering crescent, whilst a flowing veil, bespangled with stars, reaches to her feet, and a long robe completely envelops her.

Artemis's attributes are the bow, quiver, and spear. The animals sacred to her are the doe, dog, bear, and wild boar.

Artemis resented any sacrilege or intrusion upon her privacy. A remarkable instance of this is seen in the fate that befell the famous hunter Actaeon, who happening one day to see Artemis and her attendants bathing, imprudently ventured to approach the spot. The goddess, incensed at his audacity, sprinkled him with water, and transformed him into a stag, whereupon he was torn in pieces and devoured by his own dogs.

The CALYDONIAN BOAR-HUNT

Oeneus, king of Calydon in Ætolia, also incurred the displeasure of Artemis, by neglecting to include her in a general sacrifice to the gods that he had offered up out of gratitude for a bountiful harvest. The goddess, enraged at this neglect, sent a wild boar of extraordinary size and prodigious strength that destroyed the sprouting grain, laid waste to the fields, and threatened the inhabitants with famine and death. At this juncture, Meleager, the brave son of Oeneus, returned from the Argonautic expedition, and finding his country ravaged by this dreadful scourge, entreated the assistance of all the celebrated heroes of the age to join him in hunting the ferocious monster. Among the most famous of those who responded to his call were Jason, Castor and Pollux, Idas and Lynceus, Peleus, Telamon, Admetus, Perithous, and Theseus. The brothers of Althea, wife of Oeneus, joined the hunters, and Meleager also enlisted into his service the fleet-footed huntress Atalanta.

The father of this maiden was Schoeneus, an Arcadian, who, disappointed at the birth of a daughter when he had particularly desired a son, had exposed her on the Parthenian Hill, where he left her to perish. Here she was nursed by a she-bear, and at last found by some hunters, who reared her, and gave her the name of Atalanta. As the maiden grew up, she became an ardent lover of the chase, and was alike distinguished for her beauty and courage. Though often wooed, she led a life of strict celibacy, an oracle having predicted that inevitable misfortune awaited her should she give herself in marriage to any of her numerous suitors.

Many of the heroes objected to hunting in the company of a maiden; but Meleager, who loved Atalanta, overcame their opposition, and the valiant band set out on their expedition. Atalanta was the first to wound the boar with her spear, but not before two of the heroes had met their death from his fierce tusks. After a long and desperate encounter, Meleager succeeded in killing the monster, and presented the head and hide to Atalanta as trophies of the victory.

The uncles of Meleager, however, forcibly took the hide from the maiden, claiming their right to the spoil as next of kin, if Meleager resigned it. Artemis, whose anger was still unappeased, caused a violent quarrel to arise between uncles and nephew, and, in the struggle that ensued, Meleager killed his mother's brothers, and then restored the hide to Atalanta. When Althea beheld the dead bodies of her slain brothers, her grief and anger knew no bounds. She swore to revenge their deaths on her own son, and unfortunately for him, the instrument of vengeance lay ready to her hand.

OVERLEAF: *The Calydonian Boar Hunt*, Peter Paul Rubens, c. 1611–1612. Meleager spears the giant boar Artemis created, while his chaste love, the huntress Atalanta, looks on.

At the birth of Meleager, the Moirae, or Fates, had entered the house of Oeneus, and pointing to a piece of wood then burning on the hearth, declared that as soon as it was consumed the babe would surely die. On hearing this, Althea seized the brand, laid it up carefully in a chest, and henceforth preserved it as her most precious possession. But now, love for her son giving place to the resentment she felt against the murderer of her brothers, she threw the fatal brand into the devouring flames. As it consumed, the vigor of Meleager

wasted away, and when it was reduced to ashes, he expired. Repenting too late the terrible effects of her rash deed, Althea, in remorse and despair, took away her own life.

The news of the courage and intrepidity displayed by Atalanta in the famous boar-hunt being carried to the ears of her father caused him to acknowledge his long-lost child. Urged by him to choose one of her numerous suitors, she consented to do so, but made it a condition that he alone who could outstrip her in a race should beccome her husband, whilst those she defeated should be put to death by her, with the lance that she bore in her hand.

Thus many suitors perished, for the maiden was unequalled for swiftness of foot, but at last a beautiful youth, named Hippomenes, who had vainly endeavored to win her love by his assiduous attentions in the chase, ventured to enter the fatal lists. Knowing that only by stratagem could he hope to be successful, he obtained, by the help of Aphrodite, three golden apples from the garden of the Hesperides, which he threw down at intervals during his course. Atalanta, secure of victory, stooped to pick up the tempting fruit, and, in the meantime, Hippomenes arrived at the goal.

He became the husband of the lovely Atalanta, but forgot, in his newly found happiness, the gratitude that he owed to Aphrodite, and the goddess withdrew her favor from the pair. Not long after, the prediction that foretold misfortune to Atalanta in the event of her marriage was verified, for she and her husband, having strayed unsanctioned into a sacred grove of Zeus, were both transformed into lions.

OPPOSITE: ***Death of Meleager*, François Boucher, c. 1727. Meleager's mother Althea killed him with a cursed piece of burning wood. Even though she did it out of grief at Meleager's killing of her brothers, she so regretted her decision that she immediately killed herself.**

The BRAURONIAN ARTEMIS

In ancient times, the country later called Crimea was known by the name of the Taurica Chersonnesus. It was colonized by Greek settlers, who, finding that the Scythian inhabitants had a native divinity somewhat resembling their own Artemis, identified her with the Huntress Goddess of the mother-country. The worship of this Taurian Artemis was attended with the most barbarous practices, for, in accordance with a law that she had enacted, all strangers, whether male or female, landing or shipwrecked on her shores, were sacrificed upon her altars. It is supposed that this decree was issued by the Taurian Goddess of Chastity to protect the purity of her followers by keeping them apart from foreign influences.

The EPHESIAN DIANA

The Ephesian Artemis, known to us as "Diana of the Ephesians," was a very ancient Asiatic divinity of Persian origin called Metra,[25] whose worship the Greek colonists found already established when they first settled in Asia Minor, and whom they identified with their own Greek Artemis, though she really possessed but one single attribute in common with their home deity.

Metra was a twofold divinity, and represented, in one phase of her character, all-pervading love; in the other she was the light of heaven; and as Artemis, in her character as Selene, was the only Greek female divinity who represented celestial light, the Greek settlers, according to their custom of fusing foreign deities into their own, seized at once

25 Also called Anaitis-Aphroditis.

upon this point of resemblance, and decided that Metra should henceforth be regarded as identical with Artemis.

In her character as the love that pervades all nature, and penetrates everywhere, they believed her also to be present in the mysterious realm of shades, where she exercised her benign sway, replacing to a certain extent that ancient divinity Hecate, and partly usurping also the place of Persephone, as mistress of the lower world. Thus they believed that it was she who permitted the spirits of the departed to revisit the Earth, in order to communicate with those they loved and to give them timely warning of coming evil. In fact, this great, mighty, and omnipresent power of love, as embodied in the Ephesian Artemis, was believed by the great thinkers of old to be the ruling spirit of the universe, and it was to her influence that all the mysterious and beneficent workings of nature were ascribed.

There was a magnificent temple erected to this divinity at Ephesus (a city of Asia Minor), that was ranked among the Seven Wonders of the World, and was unequalled in beauty and grandeur. The interior of this edifice was adorned with statues and paintings, and contained 127 columns, sixty feet in height, each column having been placed there by a different king. The wealth deposited in this temple was enormous, and the goddess was here worshipped with particular awe and solemnity. In the interior of the edifice stood a statue of her, formed of ebony, with lions on her arms and turrets on her head, whilst a number of breasts indicated the fruitfulness of the earth and of nature.

OPPOSITE: *Diana and Her Nymphs on the Hunt*, workshop of Peter Paul Rubens, c. 1627–1628. Diana, in blood red, takes charge of the hunt while a satyr tries to steal a kiss from one of her nymphs.

Ctesiphon was the principal architect of this world-renowned structure, which, however, was not entirely completed till 220 CE after the foundation stone was laid. But the labor of centuries was destroyed in a single night; for a man called Herostratus, seized with the insane desire of making his name famous to all succeeding generations, set fire to it and completely destroyed it.[26] So great was the indignation and sorrow of the Ephesians at this calamity that they enacted a law forbidding the incendiary's name to be mentioned, thereby however defeating their own object, for thus the name of Herostratus has been handed down to posterity, and will live as long as the memory of the famous temple of Ephesus.

The ROMAN DIANA

The Diana of the Romans was identified with the Greek Artemis, with whom she shares that peculiar tripartite character, which so strongly marks the individuality of the Greek goddess. In heaven she was Luna (the Moon), on Earth Diana (the Huntress Goddess), and in the lower world Persephone (Proserpine); but, unlike the Ephesian Artemis, Diana, in

26 This occurred during the night Alexander the Great was born.

her character as Proserpine, carries with her into the lower world no element of love or sympathy; she is, on the contrary, characterized by practices altogether hostile to man, such as the exercise of witchcraft, evil charms, and other antagonistic influences, and is, in fact, the Greek Hecate, in her later development.

The statues of Diana were generally erected at a point where three roads met, for which reason she is called Trivia (from *tri*, "three," and *via*, "way"). A temple was dedicated to her on the Aventine hill by Servius Tullius, who is said to have first introduced the worship of this divinity into Rome.

The Nemoralia, or Grove Festivals, were celebrated in her honor on the 13th of August, on the Lacus Nemorensis, or forest-buried lake, near Aricia. The priest who officiated in her temple on this spot was always a fugitive slave, who had gained his office by murdering his predecessor, and hence was constantly armed, in order that he might thus be prepared to encounter a new aspirant.

Detail from *L'Épître Othéa*, attributed to the Master of the Cité des Dames and workshop, c. 1410–1414. Artemis, with bow and arrow, hunts a stag with her nymphs and a hound.

HEPHÆSTUS § VULCAN

Vulcan at the Forge, **Marco Dente, c. 1493–1527. Industrious Hephæstus works alongside his wife Aphrodite and little Amors, or love gods, who were said to be her children and often accompanied her.**

Hephæstus, the son of Zeus and Hera and the maker of Zeus's thunderbolts, was the God of Fire in its beneficial aspect, and the presiding deity over all workmanship accomplished by means of this useful element. He was universally honored, not only as the God of all Mechanical Arts, but also as a house and hearth divinity, who exercised a beneficial influence on civilized society in general. Unlike the other Greek divinities, he was ugly and deformed, being awkward in his movements, and limping in his gait. This latter defect originated from the wrath of his father Zeus, who hurled him down from heaven for taking Hera's side in one of the domestic disagreements that so frequently arose between this royal pair.[27]

Hephæstus was a whole day falling from Olympus to Earth, where he at length alighted on the island of Lemnos. The inhabitants of the country, seeing him descending through the air, received him in their arms; but in spite of their care, his leg was broken by the fall, and he remained ever afterwards lame in one foot. Grateful for the kindness of

27 Another version with regard to the origin of this defect is that, being born ugly and deformed, Hephæstus's mother Hera, disgusted at his unsightliness, threw him violently from her lap, and it was then that his leg was broken, producing the lameness from which he suffered ever after. In this account, he fell into the sea, and was saved by the sea-nymphs Thetis and Eurynome, who kept him for nine years in a cavern beneath the ocean, where he made for them, in gratitude for their kindness, several beautiful ornaments and trinkets of rare workmanship.

the Lemnians, he henceforth took up his abode on their island, and there built for himself a superb palace, and forges for the pursuit of his avocation. He instructed the people how to work in metals, and also taught them other valuable and useful arts.

Hephæstus is usually represented as a powerful, brawny, and very muscular man of middle height and mature age; his strong uplifted arm is often raised in the act of striking the anvil with a hammer, which he holds in one hand, whilst with the other he is often turning a thunderbolt, which an eagle beside him is waiting to carry to Zeus.

OPPOSITE: *Venus at the Forge of Vulcan*. Francesco Solimena, 1704. Hephæstus bestowed upon Aphrodite (Venus) many beautiful gifts made at his forge, as well as this shield for her son Æneas.

The principal seat of Hephæstus's worship was the island of Lemnos, where he was regarded with peculiar veneration. There was also a temple on Mount Etna erected in his honor, which none but the pure and virtuous were permitted to enter. The entrance to this temple was guarded by dogs that possessed the extraordinary faculty of being able to discriminate between the righteous and the unrighteous, fawning upon and caressing the good, whilst they rushed upon all evil-doers and drove them away.

THE WORK *of* HEPHÆSTUS

It is said that the first work of Hephæstus was a most ingenious throne of gold with secret springs, which he presented to Hera. It was arranged in such a manner that, once seated, she found herself unable to move, and though all the gods endeavored to extricate her, their efforts were unavailing. Hephæstus thus revenged himself on his mother for the cruelty she had always displayed towards him, on account of his lack of comeliness and grace. Dionysus, the Wine God, contrived, however, to intoxicate Hephæstus, and then induced him to return to Olympus, where, after having released the queen of heaven from her very undignified position, he became reconciled to his parents.

He now built for himself a glorious palace on Olympus, of shining gold, and made for the other deities magnificent edifices for them to inhabit. He was assisted in his various and exquisitely skillful works of art by two female statues of pure gold, formed by his own hand, who possessed the power of motion, and always accompanied him wherever he went.

Hephæstus was an indispensable member of the Olympic assembly, where he played the part of smith, armorer, chariot-builder, and more. He not only constructed the palaces where the gods resided, but fashioned the golden shoes with which they trod the air or water, built for them their wonderful chariots, and shod with brass the horses of celestial breed, who conveyed these glittering equipages over land and sea. He made the tripods that moved of themselves in and out of the celestial halls, formed for Zeus the far-famed ægis, and erected the magnificent palace of the sun. He also created the brazen-footed bulls of Aëtes, who breathed flames from their nostrils, sent forth clouds of smoke, and filled the air with their roaring.[28] Among his most renowned works for mortals were the armor of Achilles and Æneas, the beautiful necklace of Harmonia, and the crown of Ariadne; but his masterpiece was Pandora, of whom a detailed account is given on page 196.

HEPHÆSTUS and APHRODITE

OPPOSITE: ***Mars and Venus Surprised by Vulcan*, Hendrik Goltzius, 1585. Many famous artworks depict the subject of Hephaestus finding his unfaithful wife in bed with Ares (Mars). Here Dutch artist Hendrik Goltzius, who mostly drew serious portraits of the gods that looked almost like statues, shows his representation.**

With the assistance of the Cyclops, Hephæstus forged for Zeus his wonderful thunderbolts, thus investing his mighty father with a new power of terrible import. Zeus showed his appreciation of this precious gift by bestowing upon Hephæstus the beautiful Aphrodite in marriage,[29] but this was a questionable boon; for the lovely Aphrodite, who was the personification of all grace and beauty, felt no affection for her ungainly and unattractive spouse, and amused herself by ridiculing his awkward movements and unsightly person. On one occasion especially, when Hephæstus good-naturedly took upon himself the office of cup-bearer to the gods, his hobbling gait and extreme awkwardness created the greatest mirth amongst the celestials, in which his disloyal partner was the first to join, with unconcealed merriment.

Aphrodite greatly preferred Ares to her husband, and this preference naturally gave rise to much jealousy on the part of Hephæstus, and caused them great unhappiness.

The ROMAN VULCAN

The Roman Vulcan was merely an importation from Greece that never at any time took firm root in Rome, nor entered largely into the actual life and sympathies of the nation, his worship being unattended by the devotional feeling and enthusiasm that characterized the religious rites of the other deities. He still, however, retained in Rome his Greek attributes as God of Fire, and unrivaled master of the art of working in metals, and was ranked among the twelve great gods of Olympus, whose gilded statues were arranged consecutively along the Forum. His Roman name, Vulcan, would seem to indicate a connection with the first great metal-working artificer of Biblical history, Tubal-Cain.

28 As part of his quest for the golden fleece, Jason had to yoke Aëtes's bulls and plow the fields of Ares. See page 210.

29 According to some accounts Chares was the wife of Hephæstus.

Chapter Two

SEA DIVINITIES

OPPOSITE: ***Siren*, Henri-Arthur Lefort, c. 1897. While some sea gods were benevolent, others, like the Sirens, brought death to those who dared come near.**

POSEIDON ∫ NEPTUNE

Poseidon was the son of Cronus and Rhea, and the brother of Zeus. He was God of the Sea, more particularly of the Mediterranean, and, like the element over which he presided, was of a variable disposition, now violently agitated, then calm and placid. For this reason he is sometimes represented by the poets as quiet and composed, and at others as disturbed and angry.

In the earliest ages of Greek mythology, Poseidon merely symbolized the watery element; but in later times, as navigation and intercourse with other nations engendered greater traffic by sea, Poseidon gained in importance, and came to be regarded as a distinct divinity, holding indisputable dominion over the sea and all sea divinities, who acknowledged him as their sovereign ruler. He possessed the power of causing, at will, mighty and destructive tempests, in which the billows rose mountains high, the wind became a hurricane, and land and sea were enveloped in thick mists, whilst destruction assailed the unfortunate mariners exposed to their fury. On the other hand, his alone was the power of stilling the angry waves and soothing the troubled waters, thereby granting safe voyages to mariners. For this reason, Poseidon was always invoked and propitiated by a libation before a voyage was undertaken, and sacrifices and thanksgivings were gratefully offered to him after a safe and prosperous journey by sea.

Poseidon was also the presiding deity over fishermen, and was on that account more particularly worshipped and revered in countries bordering on the seacoast, where fish naturally formed a staple commodity of trade. He was said to vent his displeasure by sending disastrous inundations that completely destroyed whole countries, and were usually accompanied by terrible marine monsters who swallowed up and devoured those whom the floods had spared. It is probable that these sea-monsters are the poetical figures that represent the demons of hunger and famine, which often accompany mass floods.

Poseidon is generally represented as resembling his brother Zeus in features, height, and general aspect; but we miss in the countenance of the Sea God the kindness and benignity that so pleasingly distinguish his mighty brother. Poseidon's eyes are bright and piercing, and the contour of his face somewhat sharper in its outline than Zeus's, thus corresponding, as it were, with his more angry and violent nature. His hair waves in dark, disorderly masses over his shoulders; his chest is broad, and his frame powerful and stalwart; he often wears a short, curling beard, and a band around his head. He usually appears standing erect in a graceful shell-chariot, drawn by hippocamps, or sea-horses, with golden manes and brazen hoofs, who bound over the dancing waves with such wonderful swiftness that the chariot scarcely touches the water. The monsters of the deep, acknowledging their mighty lord, gambol playfully around him, whilst the sea joyfully smooths a path for the passage of its all-powerful ruler.

The symbol of Poseidon's power was the fisherman's fork or trident, which resembled the arrow-headed pronged fork used by the fishermen of the Mediterranean Sea in the eel fishery, and by means of which Poseidon produced earthquakes, raised up islands from the bottom of the sea, and caused wells to spring forth out of the earth.

OPPOSITE: *Neptune with Dolphin*, Gian Lorenzo Bernini, c. 1623–1700. Poseidon was often portrayed with a trident and a dolphin, whose form he took to woo lovers. BELOW: *Neptune on a Sea Monster*, Albrecht Altdorfer, c. 1480–1538. Because he could harness the power of sea creatures as well as the sea itself, Poseidon was a formidable god for mariners and anyone who made their home along a shore.

POSEIDON'S PALACE

Although Poseidon possessed a royal residence on Mount Olympus, he only visited when his presence was required at the council of the gods. Otherwise, the god inhabited a beautiful palace at the bottom of the sea at Ægea in Eubœa that was of vast extent; in its lofty and capacious halls thousands of his followers could assemble. The exterior of the building was of bright gold, which the continual wash of the waters preserved untarnished; in the interior, lofty and graceful columns supported the gleaming dome. Everywhere fountains of glistening, silvery water played; everywhere groves and arbors of feathery-leaved sea-plants appeared, whilst rocks of pure crystal glistened with all the varied colors of the rainbow. Some of the paths were strewn with white sparkling sand, interspersed with jewels, pearls, and amber. This delightful abode was surrounded on all sides by wide fields, where there were whole groves of dark purple coralline, and tufts of beautiful scarlet-leaved plants, and sea-anemones of every tint. Here grew bright, pinky sea-weeds, mosses of all hues and shades, and tall grasses, that, growing upwards, formed emerald caves and grottoes that the Nereides loved, whilst fish of various kinds playfully darted in and out in the full enjoyment of their native element. Nor was illumination wanting in this fairy-like region, which at night was lit up by the glow-worms of the deep.

OPPOSITE: *Neptune with Two Horses on the Sea*, Cornelis Schut I, c. 1597–1655. Poseidon, most likely seen here with his wife Amphitrite, rides his chariot effortlessly across the waves.

AMPHITRITE and SCYLLA

Poseidon married a sea-nymph named Amphitrite, whom he wooed under the form of a dolphin. The sea divinities Triton, Rhoda,[1] and Benthesicyme were the children of Poseidon and Amphitrite, as well as the Cyclops.

Amphitrite, like most goddesses, had problems with her husband's fidelity, and she soon became jealous of a beautiful maiden called Scylla, who was beloved by Poseidon. In order to revenge herself, she threw some herbs into a well where Scylla was bathing, which had the effect of metamorphosing her into a monster of terrible aspect, having twelve feet, six heads with six long necks, and a voice that resembled the bark of a dog. This awful monster is said to have inhabited a cave at a very great height in the famous rock that forever bore her name,[2] and was supposed to swoop down from her rocky eminence upon every ship that passed, and with each of her six heads to secure a victim.

1 To whom the Greek island of Rhodes owes its name.

2 Scylla was a dangerous rock, much dreaded by mariners, in the Straits of Messina.

OTHER CHILDREN *of* POSEIDON

Like the other gods, Poseidon wooed his mortal lovers by taking on other forms. Poseidon was in the form of seafoam when he impregnanted Iphimedeia, who gave birth to two giant sons called Otus and Ephialtes.[3] When only nine years old, they were said to be twenty-seven cubits[4] in height and nine in breadth. These youthful giants were as rebellious as they were powerful, even presuming to threaten the gods themselves with hostilities. During the war of the Gigantomachia, they endeavored to scale heaven by piling mighty mountains one upon another. Already had they succeeded in placing Mount Ossa

3 It is worthy of notice that all sons of Poseidon were, for the most part, distinguished by great force and turbulence of character, in keeping with the element over which their father was the presiding deity. They were giants in power, and intractable, fiery, and impatient by nature, spurning all efforts to control them; in all respects, therefore, fitting representatives of their progenitor, the mighty ruler of the sea.

4 A cubit is the length from the elbow to the extremity of the middle finger, and therefore an indefinite measure, but modern usage takes it as representing a length of seventeen to eighteen inches.

on Olympus and Pelion on Ossa, when this impious project was halted by Apollo, who destroyed them with his arrows. It was supposed that had not their lives been thus cut off before reaching maturity, their sacrilegious designs would have been carried into effect.

Pelias and Neleus were also sons of Poseidon. Their mother Tyro was attached to the river divinity Enipeus, whose form Poseidon assumed to win her love. Pelias became famous afterward as the king who sent Jason on the quest for the golden fleece (as will be recounted beginning on page 206), and Neleus became the father of Nestor, who was distinguished in the Trojan War.

ORGIN *of the* HORSE

The Greeks believed that they were indebted to Poseidon for the existence of the horse, which he is said to have produced in the following manner: Athene and Poseidon both claiming the right to name Cecropia (the ancient name of Athens), a violent dispute arose that was finally settled by an assembly of the Olympian gods, who decided that whichever of the contending parties presented mankind with the most useful gift would obtain the privilege of naming the city. Upon this Poseidon struck the ground with his trident, and the horse sprang forth in all his untamed strength and graceful beauty. From the spot that Athene touched with her wand issued the olive tree, whereupon the gods unanimously awarded to her the victory, declaring her gift to be an emblem of peace and plenty, whilst that of Poseidon was thought to be a symbol of war and bloodshed. Athene accordingly called the city Athens, after herself, and it has ever since retained this name.

Poseidon tamed the horse for the use of mankind, and was believed to have taught men the art of managing horses by the bridle. The Isthmian games (so named because they were held on the Isthmus of Corinth), in which horse-and-chariot races were a distinguishing feature, were instituted in honor of Poseidon.

NEREUS

OPPOSITE: *Nereus*, Philip Galle, 1586. Unlike Poseidon, Nereus was always benevolent, and brought only gentle waves.

Nereus appears to have been the personification of the sea in its calm and placid moods, and was, after Poseidon, the most important of the sea-deities to mariners. He is represented as a kind and benevolent old man, possessing the gift of prophecy, and presiding more particularly over the Ægean Sea, of which he was considered to be the protecting spirit. There he dwelt with his wife Doris and their fifty blooming daughters, the Nereides, beneath the waves in a beautiful grotto-palace, and was ever ready to assist distressed mariners in their hour of danger.

Phls Gall. inuen. et scalp.
NEREVS.
3.

THE CYCLOPS

The Cyclops were the children of Poseidon and Amphitrite. They were a wild race of gigantic growth, similar in nature to the Earth-born Giants, and had only one eye each in the middle of their foreheads. They led a lawless life, possessing neither social manners nor fear of the gods, and worked for Hephæstus, whose workshop was said to be in the heart of the volcanic mountain Ætna.

Roman lamp, circa 1–400 CE. The decoration on this lamp depicts Odysseus hiding under a ram to escape the giant Cyclops Polyphemus.

POLYPHEMUS

The chief representative of the Cyclops was the man-eating monster Polyphemus, who fell in love with a beautiful nymph called Galatea; but, as may be supposed, his romantic addresses were not acceptable to the fair maiden, who rejected them in favor of a youth named Acis, upon which Polyphemus, with his usual barbarity, destroyed the life of his rival by throwing upon him a gigantic rock. The blood of the murdered Acis, gushing out of the rock, formed a stream that still bears his name.

Polyphemus is most well-known, however, for being outwitted by Odysseus. During his adventures, Odysseus and his companions came across the country of the Cyclops, and in it, a vast cave, into which they boldly entered. In the interior they saw, to their surprise, huge piles of cheese and great pails of milk ranged round the walls. After partaking freely of these provisions, Odysseus's companions endeavored to persuade him to return to the ship; but the hero, being curious to make the acquaintance of the owner of this extraordinary abode, ordered them to remain and await his pleasure.

Towards evening Polyphemus made his appearance, bearing an enormous load of wood upon his shoulders, and driving before him a large flock of sheep. After all his sheep had entered, the giant rolled before the entrance to the cave an enormous rock, which the combined strength of a hundred men would have been powerless to move.

Having kindled a fire of great logs of pine-wood, he was about to prepare his supper, when the flames revealed to him, in a corner of the cavern, its new occupants, who now came forward and informed him that they were shipwrecked mariners, and claimed his hospitality in the name of Zeus. But the fierce monster railed at the great ruler of

Olympus—for the lawless Cyclops knew no fear of the gods—and hardly granted a reply to the demand of the hero. To the consternation of Odysseus, the giant seized two of his companions, and, after dashing them to the ground, consumed their remains, washing down the ghastly meal with huge draughts of milk. He then stretched his gigantic limbs on the ground and soon fell fast asleep beside the fire.

Thinking the opportunity a favorable one to rid himself and his companions of their terrible enemy, Odysseus drew his sword, and, creeping stealthily forward, was about to slay the giant when he suddenly remembered that the aperture of the cave was effectually closed by the immense rock, which rendered egress impossible. He therefore wisely determined to wait until the following day, and set his wits to work in the meantime

***Forge of the Cyclopes*, Cornelis Cort, 1572. In the forge of Hephæstus, the Cyclops made the finest armor in the world.**

Detail from *L'Épître Othéa*, attributed to the Master of the Cité des Dames and workshop, c. 1410–1414. Odysseus escaped from the Cyclops Polyphemus by blinding him, or in this version of the tale, blindfolding him.

on devising a scheme by which he and his companions might make their escape.

When the giant awoke early the next morning, two more unfortunate companions of the hero were seized by him and devoured; after which Polyphemus leisurely drove out his flock, taking care to secure the entrance of the cave as before. The next evening the giant devoured two more of his victims, and when he had finished his revolting meal Odysseus stepped forward and presented him with a large measure of wine, which he had brought with him from his ship in a goat's skin. Delighted with the delicious beverage the giant inquired the name of the donor. Odysseus replied that his name was Noman, whereupon Polyphemus graciously announced that he would evince his gratitude by eating him the last.

The monster, thoroughly overcome with the powerful old liquor, soon fell into a heavy sleep, and Odysseus lost no time in putting his plans into execution. He had cut during the day a large piece of the giant's own olive staff, which he now heated in the fire, and, aided by his companions, thrust it into the eyeball of Polyphemus.

The giant made the cave resound with his howls of pain and rage. His cries being heard by his brother Cyclops, who lived in caves not far distant from his own, they soon came trooping over the hills from all sides, and assailed the door of the cave with inquiries concerning the cause of his cries and groans. But as his only reply was "No man has injured me," they concluded that he was playing a trick a them, and therefore abandoned him to his fate.

The blinded giant now groped vainly around his cave in hopes of laying hands on some of his tormentors; but wearied at length of these fruitless exertions he rolled away the rock that closed the aperture, thinking that his victims would rush out with the sheep, when it would be an easy matter to capture them. But in the meantime Odysseus had not been idle, and the intelligence of the hero was now brought into play, and proved more than a match for the giant's strength. The sheep were very large, and Odysseus, with bands of willow taken from the bed of Polyphemus, had cleverly linked them together three abreast, and under each center one had secured one of his comrades. After providing for the safety of his companions, Odysseus himself selected the finest ram of the flock, and, by clinging to the wool of the animal, made his escape. As the sheep passed out of the cave the giant felt carefully among them for his victims, but not finding them on the backs of the animals he let them pass, and thus they all escaped.

They now hastened on board their vessel, and Odysseus, thinking himself at a safe distance, shouted out his real name and mockingly defied the giant; whereupon Polyphemus seized a huge rock, and, following the direction of the voice, hurled it towards the ship, which narrowly escaped destruction. He then called upon his father Poseidon to avenge him, entreating him to curse Odysseus with a long and tedious voyage, to destroy all his ships and all his companions, and to make his return as late, as unhappy, and as desolate as possible. As Odysseus's return home was so fraught, Polyphemus had his vengence.

OCEANUS

Oceanus was the son of Uranus and Gæa. He was the personification of the ever-flowing stream, that, according to the primitive notions of the early Greeks, encircled the world, and from which sprang all the rivers

Juno Complaining to Oceanus and Thetis, **Hendrik Goltzius, 1590. Hera (Juno), in her chariot, complains to Oceanus (center), and Thetis (left), most likely about not being judged by Paris to be the fairest goddess at Thetis's wedding.**

and streams that watered the earth. He was married to Tethys, one of the Titans, and was the father of a numerous progeny called the Oceanides, who are said to have been three thousand in number. He alone, of all the Titans, refrained from taking part against Zeus in the Titanomachia, and was, on that account, the only one of the primeval divinities permitted to retain his dominion under the new dynasty.

THETIS

OPPOSITE: *Thetis Bringing the Armor to Achilles,* Benjamin West, 1804. Thetis was the mother of Achilles, the renown hero of the Trojan War. Here she brings him the greatest armor ever made by the legendary forger-god Hephæstus.

The silver-footed, fair-haired Thetis, who plays an important part in the mythology of Greece, was the daughter of Nereus. Thetis retained great influence over the mighty Zeus, which she used in favor of her renowned son, Achilles, in the Trojan War (as will be recounted on page 251).

Thetis's grace and beauty were so remarkable that Zeus and Poseidon both sought an alliance with her; but, as it had been foretold that a son of hers would gain supremacy over his father, they relinquished their intentions, and she became the wife of Peleus, son of Æacus. Like Proteus, Thetis possessed the power of transforming herself into a variety of different shapes, and when wooed by Peleus she exerted this power in order to elude him. But, knowing that persistence would eventually succeed, he held her fast until she assumed her true form. Their nuptials were celebrated with the utmost pomp and magnificence, and were honored by the presence of all the gods and goddesses, with the exception of Eris, the Goddess of Discord. As recounted beginning on page 32, Eris so resented her exclusion from the marriage festivities that she produced the golden apple that started the Trojan War.

The ORGIN of HALYCONES

Thetis played a large role in the story of Halcyone, the wife of King Ceyx. When Halcyone plunged into the sea in despair after the shipwreck and death of her husband, Thetis transformed both husband and wife into kingfisher birds (halcyones), which, with the tender affection that characterized the unfortunate couple, always fly in pairs. The idea of the ancients was that these birds brought forth their young in nests, which float on the surface of the sea in calm weather, before and after the shortest day, when Thetis was said to keep the waters smooth and tranquil for their special benefit; hence the term "halcyon days," which signifies a period of rest and untroubled felicity.

Plate from *The Wonder Book for Girls & Boys*, Walter Crane, 1892. Heracles wrestles with Proteus. Both of Proteus's sons would eventually be killed by Heracles.

PROTEUS

Proteus, more familiarly known as "the Old Man of the Sea," was a son of Poseidon, and gifted with prophetic power, but had an invincible objection to being consulted in his capacity as a seer. So, those who wished him to foretell events watched for the hour of noon, when he was in the habit of coming up to the Egyptian island of Pharos with Poseidon's flock of seals, which he tended at the bottom of the ocean. Surrounded by these creatures of the deep, he slumbered beneath the grateful shade of the rocks. This was the best moment to seize the prophet, who, in order to avoid importunities, would change himself into an infinite variety of forms. But patience gained the day; for if he were only held long enough, he became wearied at last, and, resuming his true form, gave the information desired, after which he dived down again to the bottom of the sea, accompanied by the animals he tended.

TRITON

Triton was the only son of Poseidon and Amphitrite, but he possessed little influence, being altogether a minor divinity. He is usually represented as preceding his father and acting as his trumpeter, using a conch-shell for this purpose. He lived with his parents in their beautiful golden palace beneath the sea at Ægea, and his favorite pastime was to ride over the billows on horses or sea-monsters. Triton is always represented as half man, half fish, the body below the waist terminating in the tail of a dolphin. The poets frequently make mention of Tritons, who are either the offspring or kindred of Triton.

Doorknocker with Nereid, Triton, and Putti, c. 1550. Triton, bottom right, is featured on this ancient bronze doorknocker alongside a sea-nymph and tiny love gods.

GLAUCUS

Glaucus, a fisherman who was transformed into a god, is said to have become a sea divinity in the following manner. While angling one day, he observed that the fish he caught and threw on the bank at once nibbled at the grass and then leapt back into the water. His curiosity was naturally excited, and he proceeded to gratify it by taking up a few blades of grass and tasting them. No sooner was this done than, obeying an irresistible impulse, he suddenly dived into the deep, and became a sea god.

Like most sea divinities, Glaucus was gifted with prophetic power, and each year visited all the islands and coasts with a train of marine monsters, foretelling all kinds of evil. Hence fishermen dreaded his approach, and endeavored, by prayer and fasting, to avert the misfortunes that he prophesied. He is often represented floating on the billows, his body covered with mussels, seaweed, and shells, wearing a full beard and long flowing hair, and bitterly bewailing his immortality.

WATER-NYMPHS

The streams, springs, and fountains of an ancient land bear the same relation to it that blood bears to the body; both represent the living, moving, life-awakening element, without which existence would be impossible. Hence we find among the ancient Greeks a deep feeling of attachment to the streams and waters of their native land, with each tribe regarding the rivers and springs of its individual state as beneficent powers that brought blessing and prosperity to the country. These water-nymphs were the primitive version of today's mermaids, whose existence is still believed in by some mariners, and are divided into the Oceanides (ocean-nymphs), Nereides (sea-nymphs), and Naiades (fresh-water nymphs).

The water-nymphs presided over the gentle whisper of the fountain, which lulled the senses with its low, rippling tones; the soft purling of the brook as it rushed over the pebbles; and the mighty voice of the waterfall as it dashed on in its headlong course; all these charming sights and sounds of nature corresponded to the water-nymphs' graceful appearances.

OPPOSITE: ***Glaucus*, Philip Galle, 1586. Glaucus was feared by fishermen for his evil prophecies.**
BELOW: ***A Nymph on a Dolphin*, Francesco Marti, c. 1489–1516. Because of water's importance in the life of the ancients, water-nymphs were some of their most-beloved deities.**

The OCEANIDES

The Oceanides, or ocean-nymphs, were the daughters of Oceanus and Tethys, and, like most sea divinities, were endowed with the gift of prophecy. They were personifications of those delicate vapor-like exhalations, that, in warm climates, are emitted from the surface of the sea, more especially at sunset, and are impelled forward by the evening breeze. They are accordingly represented as misty, shadowy beings, with graceful swaying forms, and robed in pale blue, gauze-like fabrics.

BELOW: *Nereid Arranging Her Necklace*, Antonie-Louis Barye, c. 1836. The Nereides, the most famous of which was Thetis, lived in the Mediterranean Sea off the coast of Greece. OPPOSITE: *Triton and Nymph*, Gabriel Huquier after François Boucher, c. 1736. The beautiful nymphs of the sea were often seen sharing seashells with Tritons.

The NEREIDES

The Nereides were the daughters of Nereus and Doris, and were nymphs of the Mediterranean Sea. They were similar in appearance to the Oceanides, but their beauty was of a less shadowy order, and was more like that of mortals. They wore flowing, pale green robes; their liquid eyes resembled, in their clear depths, the lucid waters of the sea they inhabited; and their hair floated carelessly over their shoulders, and assumed the greenish tint of the water itself, which, far from deteriorating from their beauty, greatly added to its effect. The Nereides either accompanied the chariot of the mighty God of the Sea, or followed in his train.

Lonely mariners watched the Nereides with silent awe and wondering delight as they rose from their grotto-palaces in the deep, and danced, in joyful groups, over the sleeping waves. Some, with arms entwined, followed their movements with melodies that seemed to hover over the sea, whilst others scattered liquid gems around (these being emblematical of the phosphorescent lights so frequently observed at night by travelers in southern waters).

The best known of the Nereides were Thetis, the wife of Peleus; Amphitrite, the spouse of Poseidon; and Galatea, the beloved of Acis.

The NAIADES

The Naiades were the nymphs of fresh-water springs, lakes, brooks, and rivers. As the trees, plants, and flowers owed their nourishment to their genial, fostering care, these divinities were regarded by the Greeks as special benefactors to mankind. Like all the nymphs, they possessed the gift of prophecy, for which reason many of the springs and fountains over which they presided were believed to inspire mortals who drank of their waters with the power of foretelling future events. The Naiades gave their name to Nymphæ, or water-lilies, whose broad, green leaves and yellow cups float upon the surface of the water, as though proudly conscious of their own grace and beauty.

We often hear of the Naiades forming alliances with mortals, and also of their being wooed by the pastoral deities of the woods and dales.

THE SIRENS

The Sirens were sea-nymphs, with the upper part of the body of a maiden and the lower half of a sea-bird, with wings attached to their shoulders. The Sirens were endowed with such wonderful voices that their sweet songs are said to have lured mariners to destruction, and were seemingly the personifications of those numerous rocks and unseen dangers that abound on the southwest coast of Italy.

In the tale of Odysseus we are told that the goddess Circe had warned Odysseus on no account to listen to the seductive melodies of these treacherous nymphs; for all who gave ear to their enticing strains felt an unconquerable desire to leap overboard and join them, where they either perished at their hands, or were engulfed by the waves.

Therefore, when the course

of Odysseus's ship led them past the island of the Sirens, he had filled the ears of his crew with melted wax; but the hero himself so dearly loved adventure that he could not resist the temptation of braving this new danger. By his own desire, therefore, he was lashed to the mast, and his comrades had strict orders on no account to release him until they were out of sight of the island, no matter how he might implore them to set him free.

As they neared the fatal shore they beheld the Sirens seated side by side on the verdant slopes of their island; and as their sweet and alluring strains fell upon his ear, the hero became so powerfully affected by them, that, forgetful of all danger, he entreated his comrades to release him; but the sailors, obedient to their orders, refused to unbind him until the enchanted island had disappeared from view. The danger past, the hero gratefully acknowledged the firmness of his followers, which had been the means of saving his life.

OPPOSITE: *The Sirens*, Auguste Rodin, c. 1887–1920. Mythological creatures are a favorite subject of artists. This bronze sculpture of the Sirens was crafted by Auguste Rodin, who is better known for his bronze *The Thinker*.

ABOVE: *The Sirens*, Antoni Tempesta and Wilhelm Janson, 1606. The beautiful Sirens would lure seamen to their deaths with their songs.

Chapter Three

DARK DIVINITIES

OPPOSITE: **Plate from Dante's *Inferno*, M. Gustave Doré, c. 1866. Charon, the ferryman of the dead, rows across the River Styx.**

HADES ∫ PLUTO

***Statuette of Pluto,* c. 100 BCE. Hades was similar to Zeus in appearance, but always had a serious countenance.**

Hades, or Aïdes[1], was the son of Cronus and Rhea, and the youngest brother of Zeus and Poseidon. He was the ruler of that subterranean region called Erebus, which was inhabited by the shades or spirits of the dead, and also by those dethroned and exiled deities who had been vanquished by Zeus and his allies. Hades, the grim and gloomy monarch of this lower world, was the successor of Erebus, a similar ancient, primeval divinity after whom these realms were called. In many accounts, the underworld was renamed Hades after its newer ruler.

The early Greeks regarded Hades as their greatest foe, and Homer tells us that of all the gods, he was the most detested, being the grim robber who stole from people their nearest and dearest, and eventually depriving each of them of their share in terrestrial existence. His name was so feared that it was never mentioned by mortals, who, when they invoked him, struck the earth with their hands, and in sacrificing to him turned away their faces. His sacrifices, which took place at night, consisted of black sheep, and the blood, instead of being sprinkled on the altars or received in vessels, as at other sacrifices, was permitted to run down into a trench, dug for this purpose. The officiating priests wore black robes, and were crowned with cypress.

In later times, in consequence of extended intercourse with foreign nations, new ideas became gradually introduced, and Egyptian theories with regard to an afterlife started taking root in Greece. It was then that the poets and philosophers, and more especially the teachers of the Eleusinian Mysteries, begin to inculcate the doctrine of the future

1 Also known as Aïdoneus.

Plate from Dante's *Inferno*, M. Gustave Doré, c. 1866. Unlike other gods, Hades was hideous to behold.

reward and punishment of good and bad deeds. Hades, who had hitherto been regarded as the dread enemy of mankind, who delighted in his grim office, and kept the shades imprisoned in his dominions after withdrawing them from the joys of existence, now started receiving them with hospitality and friendship, and Hermes replaced him as the god who transported the shades to Erebus.

The god Hades is usually represented as a man of mature years and stern majestic mien, bearing a striking resemblance to his brother Zeus; but the gloomy and inexorable expression on his face contrasts forcibly with that peculiar benignity that so characterizes the countenance of the mighty God of Heaven. He is seated on a throne of ebony, with his queen, the grave and sad Persephone, beside him; and wears a full beard, and long flowing black hair, which hangs straight down over his forehead; in his hand he either bears a two-pronged fork or the keys of the lower world; and at his feet sits Cerberus, his guard dog. Hades is sometimes seen in a chariot of gold, drawn by four black horses, and

Pluto, Hendrik Goltzius, c. 1594. Hades was such a dark divinity that superstition often prevented artists from depicting his face, such as in this woodcut print.

wearing on his head a helmet made for him by the Cyclops, which rendered the wearer invisible. This helmet he frequently lent to mortals and immortals.

The SHADES *of the* LOWER WORLD

The belief of the people with regard to a future state was, in the Homeric age, a sad and cheerless one. It was believed that when a mortal ceased to exist, his spirit tenanted the shadowy outline of the human form it had quitted. These shadows, or shades as they were called, were driven by Hades into his dominions, where they passed their time, some in brooding over the vicissitudes of fortune that they had experienced on Earth, others in regretting the lost pleasures they had enjoyed in life, but all in a condition of semi-consciousness, from which the intellect could only be roused to full activity by drinking the blood of the sacrifices offered to their shades by living friends, which, for a time, endowed them with their former mental vigor.

The only beings supposed to enjoy any happiness in a future state were the heroes, whose acts of daring and deeds of prowess had, during their life, reflected honor on the land of their birth; and even these, according to Homer, pined after their career of earthly activity. He tells us that when Odysseus visited the lower world at the command of Circe, and held communion with the shades of the heroes of the Trojan War, Achilles assured him that he would rather be the poorest day-laborer on Earth than reign supreme over Erebus.

The early Greek poets offer but scanty allusions to realms of the shades. Homer appears purposely to envelop them in vagueness and mystery, in order, probably, to heighten the sensation of awe inseparably connected with the lower world. In the *Odyssey,* he describes the entrance to Erebus as being beyond the furthermost edge of Oceanus, in the far west, where the Cimmerians dwelt, enveloped in eternal mists and darkness. However, the later poets mention various entrances to Erebus, which were for the most part caves and fissures. There was one in the mountain of Taenarum, another in Thesprotia, and a third, the most celebrated of all, in Italy, near the pestiferous Lake Avernus, over which it is said no bird could fly, so noxious were its exhalations.

The RIVER STYX

In the dominions of Erebus there were four great rivers, three of which had to be crossed by all the shades. These three were Acheron (sorrow), Cocytus (lamentation), and Styx (intense darkness), the sacred stream that flowed nine times round these realms.

The shades were ferried over the Styx by the grim, unshaven old boatman Charon, who only took those whose bodies had received funereal rites on Earth, and who had brought with them his indispensable toll, which was usually a small coin, placed under the tongue of a dead person for this purpose. If these conditions had not been fulfilled, the unhappy shades were left behind to wander up and down the banks for a hundred years as restless spirits.

On the opposite bank of the Styx was the tribunal of Minos, the supreme judge, before whom all shades had to appear. It was guarded by the terrible dog Cerberus, a monster with three heads, out of whose awful jaws dripped poison. The hair on his heads and back was formed of venomous snakes, and his body terminated in the tail of a dragon. Cereberus lay at full length on the ground—a formidable sentinel who permitted all

Detail from Dante's *Inferno*, Priamo della Quercia, c. 1444–1450. Dante is taken into the underworld by Charon the ferryman.

ABOVE: Detail from Dante's *Inferno*, Master of the Antiphonar of Padua, c. 1300–1350. Minos (far right) judges new souls as they arrive in Hades.
OPPOSITE: *Pluto and Proserpina*, Jan Pietersz. Saenredam, c. 1593–1594. Hades's wife was Persephone (Proserpina), who split her time between Hades and Earth. While Persephone was in Hades, the grief of her mother Demeter was said to cause fall and winter.

shades to enter, but none to return. Minos, after hearing full confession of each shade's actions whilst on Earth, pronounced the sentence of happiness or misery to which their deeds had entitled them.

The ELYSIAN FIELDS

If happiness was declared by Minos, shades would be allowed into the Elysian Fields, where the warrior found his horses and arms, the musician his lyre, and the hunter his quiver and bow. After having passed through the court of Minos, these souls proceeded to the golden palace where Hades and Persephone held their royal court, from whom they received a kindly greeting, ere they set out for the Elysian Fields that lay beyond.

This blissful region was replete with all that could charm the senses or please the imagination. The air was balmy and fragrant; rippling brooks flowed peacefully through the smiling meadows, which glowed with the varied hues of a thousand flowers; whilst the groves resounded with the joyous songs of birds. The occupations and amusements of these happy shades were of the same nature as those that they had delighted in whilst on Earth. But in a secluded vale of Elysium there flowed a gentle, silent stream, called Lethe (oblivion), whose waters had the effect of dispelling care, and producing utter forgetfulness of former events. According to the Pythagorean doctrine of the transmigration of souls, after the

3
HG.
Persephone vmbrarum Domino si blandula ridet,
Amplexuq; ambit sortitum tertia regna;
Jam tum terna ferox compescit Cerberus ora,
Jmmotaq; sedent Rhadamanthus, et Æacus vrna.

shades had inhabited Elysium for a thousand years, they were destined to animate other bodies on Earth, and before leaving Elysium they drank of the river Lethe, in order that they might enter upon their new career without any remembrance of the past.

TARTARUS

OPPOSITE: ***Tityus Punished in Hell*, Cornelis Cort, 1566. Like the rest of the Greek myths, the stories of penances paid in the underworld were imaginative and often gruesome. Here Tityus is punished for insulting Hera by having a vulture forever gnaw his liver.**

The guilty souls, after leaving the presence of Minos, were conducted to the great judgment-hall of Erebus,[2] whose massive walls of made from the legendary rock called adamant were surrounded by the river Phlegethon, the waves of which rolled flames of fire, and lit up, with their lurid glare, these awful realms. In the interior sat the dread judge Rhadamanthus, who declared to each comer the precise torments that awaited him in Tartarus, the land beyond. The wretched sinners were then seized by the Furies, who scourged them with their whips, and dragged them along to the great gate that closed the opening to Tartarus, into whose awful depths they were hurled, to suffer endless torture.

Tartarus was a vast and gloomy expanse, as far below Hades as the earth is distant from the skies. There the Titans, fallen from their high estate, dragged out a dreary and monotonous existence. There also were Otus and Ephialtes, the Giant sons of Poseidon, who, with impious hands, had attempted to scale Olympus and dethrone its mighty ruler. Also suffering in Tartarus were Sisyphus, a tyrant who killed travelers with rocks and was condemned to roll incessantly a huge block of stone up a steep hill, that, as soon as it reached the summit, always rolled back again to the plain below; Tityus, an Earth-born Giant who had insulted Hera and was doomed to have two vultures perpetually gnawing his liver; Tantalus, who killed his own son, Pelops, and served him up at one of the banquets to the gods, in order to test their omniscience, and was tortured with an ever-burning thirst that could never be satiated; Ixion, bound to an ever-revolving wheel after making advances on Hera; and the Danaïdes, the fifty daughters of King Danaus of Argos, doomed to fill water vessels full of holes (a never-ending and pointless task) in punishment for killing their husbands.

The ROMAN PLUTO

Before the introduction into Rome of the religion and literature of Greece, the Romans had no belief in a realm of future happiness or misery, corresponding to the Greek Erebus;

2 The shades of those mortals whose lives had neither been distinguished by virtue nor vice were condemned to a monotonous, joyless existence in the Asphodel Meadows of Erebus.

hence they had no God of the lower world identical with Hades. They believed that there was, in the center of the Earth, a vast, gloomy, and impenetrably dark cavity called Orcus, that formed a place of eternal rest for the dead. But with the introduction of Greek mythology, the Roman Orcus became the Greek Erebus/Hades, and all the Greek notions with regard to a future state now were established with the Romans, who worshipped Hades under the name of Pluto, his other appellations being Dis (from dives, rich) and Orcus, from the dominion over which he ruled.

ARES ∫ MARS

***Venus and Mars*, Palma il Giovane, c. 1605–1609. Aphrodite (Venus) and Ares were secret lovers, later discovered by Aphrodite's husband Hephæstus. Here Eros helps Ares disrobe while Aphrodite waits in bed.**

Ares, the son of Zeus and Hera, was the God of War, who gloried in strife for its own sake; he loved the tumult and havoc of the battlefield, and delighted in slaughter and extermination; in fact he presents no benevolent aspect who acts favorably upon human life.

Ares is represented as a man of youthful appearance; his tall muscular form combines great strength with wonderful agility. In his right hand he bears a sword or a mighty lance, while on the left arm he carries his round shield. His demoniacal surroundings are Terror and Fear; Enyo, the Goddess of the War-Cry; Keidomos, the demon of the noise of battles; and Eris (Contention), his twin-sister and companion, who always precedes his chariot when he rushes to the fight, this being evidently a simile of the poets to express the fact that war follows contention.

The attributes of this divinity are the helmet, shield, and spear. The animals consecrated to him were the wolf, horse, vulture, and woodpecker. Epic poets, in particular, represent the God of Battles as a wild ungovernable warrior, who passes through armies of men like a whirlwind, hurling to the ground the brave and cowardly alike; destroying chariots and helmets, and triumphing over the terrible desolation that he produces.

Ares appears to have been an object of aversion to all the gods of Olympus, Aphrodite alone excepted (they were lovers). As the son of Hera, he inherited from his mother the strongest feelings of independence and contradiction, and as he took delight in upsetting that peaceful course of state-life that it was pre-eminently the care of Zeus to establish, he was naturally disliked and even hated by him.

ARES and DIOMEDES

In all the myths concerning Ares, his sister Athene always appears in opposition to him, endeavoring by every means in her power to defeat his bloodthirsty designs. Thusly she assisted the divine hero Diomedes at the siege of Troy to overcome Ares in battle, and so well did he profit by her timely aid that he succeeded in wounding the sanguinary War God, who made his exit from the field, roaring like ten thousand bulls.

After being wounded by Diomedes, Ares complained to his father, but received no sympathy from the otherwise kindly and beneficent ruler of Olympus, who thus angrily addressed him: "Do not trouble me with thy complaints, thou who art of all the gods of Olympus most hateful to me, for thou delightest in naught save war and strife. The very spirit of thy mother lives in thee, and wert thou not my son, long ago wouldst thou have lain deeper down in the bowels of the Earth than the son of Uranus."

The SLAYING of HARLIRRHOTHIOS

Ares upon one occasion incurred the anger of Poseidon by slaying his son Halirrhothios, who had insulted Alcippe, Ares's daughter. For this deed, Poseidon summoned Ares to appear before the tribunal of the Olympic gods, which was held upon a hill in Athens. Ares was acquitted, and this event was supposed to have given rise to the name Areopagus (or Hill of Ares), which afterward became famous as a court of justice. In the Gigantomachia,[3] Ares was defeated by the Aloidæ, the two Giant sons of Poseidon, who put him in chains, and kept him in prison for thirteen months.

---

3 As recounted on page 10.

The ROMAN MARS

The Roman divinity most closely resembling the Greek Ares, and identified with him, was called Mars, Mamers, and Marspiter (or Father Mars).

The earliest Italian tribes, who were mostly engaged in the pursuit of husbandry, regarded this deity more especially as the God of Spring, who vanquished the powers of winter and encouraged the peaceful arts of agriculture. But with the Romans, who were an essentially warlike nation, Mars gradually lost his peaceful character, and, as God of War, attained, after Jupiter, the highest position among the Olympic gods. The Romans looked upon him as their special protector, and declared him to have been the father of Romulus and Remus, the founders of their city.

But although he was especially worshipped in Rome as God of War, he still continued to preside over agriculture, and was also the protecting deity who watched over the welfare of the state. The assistance and protection of the God of War was always solemnly invoked before the departure of a Roman army for the field of battle, and any reverses of fortune were invariably ascribed to his anger, which was accordingly propitiated by means of extraordinary sin-offerings and prayers.

***The Triumph of Mars*, Antoine Caron, c. 1570. Though he was also the God of Agriculture, Ares was most often depicted in art as the revered God of War.**

NIKE § VICTORIA

Nike, the Goddess of Victory, was the daughter of the Titan Pallas, and of Styx, the presiding nymph of the river of that name in the lower world.

In her statues, Nike somewhat resembles Athene, but may easily be recognized by her large, graceful wings and flowing drapery, which is negligently fastened on the right shoulder, and often only partially concealing her lovely form. In her left hand, she often holds aloft a crown of laurel, and in the right, a palm branch. In ancient sculpture, Nike is usually represented in connection with colossal statues of Zeus or Athene, in which case she is life-sized, and stands on a ball, held in the open palm of the deity she accompanies. Sometimes she is represented engaged in inscribing the victory of a conqueror on his shield, her right foot being slightly raised and placed on a ball.

A celebrated temple was erected to this divinity on the Acropolis at Athens.

The ROMAN VICTORIA

Under the name of Victoria, Nike was highly honored by the Romans, with whom love of conquest was an all-absorbing characteristic. There were several sanctuaries in Rome dedicated to her, the principal of which was on the capitol, where it was the custom of generals, after success had attended their arms, to erect statues of the goddess in commemoration of their victories. The most magnificent of these statues was that raised by Augustus after the battle of Actium.

A festival was celebrated in honor of Nike on the 12th of April.

***Monument to Ukraine Independence*, Alexander Ridny and Anna Ivanova, 2012. Nike is an appropriate subject for this statue in Constitution Square in Kharkov, Ukraine, which was made to replace a statue of a past regime.**

CIRCE

***Circe and Her Lovers in a Landscape*, Dosso Dossi, c. 1525. Circe was a powerful sorceress who was known to transform her lovers into animals.**

Circe was the Goddess of Charms and Magic Arts, the daughter of the Sun God Helios and the sea-nymph Perse. Circe was a beautiful enchantress and renowned sorceress who was brutal to her enemies (often turning them into animals), but also had the ability to purify one from the sins of a crime.

Circe was said to live on an island that bore her name, in a magnificent marble palace, which was situated in the most charming and fertile valley of the island. The entrance to her abode was guarded by wolves and lions, tame and harmless as lambs, who were, in fact, human beings who, by the wicked arts of the sorceress, had been thus transformed. Inside were wide and spacious halls of tessellated marble objects of wealth and beauty, soft and luxuriant couches studded with silver; and the finest vessels of pure gold for every banquet. Inside, Circe would sing a sweet melody in her enchanting voice, as she sat at her work, weaving a web such as immortals alone could produce.

CIRCE and ODYSSEUS

Homer tells us in the *Odyssey* that, during their long journey home from the Trojan War, Odysseus's companions stopped at the isle of Circe for provisions, and were graciously invited by the wicked goddess to enter her home. All of the men, save the prudent and cautious Eurylochus, accepted the invitation. While the unsuspecting guests were abandoning themselves to the pleasures of the table, the enchantress was secretly working their ruin; for the wine-cup that was presented to them was drugged with a potent elixir, after partaking of which the sorceress touched them with her magic wand, and they were immediately transformed into swine, still, however, retaining their human senses.

Detail from *L'Épître Othéa*, attributed to the Master of the Cité des Dames and workshop, c. 1410–1414. Circe uses her magic arts to turn Odysseus's men into swine.

When Odysseus heard from Eurylochus of the terrible fate that had befallen his companions, he set out to rescue them. On his way to the palace of the sorceress he met a fair youth bearing a wand of gold, who revealed himself to be Hermes, the divine messenger of the gods. He gently reproached the hero for his temerity in venturing to enter the abode of Circe unprovided with an antidote against her spells, and presented him with a peculiar herb called moly, assuring him that it would inevitably counteract the baneful arts of the fell enchantress. Hermes warned Odysseus that Circe would offer him a draught of drugged wine with the intention of transforming him as she had done his companions. He bade him drink the wine, the effect of which would be completely

***Circe Offers the Fatal Cup,* attributed to Giulio di Antonio Bonasone, c. 1543. Circe offers a poisoned cup of wine to the companions of Odysseus.**

nullified by the herb which he had given him, and then rush boldly at the sorceress as though he would take her life, whereupon her power over him would cease, she would recognize her master, and grant him whatever he might desire.

Circe received the hero with all the grace and fascination at her command, and presented him with a draught of wine in a golden goblet. This he readily accepted, trusting to the efficacy of the antidote. Then, in obedience to the injunction of Hermes, he drew his sword from its scabbard and rushed upon the sorceress as though he would slay her.

When Circe found that her devious plans were, for the first time, frustrated, and that a mortal had dared to attack her, she knew that it must be the great Odysseus who stood before her, whose visit to her abode had been foretold to her by Hermes. At his solicitation she restored to his companions their human forms, promising at the same time that henceforth the hero and his comrades should be free from her enchantments.

But all warnings and past experience were forgotten by Odysseus when Circe commenced to exercise upon him her fascinations and blandishments. At her request his companions took up their sojourn in the island, and he himself became the guest and slave of the enchantress for a whole year; and it was only at the earnest admonition of his friends that he was at length induced to free himself from her toils.

Circe had become so attached to the gallant hero that it cost her a great effort to part with him, but having vowed not to exercise her magic spells against him, she was powerless to detain him further. The goddess now warned him that his future would be beset with many dangers, and commanded him to consult the blind old seer Tiresias[4] in the realm of Hades concerning his future destiny. She then loaded his ship with provisions for the voyage, and reluctantly bade him farewell.

4 Tiresias alone, of all the shades, was in full possession of his mental vigor.

THE HARPIES

The Harpies, along with the Furies, were employed by the gods as instruments for the punishment of the guilty. They were three female divinities, daughters of Thaumas and Electra, called Aello, Ocypete, and Celæno, and were represented with the heads of fair-haired maidens and the bodies of vultures. They were perpetually devoured by the pangs of insatiable hunger, which caused them to torment their victims by robbing them of

Plate from Dante's *Inferno*, M. Gustave Doré, c. 1866. The terrifying Harpies had the heads of women and the bodies of vultures.

Detail from ***Divina Commedia***, **Giovanni di Paolo, c. 1450. The harpies swarm above the trees in the Wood of Suicide in this illuminated edition of Dante's *Inferno*.**

their food; this they either devoured with great gluttony, or defiled in such a manner as to render it unfit to be eaten.

Their wonderfully rapid flight far surpassed that of birds, or even of the winds themselves. If any mortal suddenly and unaccountably disappeared, the Harpies were believed to have carried him off. Thus they were supposed to have borne away the daughters of King Pandareos to act as servants to the Furies.

The Harpies would appear to be personifications of sudden tempests, that, with ruthless violence, sweep over whole districts, carrying off or injuring all before them.

THE FURIES

The Furies, or Erinyes, were female divinities who personified the torturing pangs of an evil conscience, and the remorse that inevitably follows wrong-doing.

Their names were Alecto, Megæra, and Tisiphone, and their origin was variously accounted for. According to Hesiod, they sprang from the blood of Uranus when wounded by Cronus, and were hence supposed to be the embodiment of all the terrible imprecations that the defeated deity called down upon the head of his rebellious son. According to other accounts they were the daughters of Nyx (Night).

The Furies are frequently represented with wings; their bodies are black, blood drips from their eyes, and snakes twine in their hair. In their hands they bear either daggers, scourges, torches, serpents, or, if pursuing Orestes (whose tale will be recounted on pages 262–263), mirrors that they held up to his horrified gaze.

These divinities were also called Eumenides, which signified the "well-meaning" or "soothed goddesses." This appellation was given to them because they were so feared and dreaded that people dared not call them by their proper title, and hoped by this means to propitiate their wrath.

The Furies were among those deities of the lower world, where they were employed by Hades and Persephone to chastise and torment those shades who, during their earthly career, had committed crimes, and had not been reconciled to the gods before descending to Hades. But their sphere of action was not confined to the realm of shades, for they appeared upon Earth as the avenging deities who relentlessly pursued and punished murderers, perjurers, those who had failed in duty to their parents or in hospitality to strangers, and those who had lost respect due to old age. Nothing escaped the piercing glances of these terrible divinities, from whom flight was unavailing and for whom no corner of the Earth was so remote as to be beyond their reach; nor did any mortal dare to offer to their victims an asylum from their persecutions.

In later times, the Furies came to be regarded as salutary agencies, who, by severely punishing sin, upheld the cause of morality and social order, and thus contributed to the welfare of mankind. They then lost their awe-inspiring aspect, and were represented, more especially in Athens, as earnest maidens, dressed,

Paestan red-figure neck amphora, attributed to Asteas, c. 340 BCE. On this ancient vessel, Orestes is poised to slay his mother, Clytemnæstra, while one of the Furies (with snakes in her hands and hair) looks on.

like Artemis, in short tunics suitable for the chase, but still retaining, in their hands, the wand of office in the form of a snake.

Their sacrifices consisted of black sheep and a libation composed of a mixture of honey and water, called nephalia. A celebrated temple was erected to the Eumenides at Athens, near the Areopagus.

THE FATES ∫ PARCÆ

***The Three Fates,* Jacob Matham, 1588. When the Fates spent time at Mount Olympus, they wore crowns, but took them off in favor of dark robes when in Hades.**

The ancients believed that the duration of human existence and the destinies of mortals were regulated by three sister-goddesses, called Clotho, Lachesis, and Atropos, who were the daughters of Zeus and Themis and called the Fates or Moiræ.

The power that these deities wielded over the fates of men was significantly indicated under the figure of a thread, which they spun out for the life of each human being from his birth to the grave. This occupation they divided amongst them. Clotho wound the flax round the distaff, ready for her sister Lachesis, who span out the thread of life, which Atropos, with her scissors, relentlessly snapped asunder when the life of an individual was about to terminate.

The Fates were mentioned as assisting the Charities to conduct Persephone to the upper world at her periodical reunion with her mother, Demeter. They also appeared in company with Eileithyia, Goddess of Birth. It was considered the function of the Fates to indicate to the Furies the precise torture that the wicked should undergo for their crimes.

Homer speaks of one Moira only, the daughter of Nyx (Night), who represents the moral force by which the universe is governed, and to whom both mortals and immortals were forced to submit, Zeus himself being powerless to avert her decrees; but in later times this conception of one inexorable, all-conquering Fate became amplified by the poets into that above described, and the Moiræ were henceforth the special presiding deities over the lives and deaths of mortals.

The Moiræ are represented by the poets as stern, inexorable female divinities, aged, hideous, and also lame, which is evidently meant to indicate the slow and halting march of destiny, which they controlled. Painters and sculptors, on the other hand, depicted them as beautiful maidens of a grave but kindly aspect.

When represented at the feet of Hades in the lower world they are clad in dark robes; but when they appear in Olympus they wear bright garments, bespangled with stars, and are seated on radiant thrones, with crowns on their heads.

7.
HG. Inuent.
Cuncta penes Parcas, Diuumq; hominumq; potestas,
Factaq; voluuntur, quicquid et orbis agit.
Illis imperium curę est, sceptrumq́, ligoq;
Illarum in manibus vitaq; morsq; sita est.

NEMESIS

ABOVE: **Engraved Roman gem, c. 100–200 CE. This ancient gem carved from red jasper shows Nemesis with her signature wheel of justice and wings of vengeance.**

OPPOSITE: ***Nemesis (the Great Fortune)*, Albrecht Dürer, c. 1501–1502. When not riding her wheel of justice, Nemesis was seen in a chariot pulled by griffins.**

Nemesis, the daughter of Nyx, represented that power that adjusts the balance of human affairs by awarding to each individual the fate that his actions deserve. Nemesis is frequently called Adrastia, and also Rhamnusia, from Rhamnus in Attica, the chief seat of her worship, which contained a celebrated statue of the goddess. Homer makes no mention of Nemesis; it is therefore evident that she was a conception of later times, when the concept of morality became more prominent in the Greek nation.

Nemesis is represented as a beautiful woman of thoughtful and benign aspect and regal bearing; a diadem crowns her majestic brow, and she bears in her hand a rudder, balance, and cubit—fitting emblems of the manner in which she guides, weighs, and measures all human events. She is also sometimes seen with a wheel, to symbolize the rapidity with which she executes justice. As the avenger of evil she appears winged, bearing in her hand either a scourge or a sword, and seated in a chariot drawn by griffins.

Nemesis rewarded humble, unacknowledged merit, punished crime, deprived the worthless of undeserved good fortune, humiliated the proud and overbearing, and visited all evil on wrong-doers; thus maintaining that proper balance of things, which the Greeks recognized as a necessary condition of all civilized life. But though Nemesis, in her original character, was the distributor of rewards as well as punishments, the world was so full of sin that she found but little occupation in her first capacity, and hence became finally regarded as the avenging goddess only.

We have seen a striking instance of the manner in which this divinity punishes the proud and arrogant in the story of Niobe (as told on page 81). Though Apollo and Artemis killed Niobe's children for insulting Apollo, it was Nemesis who prompted the deed, and presided over its execution.

NYX & NOX

Nyx, the daughter of Chaos, being the personification of Night, was, according to the poetic ideas of the Greeks, considered to be the mother of everything mysterious and inexplicable, such as death, sleep, and dreams. She became united to Hades, and their children were Aether and Hemera (Air and Daylight), evidently a simile of the poets to indicate that darkness always precedes light.

Nyx inhabited a palace in the dark regions of the lower world, and is represented as a beautiful woman, seated in a chariot, drawn by two black horses. She is clothed in dark robes, often wears a long veil, and is accompanied by the stars, which follow in her train.

Detail of *Goddess of Night* fountain, c. 1889. Nyx is accompanied by two small figures, possibly two of her children, in this statue atop a fountain in Gurzuf, Crimea.

THANATOS (MORS) and HYPNUS (SOMNUS)

Two other children of Nyx were Thanatos (Death) and his twin-brother Hypnus (Sleep). Their dwelling was in the realm of shades, and when they appeared among mortals, Thanatos was feared and hated as the enemy of mankind, whose hard heart knew no pity, whilst his brother Hypnus was universally loved and welcomed as their kindest and most beneficent friend.

But though the ancients regarded Thanatos as a gloomy and mournful divinity, they did not represent him with any exterior repulsiveness. On the contrary, he appears as a beautiful youth, who holds in his hand an inverted torch, emblematic of the light of life being extinguished, whilst his disengaged arm is thrown lovingly round the shoulder of his brother Hypnus. Hypnus is sometimes depicted standing erect with closed eyes; at others he is in a recumbent position beside his brother Thanatos, and usually bears a poppy-stalk in his hand.

***Nox (Goddess of Night)*, Hendrik Goltzius, c. 1588–1590. Nox was said to be the mother of many of the dark divinities.**

A most interesting description of the abode of Hypnus is given by Ovid in his *Metamorphoses*. He tells us how the God of Sleep dwelt in a mountain cave near the realm of the Cimmerians, which the sun never pierced with its rays. No sound disturbed the stillness, no song of birds, not a branch moved, and no human voice broke the profound silence that reigned everywhere. From the lowermost rocks of the cave issued the river Lethe, and one might almost have supposed that its course was arrested, were it not for the low, monotonous hum of the water, which invited slumber. The entrance was partially hidden by innumerable white and red poppies, which Mother Night had gathered and planted there, and from the juice of which she extracted drowsiness, which she scattered in liquid drops all over the earth as soon as the Sun God had sunk to rest each night.

Homer describes the House of Dreams as having two gates: one, whence issued all deceptive and flattering visions, being formed of ivory; the other, through which proceeded those dreams that are fulfilled, of horn.

In the center of the cave stood a couch of blackest ebony, with a bed of down, over which was laid a coverlet of sable hue. Here Hypnus himself reposed, and he could not resist his own power; for though he may have roused himself for a while, he would soon succumb to the drowsy influences that surrounded him.

These influences were idle dreams, more numerous than the sands of the sea, and they took innumerable forms. Chief among them was Morpheus, a changeling god who assumed any shape or form he pleased.

Morpheus was the son of Hypnus, and is always represented winged, and appears sometimes as a youth, sometimes as an old man. In his hand he bears a cluster of poppies, and as he stepped with noiseless footsteps over the earth, he gently scattered the seeds of this sleep-producing plant over the eyes of weary mortals.

THE GORGONS

OPPOSITE: **Plate from *The Wonder Book for Girls & Boys*, Walter Crane, 1892. Perseus slew the Gorgon Medusa to prove himself.**

The Gorgons—Stheno, Euryale, and Medusa—were the three daughters of Phorcys and Ceto, and were the personification of those benumbing and petrifying sensations that result from sudden and extreme fear.

The Gorgons were frightful winged monsters whose bodies were covered with scales; hissing, wriggling snakes clustered around their heads instead of hair; their hands were of brass; their teeth resembled the tusks of a wild boar; and their whole aspect was so appalling that they are said to have turned into stone all who beheld them. These terrible sisters were said to dwell in that remote and mysterious region in the Far West, beyond the sacred stream of Oceanus.

The Gorgons were the servants of Hades, who made use of them to terrify and overawe shades (the dead), doomed to be kept in a constant state of unrest as a punishment for their misdeeds, whilst the Furies, on their part, scourged them with their whips and tortured them incessantly.

MEDUSA

The most celebrated of the three Gorgons was Medusa, who alone was mortal. It is well to observe that when the Gorgons are spoken of in the singular, it is Medusa who is alluded to. Medusa was the mother of Pegasus and of Chrysaor, who was father of the three-headed, winged Giant Geryones, who was slain by Heracles. Medusa was originally

a golden-haired and very beautiful maiden, who, as a priestess of Athene, was devoted to a life of celibacy; but, being wooed by Poseidon, whom she loved in return, she forgot her vows, and became united to him in marriage.

For this offense she was punished by the goddess in a most terrible manner. Each wavy lock of her beautiful hair, which had so charmed her husband, was changed into a venomous snake; her once gentle, love-inspiring eyes now became blood-shot, furious orbs, which excited fear and disgust in the mind of the beholder; whilst her former rosy hue and milk-white skin assumed a loathsome greenish tinge. Seeing herself thus transformed into so repulsive an object, Medusa fled from her home, never to return. Wandering about, abhorred, dreaded, and shunned by all the world, she now developed an inner character worthy of her outward appearance. In her despair she fled to Africa, where, as she passed restlessly from place to place, infant snakes dropped from her hair, and thus, according to the belief of the ancients, that country became the hotbed of these venomous reptiles. With the curse of Athene upon her, she turned into stone whomsoever she gazed upon, till at last, after a life of nameless misery, deliverance came to her in the shape of death at the hands of Perseus as recounted on pages 202–203.

***Medusa*, Vincenzo Gemito, 1911. This relief made from partially gilt silver shows the hideous Gorgon Medusa.**

THE GRÆÆ

The Grææ, who acted as servants to their sisters the Gorgons, were also three in number; their names were Pephredo, Enyo, and Dino.

In their original conception they were merely personifications of kindly and venerable old age, possessing all its benevolent attributes without its natural infirmities. They were old and gray from their birth, and so they ever remained. In later times, however, they came to be regarded as misshapen females, decrepit, and hideously ugly, having only one eye, one tooth, and one gray wig amongst them, which they lent to each other when one of them wished to appear before the world.

When Perseus entered upon his expedition to slay Medusa, he repaired to the abode of the Grææ, in the far west, to inquire the way to the Gorgons, and on their refusing to give any information, he deprived them of their one eye, tooth, and wig, and did not restore them until he received the necessary directions.

Bellona, **Andrea Schiavone, c. 1510–1563. Enyo (Bellona), the Goddess of Destruction, was just as ferocious as her male counterpart, Ares.**

ENYO (BELLONA)

Enyo, the most well-known of the Grææ, was the Goddess of Destruction. In many poems she is conflated with Eris (Contention), the twin-sister of Keidomos.

Intimately associated with Ares in his character as God of War, Enyo is usually seen accompanying him, guiding his chariot. Enyo often appears on the battlefield inspired with mad rage, cruelty, and the love of extermination.

Enyo is portrayed in full armor, angry and menacing, with disheveled hair, and bearing a whip in one hand, and a lance in the other. When portrayed as Eris she often brandishes a dagger and a hissing adder in one hand, whilst in the other she carries a burning torch. Her dress is torn and disorderly, and her hair intertwined with venomous snakes.

This divinity was never invoked by mortals, except when they desired her assistance for the accomplishment of evil purposes.

MOMUS

Momus, another son of Nyx, was the God of Raillery and Ridicule, who delighted to criticize, with bitter sarcasm, the actions of gods and men, and contrived to discover in all things some defect or blemish. Thus when Prometheus created the first man, Momus considered his work incomplete because there was no aperture in the breast through which his inmost thoughts might be read. He also found fault with a house built by Athene because, being unprovided with the means of locomotion, it could never be removed from an unhealthy locality. Aphrodite alone defied his criticism, for, to his great chagrin, he could find no fault with her perfect form.[5]

In what manner the ancients represented this god is unknown. In modern art he is depicted like a king's jester, with a fool's cap and bells.

SPHINX

Sphinx & Pyramids, Egypt, **c. 1934–1939. This statue of the Sphinx in Giza, Egypt, is not only the oldest monument in the world still standing, it's one of the largest.**

The Sphinx was an ancient Egyptian divinity who personified wisdom and the fertility of nature. She is represented as a couchant lion, with the head and bust of a woman, and wears a peculiar sort of hood, which completely envelops her head and falls down on either side of the face.

Transplanted into Greece, this sublime and mysterious Egyptian deity degenerated into an insignificant, yet malignant

5 According to another account, Momus discovered that Aphrodite made a noise when she walked.

power, and though she also dealt in mysteries, they were, as we shall see, of a totally different character, and altogether hostile to human life.

The Sphinx is represented, according to Greek genealogy, as having wings and a smaller aspect than the Egyptian Sphinx, and as the offspring of Typhon and Echidna, a bloodthirsty half maiden, half serpent. Hera, being upon one occasion displeased with the Thebans, sent them the Sphinx as a punishment for their offenses. Taking her seat on a rocky eminence near the city of Thebes, commanding a pass that the Thebans were compelled to traverse in their usual way of business, she propounded to all comers a riddle, and if they failed to solve it, she tore them into pieces.

Red-figure lekythos showing seated Sphinx, c. 470 BCE. The Sphinx is known primarily as an Egyptian deity, but eventually was adapted in a lesser form by the Greeks, as seen on the side of the ancient terracotta vessel.

During the reign of King Creon, so many people fell sacrifice to this monster that he determined to use every effort to rid the country of so terrible a scourge. On consulting the oracle of Delphi, he was informed that the only way to destroy the Sphinx was to solve one of her riddles, when she would immediately precipitate herself from the rock on which she was seated.

Creon, accordingly, made a public declaration to the effect that whoever could give the true interpretation of a riddle propounded by the monster should obtain the crown, and the hand of his sister Jocaste. Œdipus offered himself as a candidate, and proceeding to the spot where she kept guard, received from her the following riddle for solution: “What creature goes in the morning on four legs, at noon on two, and in the evening on three?” Œdipus replied that it must be man, who during his infancy creeps on all fours, in his prime walks erect on two legs, and when old age has enfeebled his powers, calls a staff to his assistance, and thus has (as it were) three legs.

The Sphinx no sooner heard this reply, which was the correct solution of her riddle, than she flung herself over the precipice, and perished in the abyss below.

Chapter Four

MINOR DIVINITIES

OPPOSITE: ***A Young Girl Defending Herself Against Eros*****, William Adolphe Bouguereau, c. 1880. Eros was one of the most popular of the minor divinities, showing up in love stories and paintings through the ages.**

HERMES ∫ MERCURY

Hermes was the swift-footed messenger and trusted ambassador of all the gods, and conductor (transporter) of shades to Hades. He presided over the rearing and education of the young, and encouraged gymnastic exercises and athletic pursuits, for which reason all gymnasiums and wrestling schools throughout Greece were adorned with his statues. He is said to have invented the alphabet, and to have taught the art of interpreting foreign languages, and his versatility, sagacity, and cunning were so extraordinary that Zeus invariably chose him as his attendant when, disguised as a mortal, he journeyed on Earth.

Hermes was worshipped as God of Eloquence, most probably from the fact that, in his office as ambassador, this faculty was indispensable to the successful issue of the negotiations with which he was entrusted. He was regarded as the god who granted increases and prosperity to flocks and herds, and, on this account, was worshipped with special veneration by herdsmen.

OPPOSITE: ***Mercury and Argus*, Carel Fabritius, c. 1645–1647. At the request of Hera, Hermes killed the hundred-eyed Giant Argus Panoptes, who was guarding Io, Zeus's lover who had been transformed into a white cow.** BELOW: **Medal of seated Mercury, c. 1500–1599. This bronze coin from Italy features Hermes on one side.**

In ancient times, trade was conducted chiefly by means of the exchange of cattle. Hermes, therefore, as God of Herdsmen, came to be regarded as the protector of merchants, and, as ready wit and adroitness are valuable qualities both in buying and selling, he was also looked upon as the patron of artifice and cunning. Indeed, so deeply was this notion rooted in the minds of the Greek people that he was popularly believed to also be the God of Thieves, and of all persons who live by their wits.

As the patron of commerce, Hermes was the promoter of intercourse among nations; hence, he was essentially the God of Travelers, over whose safety he presided, and he severely punished those who refused assistance to a lost or weary wayfarer. He was also guardian of streets and roads, and his statues, called herms (which were pillars of stone surmounted by a head of Hermes), were placed at cross-roads, and frequently in streets and public squares.

Being the God of Grain and all undertakings in which gain was a feature, he was worshipped as the giver of wealth and good luck, and any unexpected stroke of fortune was attributed to his influence. He also presided over the game of dice, in which he is said to have been instructed by Apollo.

In his statues, Hermes is represented as a beardless youth, with broad chest and graceful but muscular limbs; his face is handsome and intelligent, and a genial smile of kindly benevolence plays round his delicately chiseled lips. As messenger of the gods he wears a winged hat and sandals, and bears in his hand the Caduceus (or herald's staff). As God of Eloquence, he is often represented with chains of gold hanging from his lips, whilst, as the patron of merchants, he bears a purse in his hand.

The ROLES *of* HERMES

As messenger of the gods, we find Hermes employed on all occasions requiring special skill, tact, or dispatch. Thus he brought Hera, Athene, and Aphrodite to Paris, led Priam to Achilles to demand the body of Hector, bound Prometheus to Mount Caucasus, secured Ixion to the eternally revolving wheel, destroyed Argus Panoptes, the hundred-eyed guardian of Io, and other such feats.

As conductor of shades, Hermes was always invoked by the dying to grant them a safe and speedy passage across the Styx. He also possessed the power of bringing back departed spirits to the upper world, and was, therefore, the mediator between the living and the dead.

The poets relate many amusing stories of the youthful tricks played by this mischief-loving god upon the other immortals. For instance, he had the audacity to extract Medusa's head from the shield of Athene, which he playfully attached to the back of Hephæstus; he also stole the girdle of Aphrodite; and deprived Artemis of her arrows and Ares of his spear, but these acts were always performed with such graceful dexterity, combined with such perfect good humor, that even the gods and goddesses he provoked were fain to pardon him, and he became a universal favorite with them all.

HERMES *and the* CATTLE *of* APOLLO

OPPOSITE: *Battus Changed into a Stone*, after Hendrik Goltzius, 1590. Hermes turned shepherd Battus into stone for witnessing him stealing sheep and being untrustworthy with the secret.

Hermes was the son of Zeus and Maia, the eldest and most beautiful of the seven Pleiades (daughters of Atlas), and was born in a cave of Mount Cyllene in Arcadia. As a mere babe, he exhibited an extraordinary faculty for cunning and dissimulation. Indeed, he was a thief from his cradle, for, not many hours after his birth, he was creeping stealthily out of the cave in which he was born, in order to steal some oxen belonging to his brother Apollo, who was at this time feeding the flocks of Admetus. But he had not proceeded very far on his expedition before he found a tortoise, which he killed, and, stretching seven strings across the empty shell, invented a lyre, upon which he at once began to play with exquisite skill.

When he had sufficiently amused himself with the instrument, he placed it in his cradle, and then resumed his journey to Pieria, where the cattle of Admetus were grazing. Arriving at sunset at his destination, he succeeded in separating fifty oxen from his brother's herd, which he now drove before him, taking the precaution to cover his feet with sandals made of twigs of myrtle, in order to escape detection.

But the little rogue was not unobserved, for the theft had been witnessed by an old shepherd named Battus, who was tending the flocks of Neleus, king of Pylos (father of Nestor). Hermes, frightened at being discovered, bribed him with the finest cow in the herd not to betray him, and Battus promised to keep the secret. But Hermes, as astute as he was dishonest, determined to test the shepherd's integrity. Feigning to go away, he assumed the form of Admetus, and then returned to the spot and offered the old man two of his best oxen if he would disclose the author of the theft. The ruse succeeded, for the avaricious shepherd, unable to resist the tempting bait, gave the desired information, upon which Hermes, exerting his divine power, changed him into a lump of touchstone as a punishment for his treachery and avarice. Hermes now killed two of the oxen, which he sacrificed to himself and the other gods, and concealed the remainder in his cave. He then carefully extinguished the fire, and, after throwing his twig shoes into the river Alpheus, returned to Cyllene.

Apollo, by means of his all-seeing power, soon discovered who it was who had robbed him, and hastening to Cyllene, demanded restitution of his property. On his complaining to Maia of her son's conduct, she pointed to the innocent babe then lying, apparently fast asleep, in his cradle, whereupon Apollo angrily aroused the pretending sleeper, and charged him with the theft; but the child stoutly denied all knowledge of it, and so cleverly did he play his part that he even inquired in the most naïve manner what sort of animals cows were.

Apollo threatened to throw him into Tartarus if he would not confess the truth, but

all to no avail. At last, he seized the babe in his arms, and brought him into the presence of his august father, who was seated in the council chamber of the gods. Zeus listened to the charge made by Apollo, and then sternly demanded that Hermes state where he had hidden the cattle. The child, who was still in swaddling clothes, looked up bravely into his father's face and said, "Now, do I look capable of driving away a herd of cattle; I, who was only born yesterday, and whose feet are much too soft and tender to tread in rough places? Until this moment, I lay in sweet sleep on my mother's bosom, and have never even crossed the threshold of our dwelling. You know well that I am not guilty; but, if you wish, I will affirm it by the most solemn oaths."

As the child stood before him, looking the picture of innocence, Zeus could not refrain from smiling at his cleverness and cunning, but, being perfectly aware of his guilt, he commanded him to conduct Apollo to the cave where he had concealed the herd. Hermes, seeing that further subterfuge was useless, unhesitatingly obeyed.

But when the divine shepherd was about to drive his cattle back into Pieria, Hermes, as though by chance, touched the cords of his lyre. Hitherto Apollo had heard nothing but the music of his own three-stringed lyre and the syrinx (Pan's pipe), and, as he listened, entranced by the delightful strains of this new instrument, his longing to possess it became so great that he gladly offered the oxen in exchange, promising at the same time to give Hermes full dominion over flocks and herds, as well as over horses, and all the wild animals of the woods and forests. The offer was accepted, and, a reconciliation being thus effected between the brothers, Hermes became henceforth God of Herdsmen, whilst Apollo devoted himself enthusiastically to the art of music.

They now proceeded together to Olympus, where Apollo introduced Hermes as his chosen friend and companion, and, having made him swear by the Styx that he would never steal his lyre or bow, nor invade his sanctuary at Delphi, he presented him with the caduceus, or golden wand. This wand was surmounted by wings, and on presenting it to Hermes, Apollo informed him that it possessed the faculty of uniting in love all beings divided by hate. Wishing to prove the truth of this assertion, Hermes threw it down between two snakes that were fighting, whereupon the angry combatants clasped each other in a loving embrace, and curling round the staff, remained ever after permanently attached to it. The wand itself typified power; the serpents, wisdom; and the wings, dispatch—all qualities characteristic of a trustworthy ambassador.

The young god was now presented by his father with a winged silver cap (called a "petasus"), and also with silver wings for his feet ("talaria"), and was forthwith appointed herald of the gods, and conductor of shades to the lower world, which office had hitherto been filled by Hades.

OPPOSITE: ***Herm of Hermes*, c. 50–100 CE. Because he is the God of Travelers, Hermes lends his name to herms, which are ancient pillars with the god's head on top that marked property boundaries.**
BELOW: **Detail from *L'Épître Othéa*, attributed to the Master of the Cité des Dames and workshop, c. 1410–1414. The steadfast Agraulos blocks Hermes's way into the home of his beloved, her sister Herse.**

HERMES and HERSE

It is said that Hermes was one day flying over Athens, when, looking down into the city, he beheld a number of maidens returning in solemn procession from the temple of Athene. Foremost among them was Herse, the beautiful daughter of king Cecrops, and Hermes was so struck with her exceeding loveliness that he determined to seek an interview with her. He accordingly presented himself at the royal palace, and begged her sister Agraulos to favor his suit; but, being of an avaricious turn of mind, she refused to do so without the payment of an enormous sum of money.

It did not take the messenger of the gods long to obtain the means of fulfilling this condition, and he soon returned with a well-filled purse. But meanwhile Athene, to punish the greed of Agraulos, had caused the demon of envy to take possession of her, and the consequence was that, being unable to contemplate the happiness of her sister, she sat down before the door, and resolutely refused to allow Hermes to enter. He tried every persuasion and blandishment in his power, but she still remained obstinate. At last, his patience being exhausted, he changed her into a mass of black stone, and, the obstacle to his wishes being removed, he succeeded in persuading Herse to become his wife.

The ROMAN MERCURY

Mercury was the Roman God of Commerce and Gain. We find mention of a temple having been erected to him near the Circus Maximus as early as 495 BCE; and he had also a temple and a sacred fount near the Porta Capena. Magic powers were ascribed to the latter, and during the festival of Mercury, which took place on the 25th of May, it was the custom for merchants to sprinkle themselves and their merchandise with this holy water, in order to ensure large profits from their wares.

The Fetiales (Roman priests whose duty it was to act as guardians of the public faith) refused to recognize the identity of Mercury with Hermes, and ordered him to be represented with a sacred branch as the emblem of peace, instead of the caduceus. In later times, however, he was completely identified with the Greek Hermes.

***Mercury*, Giovanni Girolamo Frezza, after Francesco Albani, 1704. Hermes with this characteristic wing-tipped sandals and hat, holding the caduceus, a golden wand that had the ability to unite in love all those who were divided by hate.**

DIONYSUS § BACCHUS

Dionysus, also called Bacchus (from the Latin *bacca*, or berry), was the God of Wine, and the personification of the blessings of nature in general.

Representations of Dionysus are of two kinds. According to the earliest conceptions, he appears as a grave and dignified man in the prime of life; his countenance is earnest, thoughtful, and benevolent; he wears a full beard, and is draped from head to foot in the garb of an Eastern monarch. But the sculptors of a later period represent him as a youth of singular beauty, with a somewhat effeminate appearance; the expression of his countenance is gentle and winning; his limbs are supple and gracefully molded; and his hair, which is adorned by a wreath of vine or ivy leaves, falls over his shoulders in long curls. In one hand he bears the thyrsus (his spear), and in the other a drinking-cup with two handles, these being his distinguishing attributes. He is often represented riding on a panther, or seated in a chariot drawn by lions, tigers, panthers, or lynxes. These animals, as well as dolphins, serpents, and donkeys, were sacred to this god. His sacrifices consisted of goats, probably on account of their being destructive to vineyards.

Head from *Statue of Young Bacchus*, 1–50 CE. This is all that remains of an ancient bronze statue depicting a young Dionysus.

Being the God of Wine and a promoter of sociability, he rarely appears alone, but is usually accompanied by Bacchantes, satyrs, and mountain nymphs.

Dionysus was regarded as the patron of the drama, and at the state festival of the Dionysia, which was celebrated with great pomp in the city of Athens, dramatic entertainments took place in his honor, for which all the renowned Greek dramatists of antiquity composed their immortal tragedies and comedies.

He was also a prophetic divinity, and possessed oracles, the principal of which was that on Mount Rhodope in Thrace.

DIONYSUS'S CHILDHOOD and the DISCOVERY of WINE

Dionysus was the son of Zeus and Semele, and was snatched by Zeus from the devouring flames in which his mother perished when Zeus appeared to her in all the splendor of his divine glory (as recounted on pages 25–26). The motherless child was entrusted to the charge of Hermes, who conveyed him to Semele's sister, Ino. But Hera, still implacable in her vengeance over Zeus's affair with Semele, visited Athamas, the husband of Ino, with madness. The child's life being no longer safe, he was transferred to the fostering care of the nymphs of Mount Nysa. An aged satyr named Silenus, the son of Pan, took upon himself the office of guardian and preceptor to the young god, who, in his turn, became much attached to his kind tutor; hence we see Silenus always figuring as one of the chief personages in the various expeditions of the Wine God.

Dionysus passed an innocent childhood, roaming through the woods and forests, surrounded by nymphs, satyrs, and shepherds. During one of these rambles, he found a fruit growing wild, of a most refreshing and cooling nature. This was the grape, from which he subsequently learnt to extract a juice that formed a most exhilarating beverage. After his companions had partaken freely of it, they felt their whole being pervaded by an unwonted sense of pleasurable excitement, and gave full vent to their overflowing exuberance by shouting, singing, and dancing. Their numbers were soon swelled by a crowd, eager to taste a beverage productive of such extraordinary results, and anxious to join in the worship of a divinity to whom they were indebted for this new enjoyment. Dionysus, on his part, seeing how agreeably his discovery had affected his immediate followers, resolved to extend the boon to mankind in general. He saw that wine, used in moderation, would enable man to enjoy a happier and more sociable existence, and that, under its invigorating influence, the sorrowful might, for a while, forget their grief and the sick their pain. He accordingly gathered round

OPPOSITE: ***The Infant Bacchus*, Giovanni Bellini, c. 1505–1510. Dionysus was said to have discovered wine when he was just a child.**
ABOVE: ***Dionysus Attended by Two Bacchantes*, Jean-Baptiste Deschamps, c. 1865. Dionysus had legions of followers (called "Bacchantes"), not only because he always had wine, but because he promoted what many believed to be a more social and civilized lifestyle.**

him his zealous followers, and they set forth on their travels, planting the vine and teaching its cultivation wherever they went.

BACCHANALS

OPPOSITE: *Bacchanale*, Alessandro Magnasco, c. 1720–1730. Dancing, singing, and playing instruments, satyrs take part in a bacchanal amidst the ruins.

The wild revels that attended the worship of the Wine God were later called bacchanals, after his name Bacchus. At bacchanals, men, women, nymphs, satyrs, and other mythical creatures drank wine, had orgies, and partook in other behavior many found immoral. One such disapprover was Lycurgus, king of Thrace, who drove away Dionysus's attendants, the nymphs of Nysa, from his land, and so effectually intimidated Dionysus that he leapt suddenly into the sea, where he was received into the arms of the ocean nymph Thetis. But the impious king bitterly atoned his sacrilegious conduct. He was punished with the loss of his reason, and, during one of his mad paroxysms, killed his own son Dryas, whom he mistook for a vine.

As Dionysus and his followers marched through the land, celebrating as they went, they bared thyrsuses (staffs entwined with vine-branches surmounted by pinecones), and clashed together cymbals and other musical instruments. Seated in a chariot drawn by panthers, and accompanied by thousands of enthusiastic nymphs, fauns, and other revelers, it is said that Dionysus made triumphal progress through Syria, Egypt, Arabia, and India, conquering all before him, founding cities, and establishing on every side a more civilized and sociable mode of life among the inhabitants of the various countries through which he passed.

DIONYSUS *and the* PIRATES

An incident concerning Dionysus on one of his travels was a favorite subject with the classic poets. One day, as some Tyrrhenian pirates approached the shores of Greece, they beheld Dionysus, in the form of a beautiful youth, attired in radiant garments. Thinking they would secure a rich prize, they seized him, bound him, and conveyed him on board their vessel, resolving to carry him with them to Asia and there, sell him as a slave. But the fetters dropped from his limbs, and the pilot, who was the first to perceive the miracle, called upon his companions to restore the youth carefully to the spot whence they had taken him, assuring them that he was a god, and that adverse winds and storms would, in all probability, result from their impious conduct. But, refusing to part with their prisoner, they set sail for the open sea. Suddenly, to the alarm of all on board, the ship stood still, its masts and sails covered with clustering vines and wreaths of ivy-leaves. Streams of fragrant wine inundated the vessel, and heavenly strains of music were heard all around. The

crew, terrified of the Sirens but repentant too late, crowded round the pilot for protection, and entreated him to steer for the shore. But the hour of retribution had arrived. Dionysus assumed the form of a lion, whilst beside him appeared a bear, that, with a terrific roar, rushed upon the captain and tore him in pieces; the sailors, in an agony of terror, leapt overboard, and were changed into dolphins. The discreet and pious steersman was alone permitted to escape the fate of his companions, and to him Dionysus, who had resumed his true form, addressed words of kind and affectionate encouragement, and announced his name and dignity.

They now set sail, and Dionysus desired the pilot to land him at the island of Naxos, where he found the lovely Ariadne, daughter of Minos, king of Crete. She had been abandoned by Theseus on this lonely spot, and, when Dionysus now beheld her, was lying fast asleep on a rock, worn out with sorrow and weeping. Wrapt in admiration, the god stood gazing at the beautiful vision before him, and when she at length opened her eyes, he revealed himself to her, and, in gentle tones, sought to banish her grief. Grateful for his kind sympathy, coming as it did at a moment when she had deemed herself forsaken and friendless, she gradually regained her former serenity, and, yielding to his entreaties, consented to become his wife.

OPPOSITE: *Bacchus and Ariadne*, Guido Reni, c. 1619–1620. Dionysus found his wife Ariadne on the island of Naxos, where she had been abandoned by Theseus.

KING MIDAS and the GOLDEN TOUCH

Among the most noted stories about Dionysus is when he bestowed the golden touch upon Midas,[1] the wealthy king of Phrygia who was given the ears of an ass by Apollo (as related on page 81). It began when Silenus, the tutor and friend of Dionysus, being in an intoxicated condition, strayed into the rose-gardens of King Midas, where he was found by the king's attendants, who bound him with roses and conducted him to the presence of their royal master. Midas treated the aged satyr with the greatest consideration, and, after entertaining him hospitably for ten days, led him back to Dionysus, who was so grateful for the kind attention shown to his old friend that he offered to grant Midas any favor he chose to demand. Whereupon the avaricious monarch, not content with his boundless wealth, and still thirsting for more, desired that everything he touched might turn to gold.

The request was complied with in so literal a sense that the now wretched Midas bitterly repented his folly and greed, for, when the pangs of hunger assailed him, and he tried to appease his cravings, the food became gold so he could not swallow it; as he raised the cup of wine to his parched lips, the sparkling draught was changed into the metal he

1 Midas was the son of Cybele and Gordius, the king who tied the celebrated and intricate knot.

Plate from *The Wonder Book for Girls & Boys,* Walter Crane, 1892. Midas bathes in the river Pactolus to rid himself of the golden touch bestowed upon him by Dionysus.

had so coveted; and when at length, wearied and faint, he stretched his aching frame on his hitherto luxurious couch, this also was transformed into the substance that had now become the curse of his existence.[2] The despairing king at last implored the god to take back the fatal gift, and Dionysus, pitying his unhappy plight, told him to bathe in the river Pactolus, a small stream in Lydia, in order to lose the power that had become the bane of his life. Midas joyfully obeyed, and was at once freed from the consequences of his avaricious demand, and from this time forth the sands of the river Pactolus have ever contained grains of gold.

2 In some versions of the story, Midas even turns his own daughter into gold.

EROS § CUPID

According to Hesiod's *Theogony*, Eros, the divine spirit of love, sprang forth from Chaos, while all was still in confusion, and by his beneficent power reduced to order and harmony the shapeless, conflicting elements, that, under his influence, began to assume distinct forms. This ancient Eros is represented as a full-grown and very beautiful youth, crowned with flowers, and leaning on a shepherd's crook.

Head of Eros, 100–200 CE. Eros was at first represented as a young man with a shepherd's crook, but is better known by his later likeness, a young boy with rounded cheeks and a quiver full of arrows.

In the course of time, however, this beautiful conception gradually faded away, and though occasional mention still continues to be made of the Eros of Chaos, he is mostly replaced by the son of Aphrodite, the popular, mischief-loving little God of Love, so familiar to us all.

Eros is represented as a lovely boy, with rounded limbs, and a merry, roguish expression. He has golden wings, and a quiver slung over his shoulder, which contains his magical and unerring arrows; in one hand he bears his golden bow, and in the other, a torch. He is also frequently depicted riding on a lion, dolphin, or eagle, or seated in a chariot drawn by stags or wild boars, undoubtedly emblematic of the power of love as the subduer of all nature, even of the wild animals.

In one of the myths concerning Eros, Aphrodite is described as complaining to Themis that her son, though so beautiful, did not appear to increase in stature; whereupon Themis suggested that his small proportions were probably attributable to the fact of his being always alone, and advised his mother to let him have a companion. Aphrodite accordingly gave him, as a playfellow, his younger brother Anteros (Requited Love), and soon had the gratification of seeing the little Eros begin to grow and thrive; but, curious to relate, this desirable result only continued as long as the brothers remained together, for the moment they were separated, Eros shrank once more to his original size.

By degrees the conception of Eros became multiplied and we hear of little love gods (Amors), who appear under the most charming and diversified forms. These love gods, who afforded to artists inexhaustible subjects for the exercise of their imagination, are

represented as being engaged in various occupations, such as hunting, fishing, rowing, driving chariots, and even busying themselves in mechanical labor.

EROS *and* PSYCHE

Perhaps no myth is more charming and interesting than that of Eros and Psyche, which is as follows: Psyche, the youngest of three princesses, was so transcendently beautiful that Aphrodite herself became jealous of her, and no mortal dared to aspire to the honor of her hand. As her sisters, who were by no means equal to her in attractiveness, were married, and Psyche still remained unwedded, her father consulted the oracle of Delphi, and, in obedience to the divine response, caused her to be dressed as though for the grave, and conducted her to the edge of a yawning precipice. No sooner was she alone than she felt herself lifted up and wafted away by the gentle west wind Zephyrus, who transported her to a verdant meadow, in the midst of which stood a stately palace, surrounded by groves and fountains.

OPPOSITE: *The Father of Psyche Consulting the Oracle of Apollo*, Baron François-Pascal-Simon Gérard, c. 1796. Psyche hears her fate while Eros looks on in the corner. BELOW: *Striding Cupid*, c. 1–300 CE. Depictions of Eros became so plentiful that they grew into many different love gods with separate personalities and skills, known as Amors.

Here dwelt Eros, the God of Love, in whose arms Zephyrus deposited his lovely burden. Eros, himself unseen, wooed her in the softest accents of affection; but warned her, as she valued his love, not to endeavor to behold his form. For some time Psyche was obedient to the injunction of her immortal spouse, and made no effort to gratify her natural curiosity; but, unfortunately, in the midst of her happiness she was seized with an unconquerable longing for the society of her sisters, and, in accordance with her desire, they were conducted by Zephyrus to her fairy-like abode. Filled with envy at the sight of her felicity, they poisoned her mind against her husband, and telling her that her unseen lover was a frightful monster, they gave her a sharp dagger, which they persuaded her to use for the purpose of delivering herself from his power.

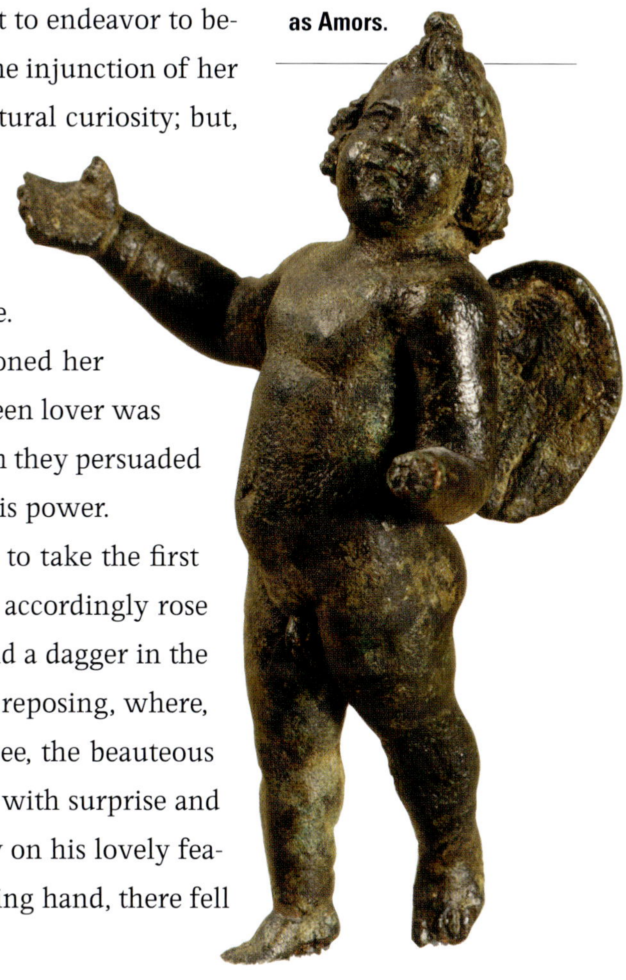

After the departure of her sisters, Psyche resolved to take the first opportunity of following their malicious counsel. She accordingly rose in the dead of night, and taking a lamp in one hand and a dagger in the other, stealthily approached the couch where Eros was reposing, where, instead of the frightful monster she had expected to see, the beauteous form of the God of Love greeted her view. Overcome with surprise and admiration, Psyche stooped down to gaze more closely on his lovely features, when, from the lamp that she held in her trembling hand, there fell a drop of burning oil upon the shoulder of the sleeping god, who instantly awoke, and seeing Psyche standing over him with the instrument of death in her hand, sorrowfully reproached her for her treacherous designs, and, spreading out his wings, flew away.

In despair at having lost her lover, the unhappy Psyche endeavored to put an end to her existence by throwing herself into the nearest river; but instead of closing over her, the waters bore her gently to the opposite bank, where Pan (the God of Shepherds) received her, and consoled her with the hope of becoming eventually reconciled to her husband.

OPPOSITE: *Venus with Cupid Stealing Honey*, Lucas Cranach the Elder, 1530. Eros with his mother, Aphrodite. In the poem "Cupid Stealing Honey" by the classical Greek poet Theocritus, Eros complains to Aphrodite about receiving bee stings, and she replies that they feel the same as the stings of his love arrows.

Meanwhile her wicked sisters, in expectation of meeting with the same good fortune that had befallen Psyche, placed themselves on the edge of the rock, but were both precipitated into the chasm below.

Psyche herself, filled with a restless yearning for her lost love, wandered all over the world in search of him. At length she appealed to Aphrodite to take compassion on her; but the Goddess of Beauty, still jealous of her charms, imposed upon her the hardest tasks, the accomplishment of which often appeared impossible. In these she was always assisted by invisible, beneficent beings, sent to her by Eros, who still loved her, and continued to watch over her welfare.

Psyche had to undergo a long and severe penance before she became worthy to regain the happiness that she had so foolishly trifled away. At last Aphrodite commanded her to descend into the under world, and obtain from Persephone a box containing all the charms of beauty. Psyche's courage now failed her, for she concluded that death must, by necessity, precede her entrance into the realm of shades.

About to abandon herself to despair, she heard a voice that warned her of every danger to be avoided on her perilous journey, and instructed her with regard to certain precautions to be observed. These were as follows: not to omit to provide herself with the ferryman's toll for Charon and the cake to pacify Cerberus, also to refrain from taking any part in the banquets of Hades and Persephone, and, above all things, to bring the box of beauty charms unopened to Aphrodite. In conclusion, the voice assured her, compliance with the above conditions would insure for her a safe return to the realms of light.

But, alas, Psyche, who had implicitly followed all injunctions, could not withstand the temptation of the last condition; and, hardly had she quitted the lower world, when, unable to resist the curiosity that devoured her, she raised the lid of the box with eager expectation. But, instead of the wondrous charms of beauty that she expected to behold, there issued from the casket a dense black vapor, which had the effect of throwing her into a death-like sleep, out of which Eros, who had long hovered round her unseen, at length awoke her with the point of one of his golden arrows. He gently reproached her with this

DVM PVER ALVEOLO FVRATVR MELLA CVPIDO
FVRANTI DIGITVM CVSPIDE FIXIT APIS
SIC ETIAM NOBIS BREVIS ET PERITVRA VOLVPTAS
QVAM PETIMVS TRISTI MIXTA DOLORE NOCET

second proof of her curiosity and folly, and then, having persuaded Aphrodite to be reconciled to his beloved, he induced Zeus to admit her among the immortal gods.

Their reunion was celebrated amidst the rejoicings of all the Olympian deities. The Graces shed perfume on their path, the Hours sprinkled roses over the sky, Apollo added the music of his lyre, and the Muses united their voices in a glad chorus of delight.

This myth would appear to be an allegory that signifies that the soul, before it can be reunited to its original divine essence, must be purified by the chastening sorrows and sufferings of its earthly career.[3]

PAN § FAUNUS

Pan was the God of Fertility, and the special patron of shepherds and huntsmen; he presided over all rural occupations, was chief of the satyrs, and head of all rural divinities.

According to common belief, he was the son of Hermes and a wood-nymph, and came into the world with horns sprouting from his forehead; a crooked nose; pointed ears; and

3 The word Psyche signifies "butterfly," the emblem of the soul in ancient art.

a goat's beard, tail and feet; and presented altogether so repulsive an appearance that, at the sight of him, his mother fled in dismay.

Hermes, however, took up his curious little offspring, wrapped him in a hare skin, and carried him in his arms to Olympus. The grotesque form and merry antics of the little stranger made him a great favorite with all the immortals, especially Dionysus; and they bestowed upon him the name of Pan (All), because he had delighted them all.

The artists of later times somewhat toned down the original very unattractive conception of Pan, as above described, and merely represent him as a young man, hardened by the exposure to all weathers that a rural life involves, and bearing in his hand the shepherd's crook and syrinx flute—these being his usual attributes—whilst small horns project from his forehead. He is either undraped, or wears merely the light cloak called the chlamys.

Pan was regarded by shepherds as their most valiant protector, who defended their flocks from the attacks of wolves. The shepherds of these early times, having no fenced enclosures, were in the habit of gathering together their flocks in mountain caves to protect them against the inclemency of the weather, and also to secure them at night against the attacks of wild animals; these caves, which were very numerous in the mountain districts of Arcadia and Bœotia, were therefore all consecrated to Pan.

OPPOSITE: *Pan and Nymphs*, Ignaz Elhafen, c. 1690–1695. Pan was often surrounded by nymphs of the woodlands, who loved to dance around him as he played his syrinx, or pan flute.

ABOVE: Applique depicting the head of Pan, c. 100 BCE. The hole in the cheek of this ancient ivory head of Pan indicated that it was originally attached to something else, possibly a piece of furniture.

Pan was equally beloved by huntsmen, being himself a great lover of the woods, which afforded to his cheerful and active disposition full scope, and in which he loved to range at will. He was regarded as the patron of the chase, and should rural sportsmen return from an unsuccessful day's sport, they beat, in token of their displeasure, the wooden image of Pan, which always occupied a prominent place in their dwellings.

Pan was gifted with the power of prophecy, which he is said to have imparted to Apollo, and he possessed a well-known and very ancient oracle in Arcadia, in which state he was most especially worshipped.

After the introduction of Pan into the worshiping of Dionysus, we hear of a number of little Pans (Panisci), who are sometimes confounded with the satyrs.

PAN *the* NOISEMAKER

Pan's favorite haunts were grottoes, and his delight was to wander in uncontrolled freedom over rocks and mountains, following his various pursuits, ever cheerful, and usually very noisy. He was a great lover of music, singing, dancing, and all pursuits that enhance the pleasures of life; and hence, in spite of his repulsive appearance, we see him surrounded with nymphs of the forests and dales, who loved to dance round him to the cheerful music of his pipe, the syrinx.

All sudden and unaccountable sounds that startle travelers in lonely spots were attributed to Pan, who possessed a frightful and most discordant voice; hence the term "panic" to indicate sudden fear. The Athenians ascribed their victory at Marathon to the alarm that he created among the Persians by his terrible voice.

As it is customary in all tropical climates to nap during the heat of the day, Pan is represented as greatly enjoying his afternoon sleep in the cool shelter of a tree or cave, and also as being highly displeased at any sound that disturbed his slumbers, for which reason the shepherds were always particularly careful to keep unbroken silence during these hours, whilst they themselves indulged in a quiet siesta.

OPPOSITE: *Pan and Syrinx*, Jean-François de Troy, c. 1722–1724. With Pan's frightening countenance, it's no wonder the wood nymph Syrinx was so terrified of his advances that he she hid from him. The gods turned her into a reed, which Pan made into his legendary flute and named after her.

PAN *and* SYRINX

The myth concerning the origin of Pan's pipe is as follows: Pan became enamored of a beautiful nymph called Syrinx, who, appalled at his terrible appearance, fled from the pertinacious attentions of her unwelcome suitor. He pursued her to the banks of the river Ladon, when, seeing his near approach, and feeling escape impossible, she called on the gods for assistance, who, in answer to her prayer, transformed her into a reed, just as Pan was about to seize her. Whilst the love-sick Pan was sighing and lamenting his unfortunate fate, the winds gently swayed the reeds, and produced a murmuring sound as of one complaining. Charmed with the soothing tones,

he endeavored to reproduce them himself, and after cutting seven of the reeds of unequal length, he joined them together, and succeeded in producing the pipe, which he called the syrinx, in memory of his lost love.

The ROMAN FAUNUS

The Romans had an old Italian divinity called Faunus, who, as the God of Shepherds, was identified with the Greek Pan, and was represented in a similar manner.

Faunus was frequently called Inuus (the fertilizer), or Lupercus (the one who wards off wolves). Like Pan, he possessed the gift of prophecy, and was the presiding spirit of the woods and fields; he also shared with his Greek prototype the faculty of alarming travelers in solitary places. Bad dreams and evil apparitions were attributed to Faunus, and he was believed to enter houses stealthily at night for this purpose.

Fauna was the wife of Faunus, and participated in his functions.

TYCHE & FORTUNA

Fortuna, c. 100–400 CE. Tyche is portrayed in this bronze sculpture with her signature cornucopia.

Tyche personified that peculiar combination of circumstances that we call luck or fortune, and was considered to be the source of all unexpected events in human life, whether good or evil. If a person succeeded in all he undertook without possessing any special merit of his own, Tyche was supposed to have smiled on his birth. If, on the other hand, undeserved ill-luck followed him through life, and all his efforts resulted in failure, it was ascribed to her adverse influence.

The Goddess of Fortune is variously represented. Sometimes she is depicted bearing in her hand two rudders, with one of which she steers the bark of the fortunate, and with the other that of the unfortunate among mortals. In later times she appears blindfolded, and stands on a ball or wheel, indicative of the fickleness and ever-revolving changes of fortune. She frequently bears a sceptre and cornucopia, or horn of plenty,[4] and is usually winged. In her temple at Thebes, she is represented holding the infant Plutus in her arms, to symbolize her power over riches and prosperity.

Tyche was worshipped in various parts of Greece, but more particularly by the Athenians, who believed in her special predilection for their city.

The ROMAN FORTUNA

Tyche was worshipped in Rome under the name of Fortuna, and held a position of much greater importance among the Romans than the Greeks.

In later times, Fortuna is never represented either winged or standing on a ball; she merely bears the cornucopia. It is evident, therefore, that she had come to be regarded as the Goddess of Good Luck only, who brings blessings to man, and not, as with the Greeks, as the personification of the fluctuations of fortune.

4 One of the horns of the goat Amalthea, broken off by Zeus, and supposed to possess the power of filling itself with whatsoever its owner desired.

Plate from *The Wonder Book for Girls & Boys*, Walter Crane, 1892. Pegasus being ridden by Bellerophon, the only mortal to ever mount him.

PEGASUS

Pegasus was a beautiful winged horse who sprang from the body of Medusa when she was slain by the hero Perseus, the son of Zeus and Danaë. Spreading out his wings, he immediately flew to the top of Mount Olympus, where he was received with delight and admiration by all the immortals. A place in his palace was assigned to him by Zeus, who employed him to carry his thunder and lightning. Pegasus permitted none but the gods to mount him, except in the case of Bellerophon, whom, at the command of Athene, he carried aloft in order that he might slay the Chimæra with his arrows (as will be recounted on page 238).

The later poets represent Pegasus as being at the service of the Muses, and for this reason he is more celebrated in modern times than in antiquity. He would appear to represent that poetical inspiration that tends to develop man's higher nature and causes the mind to soar heavenwards.

The ORIGIN *of the* FOUNTAIN HIPPOCRENE

The only mention by the ancients of Pegasus in connection with the Muses is the story of his having produced the famous fountain Hippocrene with his hoofs. It is said that during their contest with the Pierides (which will be recounted on page 185), the Muses played and sang on the summit of Mount Helicon with such extraordinary power and sweetness that heaven and Earth stood still to listen, whilst the mountain raised itself in joyous ecstasy towards the abode of the celestial gods. Poseidon, seeing his special function thus interfered with, sent Pegasus to check the boldness of the mountain in daring to move without his permission. When Pegasus reached the summit, he stamped the ground with his hoofs, and out gushed the waters of Hippocrene, afterwards renowned as the sacred fount where the Muses quaffed their richest draughts of inspiration.

Bed Hanging with Pegasus and the Nine Muses, c. 1700. Pegasus was a precursor to the modern-day unicorn, which has wings and a horn.

THE MUSES

***The Muses Urania and Calliope*, Simon Vouet and studio, c. 1634. Urania, the Muse of Astrology, is depicted in blue robes with a crown of stars, while Calliope, the Muse of Song and Poetry, sits with a book in her hands.**

Of all the Olympic deities, none occupy a more honored position than the Muses, the nine beautiful daughters of Zeus and Mnemosyne. It is said that they were created by Zeus in answer to a request on the part of the victorious deities, after the war with the Titans, that some special divinities should be called into existence in order to commemorate in song the glorious deeds of the Olympian gods.

In their original signification, they presided merely over music, song, and dance; but with the progress of civilization, the arts and sciences claimed their special presiding divinities, and we see these graceful creations in later times sharing amongst them various functions, such as poetry and astronomy.

The Muses were honored alike by mortals and immortals. In Olympus, where Apollo acted as their leader, no banquet or festivity was considered complete without their joy-inspiring presence, and on Earth no social gathering was celebrated without libations being poured out to them; nor was any task involving intellectual effort ever undertaken without earnestly supplicating their assistance. They endowed their chosen favorites with knowledge, wisdom, and understanding; they bestowed upon the orator the gift of eloquence, inspired the poet with his noblest thoughts, and the musician with his sweetest harmonies.

The Muses dwelt on the summits of Mounts Helicon, Parnassus, and Pindus, and loved to haunt the springs and fountains that gushed forth amidst these rocky heights, all of which were sacred to them and to poetic inspiration. Aganippe and Hippocrene on Mount Helicon, and the Castalian spring on Mount Parnassus, were especially sacred to the Muses. The latter flowed between two lofty rocks above the city of Delphi, and in ancient times its waters were introduced into a square stone basin, where they were retained for the use of the Pythia and the priests of Apollo.

Page from the *Regia Carmina*, c. 1335–1340. Calliope, shown here, was one of the most celebrated of the Muses.

The libations to these divinities consisted of water, milk, and honey, but never of wine.

The NINE MUSES

The Muses were nine in number, and their names and functions are as follows: Calliope, the most honored of the Muses, presided over heroic song and epic poetry, and is represented with a pencil in her hand and a slate upon her knee. Clio, the Muse of History, holds in her hand a roll of parchment, and wears a wreath of laurel. Melpomene, the Muse of Tragedy, bears a tragic mask. Thalia, the Muse of Comedy, carries in her right hand a shepherd's crook, and has a comic mask beside her. Polyhymnia, the Muse of Sacred Hymns, is crowned with a wreath of laurel. She is always represented in a thoughtful attitude, and entirely enveloped in rich folds of drapery. Terpsichore,

A Muse, Rosalba Carriera, c. 1725. Erato, one of the nine Muses, was often portrayed with a laurel-leaf crown.

the Muse of Dance and Roundelay, is represented in the act of playing on a seven-stringed lyre. Urania, the Muse of Astronomy, stands erect, and bears in her left hand a celestial globe. Euterpe, the Muse of Harmony, is represented bearing a musical instrument, usually a flute. Finally, Erato, the Muse of Love and Hymeneal Songs, wears a wreath of laurel, and is striking the cords of a lyre.

HG. Inuent.

The JEALOUSY of the MUSES

Like so many of the Greek divinities, the refined conception of the Muses was somewhat marred by the acerbity with which they punished any effort on the part of mortals to rival them in their divine powers. An instance of this is seen in the case of Thamyris, a Thracian bard, who presumed to invite them to a trial of skill in music. Having vanquished him, they not only afflicted him with blindness, but deprived him also of the power of song.

Another example of the manner in which the gods punished presumption and vanity is seen in the story of the daughters of King Pierus. Proud of the perfection to which they had brought their skill in music, they presumed to challenge the Muses themselves in the art over which they specially presided. The contest took place on Mount Helicon, and it is said that when the mortal maidens commenced their song, the sky became dark and misty, whereas when the Muses raised their heavenly voices, all nature seemed to rejoice, and Mount Helicon itself moved with exultation. The Pierides were signally defeated, and were transformed by the Muses into singing birds as a punishment for having dared to even challenge comparison with the immortals.

Undeterred by the fate of the Pierides, the Sirens also entered into a similar contest. The songs of the Muses were loyal and true, whilst those of the Sirens were the false and deceptive strains with which so many unfortunate mariners had been lured to their deaths. The Sirens were defeated by the Muses, and as a mark of humiliation, were deprived of the feathers with which their bodies were adorned.

THE GRACES

All those gentler attributes that beautify and refine human existence were personified by the Greeks under the form of the Graces, three lovely sisters, Euphrosyne, Aglaia, and Thalia, the daughters of Zeus and Eurynome (or, according to later writers, of Dionysus and Aphrodite).

OPPOSITE: ***The Three Graces,*** **Jacob Matham, 1588. The Graces, three sisters, were often portrayed with their arms lovingly intertwined.**

They are represented as beautiful, slender maidens in the full bloom of youth, with hands and arms lovingly intertwined, and are either undraped, or wear a fleecy, transparent garment of an ethereal fabric.

They portray every gentle emotion of the heart that vents itself in friendship and benevolence, and were believed to preside over those qualities that constitute grace, modesty, unconscious beauty, gentleness, kindliness, innocent joy, purity of mind and body, and eternal youth.

They not only possessed the most perfect beauty themselves, but also conferred this gift upon others. All the enjoyments of life were enhanced by their presence, and were

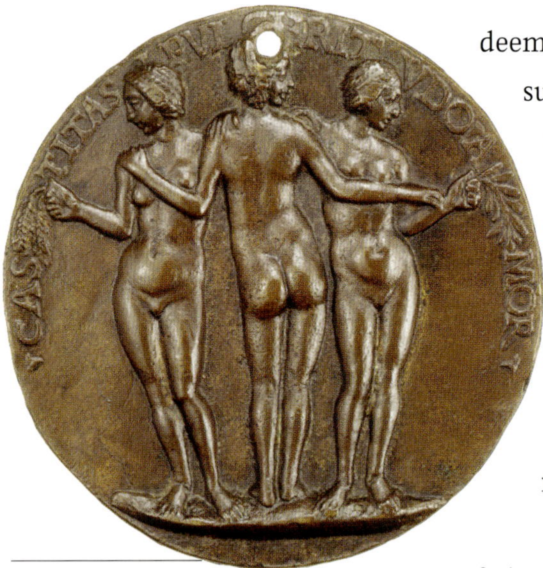

The Three Graces, attributed to Niccolò Fiorentino, c. 1486. The Graces personified the ideal woman to the Greek mind, representing grace, beauty, purity, and kindliness.

deemed incomplete without them; and wherever joy or pleasure, grace and gaiety reigned, there they were supposed to be present.

Temples and altars were everywhere erected in their honor, and people of all ages and of every rank in life entreated their favor. Incense was burnt daily upon their altars, and at every banquet they were invoked, and a libation poured out to them, as they not only heightened all enjoyment, but also by their refining influence moderated the exciting effects of wine.

Music, eloquence, poetry, and art, though the direct work of the Muses, received at the hands of the Graces an additional touch of refinement and beauty; for which reason they are always regarded as the friends of the Muses, with whom they lived on Mount Olympus.

Their special function was to act, in conjunction with the Horæ, as attendants upon Aphrodite, whom they adorned with wreaths of flowers, and she would emerge from their hands like the queen of spring, perfumed with the odor of roses and violets, and all other sweet-scented blossoms.

The Graces are frequently seen in attendance on other divinities as well; thus they carry music for Apollo and frequently accompany him, Eros, or Dionysus.

THE HORÆ ∫ SEASONS

Closely allied to the Graces were the Horæ, or Seasons, who were also represented as three beautiful maidens, daughters of Zeus and Themis. Their names were Eunomia, Dice, and Irene.

It may appear strange that these divinities, presiding over the seasons, should be but three in number, but this is quite in accordance with the notions of the ancient Greeks, who only recognized spring, summer, and autumn as seasons; nature being supposed to be wrapped in death or slumber during that cheerless and unproductive portion of the year that we call winter. In some parts of Greece, there were but two Horæ: Thallo, Goddess of the Bloom, and Carpo, Goddess of the Corn and Fruit-Bearing Season.

In their original conception, the Horæ were personifications of the clouds, and were described as opening and closing the gates of heaven, and causing fruits and flowers to spring forth, when they poured down upon them their refreshing and life-giving streams. The Horæ were always regarded as friendly toward mankind, and totally devoid of guile

***The Four Seasons*, Godfried Maes, c. 1650–1700. The Horæ, Eunomia, Dice, and Irene, are portrayed in the center of this artwork, while Hades, representing winter, sits sullenly in the corner.**

or subtlety; they were later represented as joyous, but gentle maidens, crowned with flowers, and holding each other by the hands in a round dance. When they are depicted separately as personifications of the different seasons, the Hora representing spring appears laden with flowers, that of summer bears a sheaf of corn, whilst the personification of autumn has her hands filled with clusters of grapes and other fruits. They also appear in company with the Graces in the train of Aphrodite, and are seen with Apollo and the Muses.

The Horæ were inseparably connected with all that is good and beautiful in nature. As the regular alternation of the seasons, like all of nature's other operations, demands the most perfect order and regularity, the Horæ, being the daughters of Themis, came to be regarded as the representatives of order, and the just administration of human affairs in civilized communities. Each of these graceful maidens took upon herself a separate function: Eunomia presided more especially over state life, Dice guarded the interests of individuals, whilst Irene, the gayest and brightest of the three sisters, was the light-hearted companion of Dionysus.

The Horæ were also the deities of the fast-fleeting hours, and thus presided over divisions of time both small and large. In this capacity they assisted every morning in yoking the celestial horses to the glorious chariot of the sun, which they again helped to unyoke when he sank to rest.

Plate from *The Wonder Book for Girls & Boys*, Walter Crane, 1892. Heracles stands amongst the Dryades.

THE DRYADES

Whilst the flower and meadow nymphs assumed the shapes of tiny elves and fairies, the tree-nymphs, or Dryades, partook of the distinguishing characteristics of the particular tree to whose life they were wedded.

The Hamadryades, or oak-nymphs, represented in their peculiar individuality the quiet, self-reliant power that appeared to belong essentially to the grand and lordly king of the forest. The birch-nymphs were melancholy maidens with floating hair, resembling the branches of the pale and fragile-looking trees that they inhabited. The beech-nymphs, however, were strong and sturdy, full of life and joyousness, and appeared to give the promise of faithful love and undisturbed repose, whilst their rosy cheeks, deep brown eyes, and graceful forms bespoke health, vigor, and vitality. Finally, the nymphs of the linden tree were represented as coy maidens, whose short, silver-gray dresses reached a little below the knee, and advantageously displayed their delicately formed limbs. Their sweet faces, which were shown partly averted, each revealed a pair of large blue eyes, which appeared to look at you with wondering surprise and shy mistrust; their pale, golden hair was bound by the faintest streak of rose-colored ribbon.

A Dryad, being joined to the life of the tree she inhabited, ceased to exist when it was either felled or so injured as to wither away and die.

Woodland Scene with Nymphs and a Herm, Jean-Victor Bertin, c. 1810. Dryades, or tree-nymphs, can be seen frolicking around a herm in the background of this scene by famous landscape painter Jean-Victor Bertin.

THE SATYRS & FAUNS

The satyrs were a race of woodland spirits who personified the free, wild, and untrammeled life of the forest. Their appearance was both grotesque and repulsive; they had flat broad noses, pointed ears, and little horns sprouting from their foreheads, rough shaggy skin, and small goats' tails. They led a life of pleasure and self-indulgence, followed the chase, reveled in every description of wild music and dancing, were terrible wine drinkers, and were addicted to the deep slumbers that follow heavy potations. They were no less dreaded by mortals than by the gentle woodland nymphs, who always avoided their coarse rough sports.

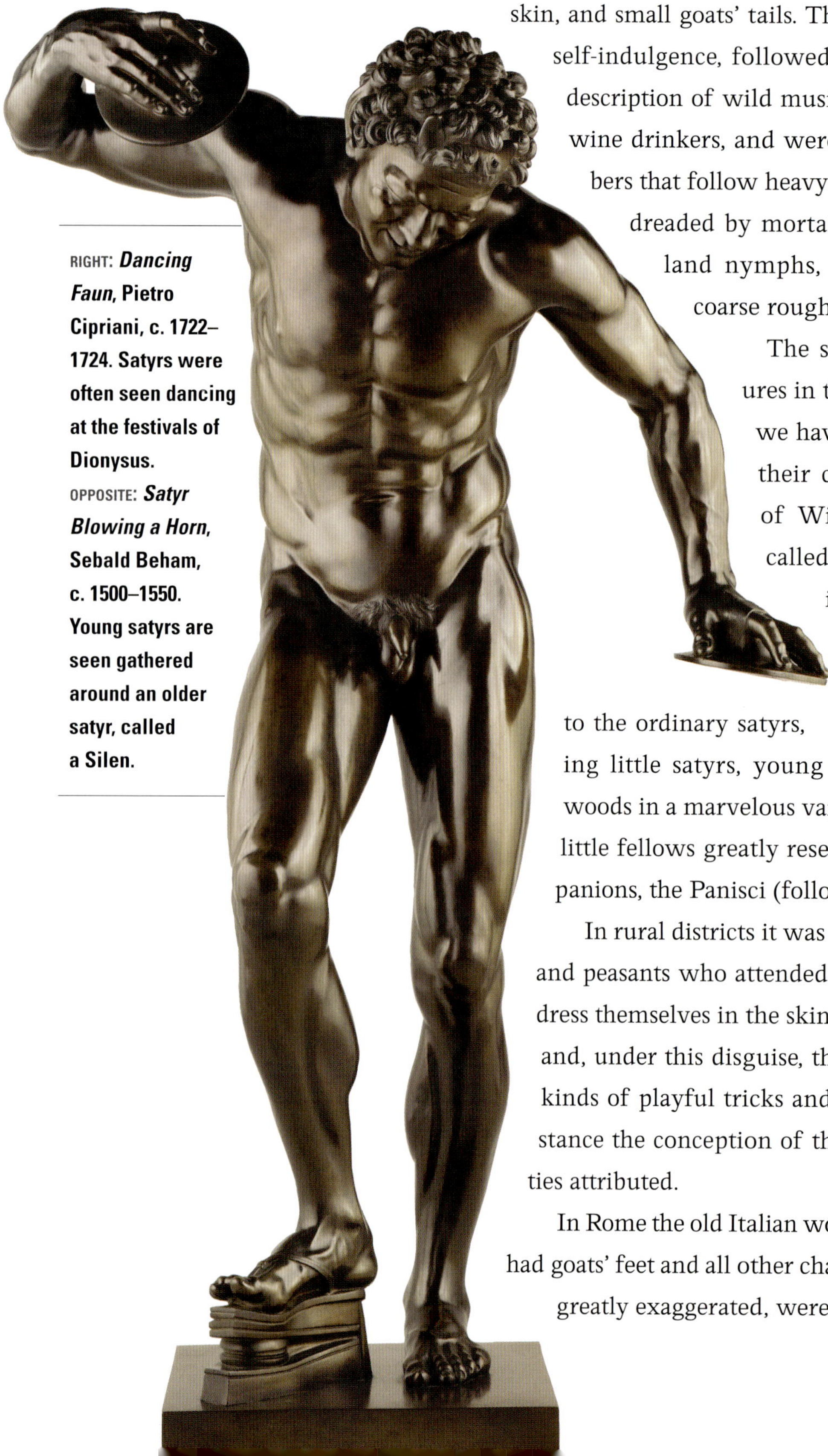

RIGHT: ***Dancing Faun*, Pietro Cipriani, c. 1722–1724. Satyrs were often seen dancing at the festivals of Dionysus.**
OPPOSITE: ***Satyr Blowing a Horn*, Sebald Beham, c. 1500–1550. Young satyrs are seen gathered around an older satyr, called a Silen.**

The satyrs were conspicuous figures in the train of Dionysus, and, as we have seen on page 163, Silenus, their chief, was tutor to the God of Wine. The older satyrs were called Silens, and are represented in antique sculpture as more nearly approaching the human form. In addition to the ordinary satyrs, artists delighted in depicting little satyrs, young imps, frolicking about the woods in a marvelous variety of droll attitudes. These little fellows greatly resemble their friends and companions, the Panisci (followers of Pan).

In rural districts it was customary for the shepherds and peasants who attended the festivals of Dionysus to dress themselves in the skins of goats and other animals, and, under this disguise, they permitted themselves all kinds of playful tricks and excesses, to which circumstance the conception of the satyrs is by some authorities attributed.

In Rome the old Italian wood divinities, the fauns, who had goats' feet and all other characteristics of the satyrs, but greatly exaggerated, were identified with them.

HSB

Chapter Five
HEROES

OPPOSITE: ***The Education of Achilles***, **Charles Clement Bervic, 1798. A young Achilles learns to use a bow and arrow from Chiron, a noble centaur who also tutored Jason and Heracles.**

PROMETHEUS

The ancient Greeks had several theories about the origin of man, but the theory of Hesiod, the oldest of all the Greek poets, was that Prometheus, the son of Iapetus, had formed man out of clay, and that Athene had breathed a soul into him. Full of love for the beings he had called into existence, Prometheus determined to elevate their minds and improve their condition in every way; he therefore taught them astronomy, mathematics, the alphabet, how to cure diseases, and the art of divination. He created this race in such great numbers

that the gods began to see the necessity of instituting certain fixed laws with regard to the sacrifices due to them, and the worship to which they considered themselves entitled from mankind in return for the protection that they accorded them. An assembly was therefore convened at Mecone in order to settle these points. It was decided that Prometheus, as the advocate of man, should slay an ox, which should be divided into two equal parts, and that the gods should select one portion that whould henceforth, in all future sacrifices, be set apart for them. Prometheus so divided the ox that one part consisted of the bones (which formed of course the least valuable portion of the animal), artfully concealed by the white fat; whilst the other contained all the edible parts, which he covered with the skin, and on the top of all he laid the stomach.

***Prometheus Creating Man*, workshop of Hendrik Goltzius. Prometheus not only created man, but gave them the important gifts of mathematics, the alphabet, and how to cure diseases.**

Zeus, pretending to be deceived, chose the heap of bones, but he saw through the stratagem, and was so angry at the deception practiced on him by Prometheus that he avenged himself by refusing to mortals the gift of fire. Prometheus, however, resolved to brave the anger of the great ruler of Olympus, and to obtain from heaven the vital spark so necessary for the further progress and comfort of the human race. He accordingly contrived to steal some sparks from the chariot of the sun, which he conveyed to Earth hidden in a hollow tube. Furious at being again outwitted, Zeus determined to have his revenge first on mankind, and then on Prometheus. To punish the former he commanded Hephæstus to mold a beautiful woman out of clay, and determined that through her instrumentality, trouble and misery should be brought into the world.

The gods were so charmed with Pandora, this graceful and artistic creation of Hephæstus, that they all determined to endow her with some special gift. Hermes bestowed on her a smooth persuasive tongue, Aphrodite gave her beauty and the art of pleasing, the Graces made her fascinating, and Athene gifted her with the possession of feminine accomplishments. Thus, she was named Pandora, which means all-gifted, having received every attribute necessary to make her charming and irresistible. Thus beautifully formed and endowed, this exquisite creature, attired by the Graces, and crowned with flowers by the Seasons, was conducted to the house of Epimetheus[1] by Hermes, the messenger of the gods.

OPPOSITE: *Prometheus,* Thomas de Leu, c. 1609. For trying to fool Zeus, Prometheus was punished by having an eagle peck at his liver for thirty years.

Now, Epimetheus had been warned by his brother not to accept any gift whatever from the gods; but he was so fascinated by the beautiful being who suddenly appeared before him that he welcomed her to his home, and made her his wife. It was not long, however, before he had cause to regret his weakness.

He had in his possession a jar of rare workmanship, containing all the blessings reserved by the gods for mankind, which he had been expressly forbidden to open. But woman's proverbial curiosity could not withstand so great a temptation, and Pandora determined to solve the mystery at any cost. Finally seeing her opportunity, she raised the lid, and immediately all the blessings that the gods had thus reserved for mankind took wing and flew away. But all was not lost. Just as Hope (which lay at the bottom) was about to escape, Pandora hastily closed the lid of the jar, and thus preserved to man that never-failing solace which helps him to bear with courage the many ills that assail him.[2]

Having punished mankind, Zeus determined to execute vengeance on Prometheus. He accordingly chained him to a rock in Mount Caucasus, and sent an eagle every day to gnaw away his liver, which grew again every night ready for fresh torments. For thirty years Prometheus endured this fearful punishment; but at length Zeus relented, and permitted his son Heracles to kill the eagle, and the sufferer was released.

1 Epimetheus signifies afterthought, Prometheus forethought.

2 There are various versions of this myth. According to some, the jar or vase was full of all "the ills that flesh is heir to."

e Charon inuentor.

ORPHEUS

OPPOSITE: ***Orpheus and Eurydice*, Jean Raoux, c. 1709. Orpheus starts to leave Hades with his wife Eurydice, as the denizens of the underworld look on.**

The renowned singer Orpheus was the son of Apollo and Calliope, the Muse of epic poetry, and, as might be expected with parents so highly gifted, was endowed with most distinguished intellectual abilities. He was a poet, a teacher of the religious doctrines known as the Orphic Mysteries, and a great musician, having inherited from his father an extraordinary genius for music. When he sang to the sweet tones of his lyre, he charmed all nature, and summoned round him the wild beasts of the forests, who, under the influence of his music, became tame and gentle as lambs. The madly rushing torrents stopped their rapid course, and the very mountains and trees moved from their places at the sound of his entrancing melodies.

Orpheus became united to a lovely nymph named Eurydice, the daughter of the sea-god Nereus, whom he fondly loved. She was no less attached to him, and their married life was full of joy and happiness. But it was only short-lived; for Aristæus,[3] the half-brother of Orpheus, having fallen in love with the beautiful Eurydice, forcibly endeavored to take her from her husband, and as she fled across some fields to elude his pursuit, she was bitten in the foot by a venomous snake, which had lain concealed in the long grass. Eurydice died of the wound, and her sorrowing husband filled the groves and valleys with his piteous and unceasing lamentations.

His longing to behold her once more became at last so unconquerable that he determined to brave the horrors of the lower world, in order to entreat Hades to restore to him his beloved wife. Armed only with his golden lyre, the gift of Apollo, he descended into the gloomy depths of Hades, where his heavenly music arrested for a while the torments of the unhappy sufferers. The stone of Sisyphus remained motionless; Tantalus forgot his perpetual thirst; the wheel of Ixion ceased to revolve; and even the Furies shed tears, and withheld for a time their persecutions.

Undismayed at the scenes of horror and suffering that met his view on every side, he pursued his way until he arrived at the palace of Hades. Presenting himself before the throne on which sat the stony-hearted king and his consort Persephone, Orpheus recounted his woes to the sound of his lyre. Moved to pity by his sweet strains, they listened to his melancholy story, and consented to release Eurydice on the condition that he should not look upon her until they reached the upper world. Orpheus gladly promised to comply with this injunction, and, followed by Eurydice, ascended the steep and gloomy path that led to the realms of life and light. All went well until he was just about to pass the

3 Aristæus was worshipped as a rural divinity in various parts of Greece, and was supposed to have taught mankind how to catch bees and utilize honey and wax

Orpheus, Marie-Alexandre-Lucien Coudray, c. 1893 . Orepheus was known for his longing, shown in his eyes even on this silver coin.

extreme limits of Hades, when, forgetting for the moment the hard condition, he turned to convince himself that his beloved wife was really behind him. The glance was fatal, and destroyed all his hopes of happiness; for, as he yearningly stretched out his arms to embrace her, she was caught back, and vanished from his sight forever.

The grief of Orpheus at this second loss was even more intense than before, and he now avoided all human society. In vain did the nymphs, his once chosen companions, endeavor to win him back to his accustomed haunts; their power to charm was gone, and music was now his sole consolation. He wandered forth alone, choosing the wildest and most secluded paths, and the hills and vales resounded with his pathetic melodies. At last he happened to cross the path of some Thracian women, who were performing the wild rites of Dionysus, and in their mad fury at his refusing to join them, they furiously attacked him, and tore him in pieces. In pity for his unhappy fate, the Muses collected his remains, which they buried at the foot of Mount Olympus, and the nightingale warbled a funeral dirge over his grave. His head was thrown into the river Hebrus, and as it floated down the stream, the lips still continued to murmur the beloved name of Eurydice.

PERSEUS

Perseus, one of the most renowned of the legendary heroes of antiquity, was the son of Zeus and Danaë, daughter of Acrisius, king of Argos. Many great heroes were descended from Perseus and his wife Andromeda, foremost among whom was Heracles, whose mother, Alcmene, was their granddaughter.

Heroic honors were paid to Perseus not only throughout Argos, but also in Athens and on the island of Seriphus. Perseus is depicted as a heroic young warrior, usually wearing Hermes's winged sandals, and often holding aloft in one hand the head of the Gorgon Medusa, who he slew.

ACRISIUS *and the* BIRTH *of* PERSEUS

An oracle having foretold to Acrisius that a son of his daughter Danaë would be the cause of his death, he imprisoned her in a tower of brass in order to keep her secluded from the world. Zeus, however, descended through the roof of the tower in the form of a shower of gold, and the lovely Danaë became his bride.

For four years Acrisius remained in ignorance of this union, but one evening as he chanced to pass by the brazen chamber, he heard the cry of a young child proceeding from within, which led to the discovery of his daughter's marriage with Zeus. Enraged at finding all his precautions unavailing, Acrisius commanded the mother and child to be placed in a chest and thrown into the sea.

But it was not the will of Zeus that they should perish. He directed Poseidon to calm the troubled waters, and caused the chest to float safely to the island of Seriphus. Dictys, brother of Polydectes, king of the island, was fishing on the seashore when he saw the chest stranded on the beach; and pitying the helpless condition of its unhappy occupants, he conducted them to the palace of the king, where they were treated with the greatest kindness. Polydectes eventually became united with Danaë, and bestowed upon Perseus an education befitting a hero.

The Sleeping Danae Being Prepared to Receive Jupiter, Hendrik Goltzius, 1603. Zeus (Jupiter) impregnated the mortal Danaë, Perseus's mother, by taking the form of a shower of gold.

When Perseus had grown and showed himself to be a legendary warrior by slaying Medusa, Acrisius, fearing the fulfilment of the oracular prediction, fled for protection to his friend Teutemias, king of Larissa. Anxious to induce the aged monarch to return to Argos, Perseus followed him thither. But here a strange fatality occurred. Whilst taking part in some funereal games, celebrated in honor of the king's father, Perseus, by an unfortunate throw of the discus, accidentally struck his grandfather, and thereby was the innocent cause of his death.

After celebrating the funereal rites of Acrisius with due solemnity, Perseus returned to Argos; but feeling loath to occupy the throne of one whose death he had caused, he exchanged kingdoms with Megapenthes, king of Tiryns, and in course of time founded the cities of Mycenæ and Midea.

Cameo gem set into a ring, c. 25 BCE–25 CE. Perseus was often seen with the head of Medusa, such as on on this ancient ring.

PERSEUS SLAYS MEDUSA

When Polydectes saw his stepson develop into a noble and manly youth, he endeavored to instill into his mind a desire to distinguish himself by the achievement of some great and heroic deed, and after mature deliberation it was decided that the slaying of the Gorgon Medusa would bring him the greatest renown.

For the successful accomplishment of Perseus's object it was necessary for him to be provided with a pair of winged sandals, a magic wallet, and the helmet of Hades, which rendered the wearer invisible, all of which were in the keeping of the nymphs, the place of whose abode was known only to the Grææ. Perseus started on his expedition, and, guided by Hermes and Athene, arrived, after a long journey, in the far-off region, on the borders of Oceanus, where dwelt the Grææ, daughters of Phorcys and Ceto. He at once applied to them for the necessary information, and on their refusing to grant it he deprived each of them of their single eye and tooth, which he only restored when they gave him full directions with regard to his route. He then proceeded to the abode of the nymphs, from whom he obtained the objects indispensable for his purpose.

Equipped with the magic helmet and wallet, and armed with a sickle, the gift of Hermes, he attached to his feet the winged sandals, and flew to the abode of the Gorgons, whom he found fast asleep. Now as Perseus had been warned by his celestial guides that whoever looked upon these weird sisters would be transformed into stone, he stood with averted face before the sleepers, and caught on his bright metal shield their triple image. Then, guided by Athene, he cut off the head of the Medusa. No sooner had he done so than from the headless trunk there sprang forth the winged steed Pegasus, and Chrysaor, the father of the winged Giant Geryones. He now hastened to elude the pursuit of the two surviving sisters, who, aroused from their slumbers, eagerly rushed to avenge the death of their sister.

His invisible helmet and winged sandals here stood him in good stead; for the former concealed him from the view of the Gorgons, whilst the latter bore him swiftly over land and sea, far beyond the reach of pursuit. In passing over the burning plains of Libya the drops of blood from the head of the Medusa oozed through his satchel, and falling on the hot sands below produced a brood of many-colored snakes, which spread all over the country.

Perseus continued his flight until he reached the kingdom of Atlas, of whom he begged rest and shelter. But as this king possessed a valuable orchard, in which every tree bore golden fruit, he was fearful lest the slayer of the Medusa might destroy the dragon that guarded it, and then rob him of his treasures. He therefore refused to grant the hospitality the hero demanded, whereupon Perseus, exasperated at the churlish repulse, produced from his bag the head of the Medusa, and holding it toward the king, transformed him into a stony mountain. Beard and hair erected themselves into forests; shoulders, hands, and limbs became huge rocks; and the head grew up into a craggy peak, which reached into the clouds.

Detail from *L'Épître Othéa*, attributed to the Master of the Cité des Dames and workshop, c. 1410–1414. Perseus slays a vicious sea dragon to win the hand of Andronmeda.

PERSEUS and ANDROMEDA

Perseus then resumed his travels. His winged sandals bore him over deserts and mountains, until he arrived at Æthiopia, the kingdom of King Cepheus. Here he found the country inundated with disastrous floods, towns and villages destroyed, and everywhere signs of desolation and ruin. On a projecting cliff close to the shore he beheld a lovely maiden chained to a rock. This was Andromeda, the king's daughter. Her mother, Cassiopea, had boasted that her beauty surpassed that of the

Nereides, and the angry sea-nymphs had appealed to Poseidon to avenge their wrongs, whereupon the God of the Sea devastated the country with a terrible inundation, which brought with it a huge monster who devoured all that came in his way.

In their distress the unfortunate Æthiopians applied to the oracle of Jupiter-Ammon, in the Libyan desert, and obtained the response that only by the sacrifice of the king's daughter to the monster could the country and people be saved.

King Cepheus, who was tenderly attached to Andromeda, at first refused to listen to this dreadful proposal; but overcome at length by the prayers and solicitations of his unhappy subjects, the heartbroken father gave up his child for the welfare of his country. Andromeda was accordingly chained to a rock on the seashore to serve as a prey for the monster, whilst her unhappy parents bewailed her sad fate on the beach below.

On being informed of the meaning of this tragic scene, Perseus proposed to Cepheus to slay the dragon, on condition that the lovely victim should become his bride. Overjoyed at the prospect of Andromeda's release, the king gladly acceded to the stipulation, and Perseus hastened to the rock, to breathe words of hope and comfort to the trembling maiden. Then assuming once more the helmet of Hades, he mounted into the air, and awaited the approach of the monster.

OPPOSITE: *Perseus Confronting Phineus with the Head of Medusa*, Sebastiano Ricci, c. 1705–1710. Once Perseus had the head of Medusa in his possession, it was his most powerful weapon. Here, some soldiers have already been transformed into stone after trying to halt Perseus's wedding at the behest of Phineus.

Presently the sea opened, and the shark-like head of the gigantic beast of the deep raised itself above the waves. Lashing his tail furiously from side to side, he leaped forward to seize his victim; but the gallant hero, watching his opportunity, suddenly darted down, and producing the head of the Medusa from his satchel, held it before the eyes of the dragon, whose hideous body became gradually transformed into a huge black rock, which remained forever a silent witness of the miraculous deliverance of Andromeda. Perseus then led the maiden to her now happy parents, who, anxious to evince their gratitude to her deliverer, ordered immediate preparations to be made for the nuptial feast.

But the young hero was not to bear away his lovely bride uncontested; for in the midst of the banquet, Phineus, the king's brother, to whom Andromeda had previously been betrothed, returned to claim his bride. Followed by a band of armed warriors, he forced his way into the hall, and a desperate encounter took place between the rivals, which might have terminated fatally for Perseus, had he not suddenly bethought himself of the Medusa's head. Calling to his friends to avert their faces, he drew it from his satchel, and held it before Phineus and his formidable bodyguard, whereupon they all stiffened into stone.

Thereafter, the head of the Medusa he presented to his divine patroness, Athene, who placed it in the center of her shield.

JASON

The hero Jason was the son of Aeson, king of Iolcus[4]. He is best known for going on a quest for the golden fleece in order to win back his homeland. The leader of the legendary Argonauts, Jason is portrayed as a bold youth, often wearing a warrior's helmet and carrying the fleece that he so heroically obtained.

Jason and the Golden Fleece, **Bertel Thorvaldsen. This replica of the original statue by Thorvaldsen can be found in the piazza that bears his name in Rome.**

JASON *and the* GOLDEN FLEECE

Aeson, Jason's father, was forced to fly from his dominions when they had been usurped by his younger brother Pelias, and with difficulty succeeded in saving the life of his young son Jason, who was at that time only ten years of age. He entrusted him to the care of the Centaur Chiron, by whom he was carefully trained in company with other noble youths, who, like himself, afterward signalized themselves by their bravery and heroic exploits. For ten years Jason remained in the cave of the Centaur, by whom he was instructed in all useful and warlike arts. But as he approached manhood, he became filled with an unconquerable desire to regain his paternal inheritance. He therefore took leave of his kind friend and preceptor, and set out for Iolcus to demand from his uncle Pelias his kingdom, which he had so unjustly usurped.

On his arrival at Iolcus he found his uncle in the marketplace, offering up

4 Jason's mother is variously accounted for.

a public sacrifice to Poseidon. When the king had concluded his offering, his eye fell upon the distinguished stranger, whose manly beauty and heroic bearing had already attracted the attention of his people. Observing that one foot was unshod, he was reminded of an oracular prediction which foretold to him the loss of his kingdom by a man wearing only one sandal. He, however, disguised his fears, conversed kindly with the youth, and drew from him his name and errand. Then pretending to be highly pleased with his nephew, Pelias entertained him sumptuously for five days, during which time all was festivity and rejoicing. On the sixth, Jason appeared before his uncle, and with manly firmness demanded from him the throne and kingdom which were his by right. Pelias, dissembling his true feelings, smilingly consented to grant his request, provided that, in return, Jason would undertake an expedition for him, which his advanced age prevented him from accomplishing himself.

Pear-shaped jug with Medea and Jason, c. 1680–1690. Jason decorates the side of this German carafe as well as the top, where he is depicted battling the dragon who guards the golden fleece.

He informed his nephew that the shade (ghost) of Phryxus had appeared to him in his dreams, and entreated him to bring back from Colchis his mortal remains and the golden fleece; the golden fleece was that of a ram that Phryxus, when alive, had sacrificed to Zeus and given to his father-in-law, King Aëtes, who had nailed it up in the Grove of Ares. An oracle having declared that the life of Aëtes depended on the safe-keeping of the fleece, he carefully guarded the entrance to the grove by placing before it an immense dragon, which never slept.

Pelias added that if Jason succeeded in obtaining for him this sacred relic, throne, kingdom, and sceptre should be his. However, he was well aware of the dangers attending such an enterprise, and hoped by this means to rid himself forever of the unwelcome intruder. Jason eagerly undertook the perilous expedition proposed to him by his uncle, and accordingly began to arrange his plans without delay, and invited the young heroes whose friendship he had formed whilst under the care of Chiron to join him in the perilous expedition. None refused the invitation, all feeling honored at being allowed the privilege of taking part in so noble and heroic an undertaking.

Jason now applied to Argos, one of the cleverest ship-builders of his time, who, under

Detail from *Roman de la Rose*, attributed to Master of the Prayer Books, c. 1490–1500. Jason, in the upper right, goes on his quest for the golden fleece while his ship, the Argo, waits on the shore.

the guidance of Athene, built for him a splendid fifty-oared galley, which was called the Argo, after the builder. In the upper deck of the vessel the goddess had imbedded a board from the speaking oak of the oracle of Zeus at Dodona, which ever retained its powers of prophecy. The exterior of the ship was ornamented with magnificent carvings, and the whole vessel was so strongly built that it defied the power of the winds and waves, and was, nevertheless, so light that the heroes, when necessary, were able to carry it on their shoulders. When the vessel was completed, the Argonauts (so called after their ship) assembled, and their places were distributed by lot; the anchor was weighed, and the ship glided like a bird out of the harbor into the waters of the great sea.

With the help of King Aëtes's daughter, the sorceress Medea, and after many heroic feats (relayed on the following pages), Jason brought back, with his new wife Medea, the golden fleece to his uncle Pelias, to the amazement of the entire kingdom. But the old king, who had never expected that Jason would return alive, crassly refused to fulfill his part of the compact, and declined to abdicate the throne. Indignant at the wrongs of her husband, Medea avenged them in a most shocking manner. She made friends with the daughters of the king, and feigned great interest in all their concerns. Having gained their confidence, she informed them that among her numerous magic arts, she possessed the power of restoring to the aged all the vigor and strength of youth, and in order to give them a convincing proof of the truth of her assertion, she cut up an old ram, which she boiled in a cauldron, whereupon, after uttering various mystic incantations, there came forth from the vessel a beautiful young lamb. She then assured them that in a similar manner they could restore to their old father his former youthful frame and vigor. The fond and credulous daughters of Pelias lent an all too willing ear to the wicked sorceress, and thus the old king perished at the hands of his innocent children.

MEDEA

Medea was the daughter of King Aëtes of Colchis, the wife of Jason, and a priestess of Hecate. A great enchantress and powerful sorceress, she was instrumental in obtaining the golden fleece. Medea stopped at nothing to get what she wanted, and many myths tell of her exacting revenge in the most gruesome of manners. She is represented as having dark hair and a chiseled, stern countenance, and is often portrayed with her chariot, which was drawn by dragons.

The MEETING of JASON and MEDEA

When Jason and the Argonauts arrived at the palace of Aëtes on their quest for the golden fleece, the news soon spread and brought the king himself to the scene, whereupon the strangers were presented to him, and were invited to a banquet that the king ordered to be prepared in their honor. All the most beautiful ladies of the court were present at this entertainment; but in the eyes of Jason none could compare with the king's daughter, the young and lovely Medea.

Detail from *Des Cleres et Nobles Femmes, De Claris Mulieribus*, attributed to Master of Boethius, c. 1400–1425. Medea casts a spell that causes slaughter while Jason sits to her right on a horse.

When the banquet was ended, Jason related to the king his various adventures, and also the object of his expedition, with the circumstances that had led to his undertaking it. Aëtes listened, in silent indignation, to this recital, and then burst out into a torrent of invectives against the Argonauts, declaring that the fleece was his rightful property, and that on no consideration would he consent to relinquish it. Jason, however, with mild and persuasive words, induced the king to promise that if the heroes could succeed in demonstrating their divine origin by the performance of some task requiring superhuman power, the fleece should be theirs.

JASON PLOWS *the* FIELDS *of* ARES

OPPOSITE: Detail from *Metamorphoses*, c. 1475–1500. With help from Medea's spells and guidance, Jason yokes King Aëtes's fire-breathing oxen to plow the fields of Ares.

The task proposed by Aëtes to Jason to obtain the golden fleece was that he should yoke the two brazen-footed, fire-breathing oxen of the king (which had been made for him by Hephæstus) to his ponderous iron plough. Having done this he must till with them the stony field of Ares, and then sow in the furrows the poisonous teeth of a dragon, from which armed men would arise. All of these he must destroy, or he himself would perish at their hands. When Jason heard what was expected of him, his heart for a moment sank within him; but he determined, nevertheless, not to flinch from his task, but to trust to the assistance of the gods, and to his own courage and energy.

Accompanied by his two friends, Telamon and Augeas, and also by Argus, the son of Chalciope, Jason returned to the Argo for the purpose of holding a consultation as to the best means of accomplishing these perilous feats. Argus explained to Jason all the difficulties of the superhuman task which lay before him, and pronounced it as his opinion that the only means by which success was possible was to enlist the assistance of the Princess Medea. His suggestion meeting with approval, he returned to the palace, and by the aid of his mother an interview was arranged between Jason and Medea, which took place, at an early hour next morning, in the temple of Hecate.

A confession of mutual attachment took place, and Medea, trembling for her lover's safety, presented him with a magic salve, which possessed the property of rendering any person anointed with it invulnerable for the space of one day against fire and steel, and invincible against any adversary however powerful. With this salve she instructed him to anoint his spear and shield on the day of his great undertaking. She further added that when, after having ploughed the field and sown the teeth, the armed men should arise from the furrows, he must on no account lose heart, but remember to throw among them a huge rock, over the possession of which they would fight among themselves, and their attention being thus diverted, he would find it an easy task to destroy them. Overwhelmed with gratitude, Jason thanked her in the most earnest manner for her wise counsel and timely aid; at the same time he offered her his hand, and promised her he would not return to Greece without taking her with him as his wife.

The next morning Aëtes, in all the pomp of state, surrounded by his family and the members of his court, repaired to a spot whence a full view of the approaching spectacle could be obtained. Soon, Jason appeared in the field of Ares, looking as noble and majestic as the God of War himself. In a distant part of the field the brazen yokes and the massive plough met his view, but as yet the dread animals themselves were nowhere to be seen. He was about to go in search of them, when they suddenly rushed out from a subterranean cave, breathing flames of fire, and enveloped him in a thick smoke.

The friends of Jason trembled; but the undaunted hero, relying on the magic powers with which he was imbued by Medea, seized the oxen one after the other by the horns, and forced them to the yoke. Near the plough was a helmet full of dragon's teeth, which he sowed as he ploughed the field, whilst with sharp pricks from his lance he compelled the monstrous creatures to draw the plough over the stony ground, which was thus speedily tilled.

While Jason was engaged sowing the dragon's teeth in the deep furrows of the field, he kept a cautious look-out lest the germinating giant brood might grow too quickly for him, and as soon as the four acres of land had been tilled he unyoked the oxen, and succeeded in frightening them so effectually with his weapons that they rushed back in terror to their subterranean stables. Meanwhile, the armed men had sprung up out of the furrows, and the whole field now bristled with lances; but Jason, remembering the instructions of Medea, seized an immense rock and hurled it into the midst of these Earth-born warriors, who immediately began to attack each other. Jason then rushed furiously upon them, and after a terrible struggle, not one of the men remained alive.

Furious at seeing his murderous schemes thus defeated, Aëtes not only perfidiously refused to give Jason the fleece he had so bravely earned, but, in his anger, determined to destroy all the Argonauts, and to burn their vessel.

MEDEA and JASON OBTAIN the GOLDEN FLEECE

***Jason Putting the Dragon to Sleep*, Wilhelm Janson, 1606. Though Jason is often given credit for killing the dragon who guarded the golden fleece, it was with Medea's potion that he put him to sleep.**

Becoming aware of the treacherous designs of her father, Medea at once took measures to stifle them. In the darkness of night she went on board the Argo, and warned the heroes of the approaching danger. She then advised Jason to accompany her without loss of time to the sacred grove, in order to possess himself of the long-coveted golden fleece. They set out together, and Medea, followed by Jason, led the way, and advanced boldly into the grove. The tall oak tree was soon discovered, from the topmost boughs of which hung the beautiful treasure. At the foot of this tree, keeping his ever-wakeful watch, lay the dreadful, sleepless dragon, who at sight of them bounded forward, opening his huge jaws.

Medea now called into play her magic powers, and, quietly approaching the monster, threw over him a few drops of a potion, which soon took effect and sent him into a deep sleep; whereupon Jason, seizing the opportunity, climbed the tree and secured the fleece. Their perilous task being now accomplished, Jason and Medea left the grove, and hastened on board the Argo, which immediately put to sea.

The DEATH of JASON

After returning the golden fleece to Pelias (as recounted on page 208), Medea and Jason fled to Corinth, where at length they found peace and tranquility, their happiness being completed by the birth of three children.

As time passed on, however, and Medea began to lose the beauty that had won her the love of her husband, he grew weary of her, and became attracted by the youthful charms of Glauce, the beautiful daughter of Creon, king of Corinth. Jason had obtained Glauce's father's consent to their union, and the wedding day was already fixed, before he disclosed to Medea that he intended to leave her and marry another. He used all his persuasive powers in order to induce her to consent to his union with Glauce, assuring her that his affection had in no way diminished, but that for the sake of the advantages which would thereby accrue to their children, he had de-

Detail of marble sarcophagus, c. 100–200 CE. This detail of the intricate relief on the side of a Roman sarcophagus most likely depicts the death of the children of Jason and Medea at Medea's hands.

cided on forming this alliance with the royal house. Though justly enraged at his deceitful conduct, Medea dissembled her wrath, and, feigning to be satisfied with this explanation, sent, as a wedding gift to her rival, a magnificent robe of cloth-of-gold. This robe was imbued with a deadly poison that penetrated to the flesh and bone of all wearers, and burned them as though with a consuming fire. Pleased with the beauty and costliness of the garment, the unsuspecting Glauce lost no time in donning it; but no sooner had she done so than the fell poison began to take effect. In vain she tried to tear the robe away; it defied all efforts to be removed, and after horrible and protracted sufferings, she expired.

Struck with madness at the loss of her husband's love, Medea next put to death her three sons, and when Jason, thirsting for revenge, left the chamber of his dead bride, and flew to his own house in search of Medea, the ghastly spectacle of his murdered children met his view. He rushed frantically to seek the murderess, but nowhere could she be found. At length, hearing a sound above his head, he looked up, and beheld Medea gliding through the air in a golden chariot drawn by dragons.

Thus ended the tale of Jason, as, in a fit of despair, he threw himself on his own sword, and perished on the threshold of his desolate and deserted home.

ABSYRTUS

OPPOSITE: *Aeetes Accepts the Dismembered Corpse of Absyrte,* René Boyvin, 1563. Absyrtus (Absyrte) was sent after his sister Medea, who cruelly had him killed and dismembered.

Absyrtus was the unfortunate son of King Aëtes and brother of Medea, known for losing his life while chasing after Jason and the golden fleece.

When Aëtes discovered the loss of his daughter and the golden fleece with her, he dispatched a large fleet under the command of Absyrtus, in pursuit of the fugitives. After some days' sail they arrived at an island at the mouth of the river Ister, where they found the Argo at anchor, and surrounded her with their numerous ships. They then dispatched a herald on board of her, demanding the surrender of Medea and the fleece.

Medea consulted Jason, and, with his consent, carried out the following stratagem. She sent a message to Absyrtus, to the effect that she had been carried off against her will, and promised that if he would meet her in the darkness of night in the temple of Artemis, she would assist him in regaining possession of the golden fleece. Relying on the good faith of his sister, Absyrtus fell into the snare, and duly appeared at the appointed place; and whilst Medea kept her brother engaged in conversation, Jason rushed forward and slew him. Then, according to a preconcerted signal, he held aloft a lighted torch, whereupon the Argonauts attacked Absyrtus and his men, put them to flight, and entirely defeated them.

The Argonauts now returned to their ship, when the prophetic board from the Dodonean oak thus addressed them: "The cruel murder of Absyrtus was witnessed by the

Erinyes, and you will not escape the wrath of Zeus until the goddess Circe has purified you from your crime. Let Castor and Pollux pray to the gods that you may be enabled to find the abode of the sorceress." In obedience to the voice, the twin brothers invoked divine assistance, and the heroes set out in search of the isle of Circe, who ultimately cleansed them of their sin.

HERACLES ∫ HERCULES

Heracles, the most renowned hero of antiquity, was the son of Zeus and Alcmene, and the great grandson of Perseus. Known for his great heroism and strength, he was celebrated by the Greeks and later the Romans, who renamed him Hercules. Heracles was revered by the gods as well; the Olympian gods testified their appreciation of his valor by sending him presents: Hermes gave him a sword, Apollo a bundle of arrows, Hephæstus a golden quiver, and Athene a coat of leather.

Heracles is portrayed as being rugged in nature with an unkempt beard and hair; he has a large torso, arms, and legs; and usually exudes a serious demeanor. Artistic representations often show him in the midst of one of his legendary labors, or with his club in his hands.

The BIRTH of HERACLES

Detail from *Hercules and Cacus,* Baccio Bandinelli, 1533. Heracles was one of the most celebrated heroes, by both poets and artists.

At the time of Heracles's birth, his mother Alcmene was living in Thebes with her husband Amphitryon, and thus the infant Heracles, son of Zeus, was born in the palace of his stepfather.

Aware of the animosity with which Hera persecuted all those who rivaled her in the affections of Zeus, Alcmene, fearful lest this hatred should be visited on her innocent child, entrusted him soon after his birth to the care of a faithful servant, with instructions to expose him in a certain field, and there leave him, feeling assured that the divine offspring of Zeus would not long remain without the protection of the gods.

Soon after the child had been thus abandoned, Hera and Athene happened to pass by the field, and were attracted by his cries. Athene pityingly took up the infant in her arms, and prevailed upon the queen of heaven to put him to her breast; but no sooner had she done so than the child caused her pain, so she angrily threw him to the ground and left the spot. Athene, moved with compassion, carried him to Alcmene, and entreated her kind offices on behalf of the poor little foundling. Alcmene at once recognized her child, and joyfully accepted the charge.

Soon afterward, Hera, to her extreme annoyance, discovered whom she had nursed, and became filled with jealous rage. She now sent two venomous snakes into the chamber of Alcmene, which crept, unperceived by the nurses, to the cradle of the sleeping child. He awoke with a cry, and grasping a snake in each hand, strangled them both. Alcmene and her attendants, whom the cry of the child had awakened, rushed to the cradle, where, to their astonishment and terror, they beheld the two reptiles dead in the hands of the infant Heracles. Amphitryon was also attracted to the chamber by the commotion, and when he beheld this astounding proof of supernatural strength, he declared that the child must have been sent to him as a special gift from Zeus. He accordingly consulted the famous seer Tiresias, who now informed him of the divine origin of his stepson, and prognosticated for him a great and distinguished future.

Hercules Strangling the Serpents, **Heinrich Aldegrever, 1550. Hera, incensed that Zeus had had Heracles with another woman, sent snakes to kill the infant. However, he strangled them with his superhuman strength.**

When Amphitryon heard of the noble destiny that awaited the child entrusted to his care, he resolved to educate him in a manner worthy of his future career. At a suitable age he himself taught him how to guide a chariot; Eurytus, how to handle the bow; Autolycus, dexterity in wrestling and boxing; and Castor, the art of armed warfare; whilst Linus, the son of Apollo, instructed him in music and letters. Heracles was an apt pupil; but undue harshness was intolerable to his high spirit, and old Linus, who was not the gentlest of teachers, one day corrected him with blows, whereupon the boy angrily took up his lyre, and, with one stroke of his powerful arm, killed his tutor on the spot.

Apprehensive lest the ungovernable temper of the youth might again involve him in similar acts of violence, Amphitryon sent him into the country, where he placed him under the charge of one of his most trusted herdsmen. Here, as he grew up to manhood, his extraordinary stature and strength became the wonder and admiration of all beholders. His aim, whether with spear, lance, or bow, was unerring, and at the age of eighteen he was considered to be the strongest as well as the most beautiful youth in all Greece.

The LABORS *of* HERACLES

Just before the birth of Heracles, Zeus, in an assembly of the gods, exultingly declared that the child who should be born on that day to the house of Perseus should rule over all his race. When Hera heard her lord's boastful announcement she knew well that it was for the child of the hated Alcmene that this brilliant destiny was designed; and in order to rob the son of her rival of his rights, she called to her aid the Birthing Goddess Eileithyia, who slowed down the birth of Heracles, and caused his cousin Eurystheus (another grandson of Perseus) to precede him into the world. And thus, as the word of the mighty Zeus was irrevocable, Heracles became the subject and servant of his cousin Eurystheus.

Even after he became the king of Mycenæ, the land of Perseus, Eurystheus was jealous over the fame of his heroic cousin, so he asserted his rights as ruler, and commanded him to undertake for him various difficult labors. The proud spirit of the hero rebelled against this humiliation, and he was about to refuse compliance, but Zeus appeared to him and told him not to rebel against the Fates. Heracles now repaired to Delphi in order to consult the oracle, and received the answer that after performing ten tasks for his cousin Eurystheus, his servitude would be at an end.

Soon afterward Heracles fell into a state of the deepest melancholy, and through the influence of his inveterate enemy, the goddess Hera, this despondency developed into raving madness, under hold of which condition he killed his own children. When he at length regained his reason he was so horrified and grieved at what he had done that he shut himself up in his chamber and avoided all intercourse with men. But in his loneliness and seclusion the conviction that work would be the best means of procuring oblivion of the past overcame him, he decided to enter, without delay, upon the tasks appointed him by Eurystheus.

The NEMEAN LIONS

OPPOSITE: *Hercules and the Nemean Lion*, c. 1550. After strangling a Nemean lion as his first labor, Heracles made an armor from the hide that could withstand a blow from any mortal enemy.

Heracles's first task was to bring to Eurystheus the skin of one of the much-dreaded Nemean lions, which ravaged the territory between Cleone and Nemea, and whose hide was invulnerable against any mortal weapon.

Heracles proceeded to the forest of Nemea, where, having discovered a lion's lair, he attempted to pierce him with his arrows; but finding these of no avail he felled him to the ground with his club, and before the animal had time to recover from the terrible blow, Heracles seized him by the neck and, with a mighty effort, succeeded in strangling him. He then made himself a coat of mail of the skin, and a new helmet of the head

of the animal. Thus attired, he so alarmed Eurystheus by appearing suddenly before him, that the king concealed himself in his palace, and henceforth forbade Heracles to enter his presence, but commanded him to receive his behests for the future through his messenger Copreus.

HERACLES SLAYS *the* HYDRA

The second labor of Hercules was to slay the Hydra, a monster serpent bristling with nine heads, one of which was immortal. This monster infested the neighborhood of Lerna, where she committed great depredations among the herds.

Heracles, accompanied by his nephew Iolaus, set out in a chariot for the marsh of Lerna, in the slimy waters of which he found her. He commenced the attack by assailing her with his fierce arrows, in order to force her to leave her lair, from which she at length emerged, and sought refuge in a wood on a neighboring hill. Heracles now rushed forward and endeavored to crush her heads by means of well-directed blows from his tremendous club; but no sooner was one head destroyed than it was immediately replaced by two others. He next seized the monster in his powerful grasp; but at this juncture a giant crab came to the assistance of the Hydra and commenced biting the feet of her assailant. Heracles destroyed this new adversary with his club, and now called upon his nephew to come to his aid. At his command Iolaus set fire to the neighboring trees, and, with a burning branch, seared the necks of the monster as Heracles cut them off, thus effectually preventing the growth of more. Heracles next struck off the immortal head, which he buried by the road-side, and

Caeretan Hydria, attributed to Eagle Painter, c. 525 BCE. On this ancient vase, Heracles battles the multi-headed Hydra.

placed over it a heavy stone. Into the poisonous blood of the monster he then dipped his arrows, which ever afterward rendered wounds inflicted by them incurable.

The HORNED HIND

Heracles's third labor was to bring the horned hind (doe) named Cerunitis alive to Mycenæ. This animal, which was sacred to Artemis, had golden antlers and hoofs of brass.

Not wishing to wound the hind, Heracles patiently pursued her through many countries for a whole year, and overtook her at last on the banks of the river Ladon; but even there he was compelled, in order to secure her, to wound her with one of his arrows, after which he lifted her on his shoulders and carried her through Arcadia. On his way he met Artemis with her brother Apollo, and the goddess angrily reproved him for wounding her favorite hind; but Heracles succeeded in appeasing her displeasure, whereupon she permitted him to take the animal alive to Mycenæ.

The Deeds of Hercules: Hercules and the Hind, **Heinrich Aldegrever, 1550. It took Hercules a whole year to capture the mythical doe with horns without killing her.**

The ERYMANTIAN BOAR

The fourth task imposed upon Heracles by Eurystheus was to bring alive to Mycenæ the boar that had laid waste the region of Erymantia, and was the scourge of the surrounding neighborhood.

On his way thither he acquired the food and shelter of a Centaur named Pholus, who received him with generous hospitality, setting before him a good and plentiful repast. When Heracles expressed his surprise that at such a well-furnished spread wine should be missing, his host explained that the wine-cellar was the common property of all the

***Hercules Slaying the Erymanthian Boar*, Gabriel Salmon, 1528. In this elaborate woodcut, Hercules slays the boar rather than capturing him alive.**

Centaurs, and that it was against the rules for a cask to be broached except when all were present to partake of it. By dint of persuasion, however, Heracles prevailed on his kind host to make an exception in his favor; but the powerful, luscious odor of the good, old wine soon spread over the mountains, and brought large numbers of Centaurs to the spot, all armed with huge rocks and fir trees. Heracles drove them back with fire-brands, and then, following up his victory, pursued them with his arrows as far as Malea, where they took refuge in the cave of the kind old Centaur Chiron.

Unfortunately, however, as Heracles was shooting at them with his poisoned darts, one of these pierced the knee of Chiron. When Heracles discovered that it was the friend of his early days that he had wounded, he was overcome with sorrow and regret. He at once extracted the arrow, and anointed the wound with a salve, the virtue of which had been taught to him by Chiron himself. But all his efforts were unavailing. The wound, imbued with the deadly poison of the Hydra, was incurable, and so great was the agony of Chiron that, at the intercession of Heracles, death was sent him by the gods; for otherwise, being immortal, he would have been doomed to endless suffering.

Pholus, who had so kindly entertained Heracles, also perished by means of one of these arrows, which he had extracted from the body of a dead Centaur. While he was quietly examining it, astonished that so small and insignificant an object should be productive of such serious results, the arrow fell upon his foot and fatally wounded him. Full of grief at this untoward event, Heracles buried him with due honors, and then set out to chase the boar.

With loud shouts and terrible cries he first drove him out of the thickets into the deep snow-drifts that covered the summit of the mountain, and then, having at length wearied him with his incessant pursuit, he captured the exhausted animal, bound him with a rope, and brought him alive to Mycenæ.

HERACLES CLEANS *the* STABLES *of* AUGEAS

After hunting the Erymantian boar Eurystheus commanded Heracles to cleanse in one day the stables of Augeas.

Augeas was a king of Elis who was very rich in herds. Three thousand of his cattle were kept near the royal palace in an enclosure where their refuse had accumulated for many years. When Heracles presented himself before the king, and offered to cleanse his stables in one day, provided he should receive in return a tenth part of the herds, Augeas, thinking the feat impossible, accepted his offer in the presence of his son Phyleus.

Near the palace were the two rivers Peneus and Alpheus, the streams of which Heracles conducted into the stables by means of a trench which he dug for this purpose, and as the waters rushed through the shed, they swept away with them the whole mass of accumulated filth.

But when Augeas heard that this was one of the labors imposed by Eurystheus, he refused the promised guerdon. Heracles brought the matter before a court, and called Phyleus as a witness to the justice of his claim, whereupon Augeas, without waiting for the delivery of the verdict, angrily banished Heracles and his son from his dominions.

CHASING *the* STYMPHALIDES

Heracles's sixth task was to chase away the Stymphalides, which were immense birds of prey who shot from their wings feathers sharp as arrows. The home of these birds was on the shore of the lake Stymphalis, in Arcadia (after which they were called), where they caused great destruction among men and cattle.

On approaching the lake, Heracles observed great numbers of them; and, while hesitating how to commence the attack, he suddenly felt a hand on his shoulder. Looking round he beheld the majestic form of Athene, who held in her hand a gigantic pair of brazen clappers made by Hephæstus, which she presented to him; whereupon he ascended to the summit of a neighboring hill, and commenced to rattle them violently. The shrill noise of these instruments was so intolerable to the birds that they rose into the air in terror, upon which he aimed at them with his arrows, destroying them in great numbers, whilst those that escaped his darts flew away, never to return.

CAPTURING *the* CRETAN BULL

The seventh labor of Heracles was to capture the Cretan bull.

Minos, king of Crete, had vowed to sacrifice to Poseidon any animal that should first appear out of the sea, so the god caused a magnificent bull to emerge from the waves in order to test the sincerity of the Cretan king. Charmed with the splendid animal sent by Poseidon, and eager to possess it, Minos placed it among his herds, and substituted as a sacrifice one of his own bulls. Hereupon Poseidon, in order to punish the greed of Minos, caused the animal to become mad, and commit such great havoc on the island as to endanger the safety of the inhabitants. When Heracles, therefore, arrived in Crete for the purpose of capturing the bull, Minos, far from opposing his design, gladly gave him permission to do so.

The hero not only succeeded in securing the animal, but tamed him so effectually that he rode on his back right across the sea as far as the Peloponnesus. He now delivered him up to Eurystheus, who at once set him at liberty, after which he became as ferocious and wild as before, roaming all over Greece into Arcadia, and was eventually killed by Theseus on the plains of Marathon.

The MARES *of* DIOMEDES

OPPOSITE: *Diomedes Devoured by Horses*, Gustave Moreau, 1866. Heracles, hiding in the background in this painting, stole away the horses of Diomedes by feeding their master to them first.

The eighth labor of Heracles was to bring to Eurystheus the mares of Diomedes, a son of Ares and king of the Bistonians, a warlike Thracian tribe. This king possessed a breed of wild horses of tremendous size and strength, whose food consisted of human flesh, and all strangers who had the misfortune to enter the country were made prisoners and flung before the horses, who devoured them.

When Heracles arrived he first captured the cruel Diomedes himself, and then threw him before his own mares, who, after devouring their master, became perfectly tame and tractable. They were then led by Heracles to the seashore, when the Bistonians, enraged at the loss of their king, rushed after the hero and attacked him. He now gave charge of the animals to his friend Abderus, and made such a furious onslaught on his assailants that they turned and fled.

But on his return from this encounter he found, to his great grief, that the mares had torn his friend in pieces and devoured him. After celebrating due funereal rites to the unfortunate Abderus, Heracles built a city in his honor, which he named after him. He then returned to Tiryns, where he delivered up the mares to Eurystheus, who set them loose on Mount Olympus, where they became the prey of wild beasts.

The GIRDLE of HIPPOLYTE

Heracles's ninth labor was to bring to Eurystheus the girdle of Hippolyte, queen of the Amazons.

The Amazons, who dwelt on the shores of the Black Sea, near the river Thermodon, were a nation of warlike women, renowned for their strength, courage, and great skill in horsemanship. Their queen, Hippolyte, had received from her father, Ares, a beautiful girdle, which she always wore as a sign of her royal power and authority, and it was this girdle which Heracles was required to place in the hands of Eurystheus, who designed it as a gift for his daughter Admete.

Foreseeing that this would be a task of no ordinary difficulty, the hero called to his aid a select band of brave companions, with whom he embarked for the Amazonian town Themiscyra. Here they were met by queen Hippolyte, who was so impressed by the extraordinary stature and noble bearing of Heracles that, on learning his errand, she at once consented to present him with the coveted girdle. But Hera, his implacable enemy, assuming the form of an Amazon, spread the report in the town that a stranger was about to carry off their queen. The Amazons at once flew to arms and mounted their horses, whereupon a battle ensued, in which many of their bravest warriors were killed or wounded. Among the latter was their most skilful leader, Melanippe, whom Heracles afterward restored to Hippolyte, receiving the girdle in exchange.

The OXEN of GERYONES

The tenth labor of Heracles was to capture the magnificent oxen belonging to the Giant Geryones (or Geryon), who dwelt on the island of Erythia in the bay of Gadria (Cadiz). This Giant, who was the son of Chrysaor, had three bodies with three heads, six hands, and six feet. He possessed a herd of splendid cattle, which were famous for their size, beauty, and rich red color. They were guarded by another Giant named Eurytion, and a two-headed dog called Orthrus.

In choosing for him a task so replete with danger, Eurystheus was in hopes that he might finally rid himself forever of his hated cousin. But the indomitable courage of the hero rose with the prospect of this difficult and dangerous undertaking.

After a long and wearisome journey he at last arrived at the western coast of Africa, where, as a monument of his perilous expedition, he was said to have erected the famous "Pillars of Hercules" on either side of the Strait of Gibraltar.[5] Here he found the intense heat so insufferable that he angrily raised his bow toward heaven, and threatened to shoot

5 One of which is known as the Rock of Gibraltar.

Oil on panel, Maerten van Heemskerck, c. 1550. The first scene in this oil painting depicts Cronus swallowing one of his children, while the rest depict feats of Hercules: the slaying of the Hydra, wrestling Antaeus, and erecting the Pillars of Hercules.

the Sun God. But Helios, far from being incensed at his audacity, was so struck with admiration at his daring that he lent to him the golden boat with which he accomplished his nocturnal transit from the west to the east, and thus Heracles crossed over safely to the island of Erythia.

No sooner had he landed than Eurytion, accompanied by his savage dog Orthrus, fiercely attacked him; but Heracles, with a superhuman effort, slew the dog and then his master. Hereupon he collected the herd, and was proceeding to the seashore when Geryones himself met him, and a desperate encounter took place in which the Giant perished.

Heracles then drove the cattle into the sea, and seizing one of the oxen by the horns, swam with them over to the opposite coast of Iberia (Spain). Then, driving his magnificent prize before him through Gaul, Italy, Illyria, and Thrace, he at length arrived, after many perilous adventures and hair-breadth escapes, at Mycenæ, where he delivered them up to Eurystheus, who sacrificed them to Hera.

Heracles had now executed his ten tasks, which had been accomplished in the space of eight years; but Eurystheus refused to include the slaying of the Hydra and the cleansing of the stables of Augeas among the number, alleging as a reason that the one had been performed by the assistance of Iolaus, and that the other had been executed for hire. He therefore insisted on Heracles substituting two more labors in their place.

The APPLES of the HESPERIDES

The eleventh task imposed by Eurystheus was to bring him the golden apples of the Hesperides, which grew on a tree presented by Gæa to Hera, on the occasion of her marriage with Zeus. This sacred tree was guarded by four maidens, daughters of Nyx, called the Hesperides, who were assisted in their task by a terrible hundred-headed dragon. This dragon never slept, and out of its hundred throats came a constant hissing sound, which effectually warned off all intruders. But what rendered the undertaking still more difficult was the complete ignorance of the hero as to the locality of the garden, and he was forced, in consequence, to make many fruitless journeys and to undergo many trials before he could find it.

He first traveled through Thessaly and arrived at the river Echedorus, where he met the Giant Cycnus, the son of Ares and Pyrene, who challenged him to single combat. In this encounter Heracles completely vanquished his opponent, who was killed in the contest; but now a mightier adversary appeared on the scene, for the War God himself came to avenge his son. A terrible struggle ensued, which lasted some time, until Zeus interfered between the brothers, and put an end to the strife by hurling a thunderbolt between them. Heracles proceeded on his journey, and reached the banks of the river Eridanus, where dwelt the nymphs, daughters of Zeus and Themis. On seeking advice from them as to his route, they directed him to the shape-shifting sea-god Nereus, who alone knew the way to the Garden of the Hesperides. Heracles found him asleep, and seizing the opportunity, held him so firmly in his powerful grasp that he could not possibly escape, so that notwithstanding his various metamorphoses he was at last compelled to give the information required. The hero then crossed

Plate from *The Fall of Princes*, c. 1450–1460. Heracles killed the dragon guarding the golden apples of the Hesperides after it had fallen asleep.

Plate from *The Wonder Book for Girls & Boys*, Walter Crane, 1892. To find the Garden of the Hesperides, Heracles had to go to the Far West, where Atlas supported the heavens on his shoulders.

over to Libya, where he engaged in a wrestling-match with king Anteos, son of Poseidon and Gæa, which terminated fatally for the king.

From thence he proceeded to Egypt, where reigned Busiris, another son of Poseidon, who (acting on the advice given by an oracle during a time of great scarcity) sacrificed all strangers to Zeus. When Heracles arrived he was seized and dragged to the altar; but the powerful demi-god burst asunder his bonds, and then slew Busiris and his son.

Resuming his journey, he now wandered on through Arabia until he arrived at Mount Caucasus, where Prometheus groaned in unceasing agony. It was at this time that Heracles shot the eagle that had so long tortured the noble and devoted friend of mankind. Full of gratitude for his deliverance, Prometheus instructed him how to find his way to that remote region in the Far West where Atlas supported the heavens on his shoulders,

Bronze medal of Britannia and Hercules, James Mudie, 1814. Because Heracles was the epitome of strength, medals often bear his likeness, even today.

near which lay the Garden of the Hesperides. He also warned Heracles not to attempt to secure the precious fruit himself, but to assume for a time the duties of Atlas, and to dispatch him for the apples.

On arriving at his destination, Heracles followed the advice of Prometheus. Atlas, who willingly entered into the arrangement, contrived to put the dragon to sleep, and then, having cunningly outwitted the Hesperides, carried off three of the golden apples, which he now brought to Heracles. But when the latter was prepared to relinquish his burden, Atlas, having once tasted the delights of freedom, declined to resume his post, and announced his intention of being himself the bearer of the apples to Eurystheus, leaving Heracles to fill his place. To this proposal the hero feigned assent, merely begging that Atlas would be kind enough to support the heavens for a few moments whilst he contrived a pad for his head. Atlas good-naturedly threw down the apples and once more resumed his load, upon which Heracles bade him adieu, and departed.

When Heracles conveyed the golden apples to Eurystheus the latter presented them to the hero, whereupon Heracles placed the sacred fruit on the altar of Athene, who restored them to the garden of the Hesperides.

HERACLES VISITS *the* REALM *of the* SHADES

The twelfth and last labor that Eurystheus imposed on Heracles was to bring up Cerberus, Hades's guard dog, from the lower world, believing that all his heroic powers would be unavailing in the realm of shades, and that in this, his last and most perilous undertaking, the hero must at length succumb and perish.

After being initiated into the Eleusinian Mysteries, and obtaining from the priests certain information necessary for the accomplishment of his task, Heracles set out for Tænarum in Lacolia, where there was an opening that led to the underworld. Conducted by Hermes, he commenced his descent into the awful gulf, where myriad shades soon began to appear, all of whom fled in terror at his approach, Meleager and Medusa alone excepted. About to strike the latter with his sword, Hermes interfered and stayed his hand, reminding him that she was but a shadow, and that consequently no weapon could avail against her.

Arrived before the gates of Hades he found Theseus and Pirithöus, who had been fixed to an enchanted rock by Hades for their presumption in endeavoring to carry off

Persephone. When they saw Heracles they implored him to set them free. The hero succeeded in delivering Theseus, but when he endeavored to liberate Pirithöus, the Earth shook so violently beneath him that he was compelled to relinquish his task.

Proceeding further, Heracles recognized Ascalaphus, who (as recounted on page 49), had revealed the fact that Persephone had swallowed the seeds of a pomegranate offered to her by her husband, which bound her to Hades forever. Ascalaphus was groaning beneath a huge rock in which Demeter, in her anger, had hurled upon him, and which Heracles now removed, releasing the sufferer.

Before the gates of his palace stood Hades, the mighty ruler of the lower world, who barred his entrance; but Heracles, aiming at him with one of his unerring darts, shot him in the shoulder, so that for the first time the god experienced the agony of mortal suffering. Heracles then demanded of him permission to take Cerberus to the upper world, and to this Hades consented on the condition that he could secure him unarmed.

Protected by his breastplate and lion's skin, Heracles went in search of the monster, whom he found at the mouth of the river Acheron. Undismayed by the hideous barking proceeding from his three heads, he

***Heracles Capturing Cerberus*, Hans Sebald Beham, 1545. For his final labor, Heracles braved the realm of the shades to capture Cerberus, Hades's guard dog.**

seized the throat with one hand and the legs with the other, and although the dragon that served as his tail bit Heracles severely, he did not relinquish his grasp. In this manner, he stowed him away to the upper world, through an opening near Troezen in Argolia.

When Eurystheus beheld Cerberus he stood aghast, and despairing of ever getting rid of his hated rival, he hid and bade Heracles to get rid of the hell-hound at once. Heracles restored him to Hades, and with this last task the subjection of Heracles to Eurystheus terminated.

LAOMEDON

Laomedon was the powerful King of Troy, whose famous city walls were built by Apollo and Poseidon when they were condemned by Zeus to temporary servitude on Earth. But, when the gods' work was completed, King Laomedon treacherously refused to give them the reward due to them. The incensed deities therefore combined to punish the offender:

Detail from *L'Épître Othéa*, attributed to the Master of the Cité des Dames and workshop, c. 1410–1414. King Laomedon meets his death at the hands of Heracles's men.

Apollo sent a pestilence that decimated the people, and Poseidon a flood, which bore with it a marine monster who swallowed in his huge jaws all that came within his reach.

The RESCUE of HESIONE

In distress over the state of Troy, Laomedon consulted an oracle, and was informed that only by the sacrifice of his daughter Hesione could the anger of the gods be appeased. Yielding at length to the urgent appeals of his people, he consented to make the sacrifice, and chained Hesione to a rock to be devoured by the monster.

However, before the lovely maiden could meet her fate, she was intercepted by Heracles, who was on his voyage home from the Amazons after obtaining the girdle of Hippolyte. When Laomedon beheld the renowned hero, whose marvelous feats of strength and courage had become the wonder and admiration of all mankind, he earnestly implored him to save his daughter from her impending doom, and to rid the country of the monster, holding out to him as a reward the horses that Zeus had presented to his grandfather Tros in compensation for robbing him of his son Ganymede.

Heracles unhesitatingly accepted the offer, and when the monster appeared, opening his terrible jaws to receive his prey, the hero, sword in hand, attacked and slew him. But the perfidious monarch once more broke faith, and Heracles, vowing vengeance, would later return with his fellow heroes, take Troy by storm, and kill Laomedon, who thus met at length the retribution he so richly deserved. Meanwhile, to Telamon, one of his bravest followers, Heracles gave Hesione, the daughter of the king, in marriage.

DEIANEIRA

Deianeira was the daughter of Œneus, king of Ætolia, and the sister of Meleager, who slew the Calydonian boar during that great hunt (as recounted beginning on page 84). She was the wife of Heracles, and ultimately caused his death.

DEIANEIRA and the CENTAUR

Three years into the marriage of Deianeira and Heracles, an unfortunate accident occurred. Heracles was one day present at a banquet given by King Œneus, when, by a sudden swing of his hand, he had the misfortune to strike on the head a youth of noble birth, who, according to the custom of the ancients, was serving the guests at table, and so violent was the blow that it caused his death. The father of the unfortunate youth, who had witnessed the occurrence, saw that it was the result of an accident, and therefore absolved the hero

from blame. But Heracles, resolved to act according to the law of the land, banished himself from the country, and bidding farewell to his father-in-law, set out for Trachin to visit his friend King Ceyx, taking Deianeira with him, along with his young son Hyllus.

In the course of their journey they arrived at the river Evenus, over which the Centaur Nessus was in the habit of carrying travelers for hire. Heracles, with his little son in his arms, forded the stream unaided, entrusting his wife to the care of the Centaur, who, charmed with the beauty of his fair burden, attempted to carry her off. But her cries were heard by her husband, who without hesitation shot Nessus through the heart with one of his poisoned arrows. The dying Centaur was now thirsting for revenge. So he called Deianeira to his side, and directed her to secure some of the blood that flowed from his wound, assuring her that if, when in danger of losing her husband's affections, she used it in the manner indicated by him, it would act as a charm, and prevent her from being supplanted by a rival. Heracles and Deianeira now pursued their journey, and after several adventures at length arrived at their destination.

The DEATH of HERACLES

Deianeira carefully preserved the blood of Nessus for many years, which she did not have occasion to use until she was informed that Heracles had stowed away with the fair maiden Iole. Fearful lest Iole's youthful charms might supplant her in the affection of her husband, and calling to mind the advice of the dying Centaur, she determined to test the efficacy of the love-charm that he had given to her.

OPPOSITE: ***Dejanira (Autumn)*, Gustave Moreau, c. 1872–1873. The Centaur Nessus clings to the angelic form of Deianeira (Dejanira) just as he's about to be pierced by Heracles's arrow.**

When Heracles halted at Cenœus with Iole in order to offer a sacrifice to Zeus, he sent to Deianeira asking for a sacrificial robe. Deianeira, taking out the vial in which she stored the blood of the Centaur, imbued the robe with a portion of the liquid, and then sent it to Heracles. The hero clothed himself with the garment, and was about to perform the sacrifice, when the hot flames rising from the altar heated the poison with which it was imbued, and soon every fiber of his body was penetrated by the deadly venom. The unfortunate hero, suffering the most fearful tortures, endeavored to tear off the robe, but it adhered so closely to his skin that all his efforts to remove it only increased his agonies.

In this pitiable condition he was conveyed to Trachin, where Deianeira, on beholding the terrible suffering of which she was the innocent cause, was overcome with grief and remorse, and hanged herself in despair. The dying hero called his son Hyllus to his side, and desired him to make Iole his wife, and then, ordering his followers to erect a funeral pyre, he mounted it and implored the bystanders to set fire to it, and thus mercifully

Shield strap fragment, Aristodamos of Argos, c. 575 BCE. Deianeira can be seen being carried off by the Centaur Nessus in the bottom portion of this ancient bronze fragment from a shield strap.

terminate his insufferable torments. But no one had the courage to obey him, until at last his friend and companion Philoctetes, yielding to his piteous appeal, lighted the pile, and received in return the bow and arrows of the hero.

Soon flames upon flames ascended, and amidst vivid flashes of lightning, accompanied by awful peals of thunder, Athene descended in a cloud, and bore her favorite hero in a chariot to Olympus.

Heracles became admitted among the immortals; and Hera, in token of her reconciliation, bestowed upon him the hand of her beautiful daughter Hebe, the Goddess of Eternal Youth.

The HERACLIDÆ

After the death of Heracles, his descendants, the Heraclidæ, were so cruelly persecuted by King Eurystheus that they spent their lives in exile, forever trying to gain back the native land of their father. They were led by Hyllus, the eldest son of Heracles and Deianeira, a warrior who commanded great armies, but was never successful in gaining back the Peloponnesus, which he regarded as his lawful patrimony; for, according to the will of Zeus, it should have been the rightful possession of his father, had Hera not maliciously defeated his plans by causing his cousin Eurystheus to precede him into the world.

Hyllus was succeeded by his son Cleodæus, who himself collected a large army and invaded the Peloponnesus once more; but he was no more successful than his father had been, and perished with all of his forces. After many eons the long-suffering descendants of the great hero finally obtained possession of their homeland under the leadership of Oxylus, and it was divided among them by lot.

BELLEROPHON

Bellerophon, or Bellerophontes, was the son of Glaucus, king of Corinth, and grandson of Sisyphus. He was a favorite of gods and mortals, with an altar erected to him in the grove of Poseidon. He is best known for slaying the Chimæra, a terrible monster.

BELLEROPHON *and the* LETTER

In consequence of an unpremeditated murder, Bellerophon was forced to flee to Tiryns, where he was kindly received by King Prœtus, who purified him from his crime. Antea, the wife of Prœtus, was so charmed with the comely youth that she fell in love with him; but Bellerophon did not return her affection, and she, in revenge, slandered him to the king with a gross misrepresentation of the facts.

The first impulse of Prœtus, when informed of the supposed conduct of Bellerophon, was to kill him; but the youth, with his gentle and winning manners, had so endeared himself to his host that he felt it impossible to take his life with his own hands. He there-

fore sent him to his father-in-law, Iobates, king of Lycia, with a letter that contained mysterious signs indicating his desire that the bearer of the missive should be put to death.

But the gods watched over the true and loyal youth, and inclined the heart of Iobates, who was an amiable prince, toward his guest. Judging by his appearance that he was of noble birth, he entertained him, according to the hospitable custom of the Greeks, in the most princely manner for nine days, and not until the morning of the tenth did he inquire his name and errand.

Bellerophon now presented to him the letter entrusted to him by Prœtus. Iobates, who had become greatly attached to the youth, was horror-struck at its contents. Nevertheless he concluded that Prœtus must have good reasons for his conduct, and that probably Bellerophon had committed a crime that deserved death. But as he could not make up his mind to murder the guest he had grown to esteem, he decided to dispatch him upon dangerous enterprises, in which he would in all probability lose his life.

BELLEROPHON and the CHIMÆRA

OPPOSITE: Plate from *The Wonder Book for Girls & Boys*, Walter Crane, 1892. Bellerophon slays the Chimæra while riding Pegasus. The hero was the only mortal whom the winged horse ever allowed himself to be ridden by.

Iobates first sent Bellerophon to kill the Chimæra, a monster that was at this time devastating the country. The fore part of its body was that of a lion, the center of a goat, and the hind part of a dragon; whilst out of its jaws issued flames of fire.

Before starting on this difficult task, Bellerophon invoked the protection of the gods, and in answer to his prayer they dispatched to his aid the immortal winged horse Pegasus, the offspring of Poseidon and Medusa. But the divine animal would not suffer himself to be caught, and at last, worn out with his fruitless exertions, Bellerophon fell into a deep sleep beside the sacred spring Pirene. Here Athene appeared to him in a dream, and presented him with a magic bridle for the purpose of capturing the divine steed. On awaking Bellerophon instinctively put out his hand to grasp it, when, to his amazement, there lay beside him the bridle of his dream, whilst Pegasus was quietly drinking at the fountain close by. Seizing him by the mane, Bellerophon threw the bridle over his head, and succeeded in mounting him without further difficulty; then rising with him into the air he slew the Chimæra with his arrows.

The TRIUMPH of BELLEROPHON

Iobates next sent Bellerophon on an expedition against the Solymans, a fierce neighboring tribe with whom he was at enmity. Bellerophon succeeded in vanquishing them, and was

then dispatched against the much-dreaded Amazons; but greatly to the astonishment of Iobates the hero again returned victorious.

Finally, Iobates placed a number of the bravest Lycians in ambush for the purpose of destroying him, but not one returned alive, for Bellerophon bravely defended himself and slew them all. Convinced at length that Bellerophon, far from deserving death, was the special favorite of the gods, who had evidently protected him throughout his perilous exploits, the king now ceased his persecutions.

Iobates admitted him to a share in the government, and gave him his daughter in marriage. But Bellerophon, having attained the summit of earthly prosperity, became intoxicated with pride and vanity, and incurred the displeasure of the gods by endeavoring to mount to heaven on his winged horse for the purpose of gratifying his idle curiosity. Zeus punished him for his impiety by sending a gadfly to sting the horse, who became so restive that he threw his rider, who was precipitated to the Earth. Filled with remorse at having offended the gods, Bellerophon fell prey to the deepest melancholy, and wandered about for the remainder of his life in the loneliest and most desolate places.

HELEN

OPPOSITE: ***Paris Being Admitted to the Bed-chamber of Helen*, Jacob de Backer, c. 1585–1590. In this artist's rendition of the story of Paris and Helen, Helen reclines in the foreground while Paris is let into her bedchamber by a servant in the back-ground.**

Helen was the daughter of Zeus and Leda, and the wife of Menelaus, king of Sparta. Helen was the loveliest woman of her time, and the most renowned heroes in Greece sought the honor of her hand; but her step-father, Tyndareus, king of Sparta, fearing that if he bestowed her in marriage on one of her numerous lovers he would make enemies of the rest, made it a stipulation that all suitors should solemnly swear to assist and defend the successful candidate, with all the means at their command, in any feud that might thereafter arise in connection with the marriage. He at length conferred the hand of Helen upon Menelaus, a warlike prince, devoted to martial exercises and the pleasures of the chase, to whom he resigned his throne and kingdom.

As we will soon see, Paris, the prince of Troy, fell in love with Helen and stole her away from Menelaus, who thereby declared war on Troy. This war-cry was unanimously responded to from one end of Greece to the other. Many of those who volunteered their services were former suitors of the fair Helen, and were therefore bound by their oath to support the cause of Menelaus; others joined from pure love of adventure, but one and all were deeply impressed with the disgrace that would attach to their country should the abduction of Helen go unpunished. Thus, after ten long years in preparation, a powerful army was collected for the expedition against Troy, which included the great heroes Agamemnon (who was the brother of Menelaus), Odysseus, and Achilles.

Even during the resulting war, Helen lived for many happy years with Paris, until his death at enemy hands, when she was given in marriage to his brother Deiphobus. But after death robbed Helen of her lover, her heart turned back yearningly toward her native country and her husband Menelaus, and so she helped Odysseus obtain the famous Palladium of Troy, a wooden likeness of Athene that was foretold to be essential for the triumph of Odysseus's forces in the Trojan War.

Once the walls of Troy fell, Menelaus sought Helen in the royal palace, and, since she was immortal, she still retained all her former beauty and fascination. They were reunited, and she sailed home with her husband to Greece.

PARIS

The Story of Oenone and Paris, **Francesco di Giorgio Martini, c. 1460–1470. Paris's first wife Œnone stands on the left and in the center of this elaborate panel, which features Paris on the right and his many exploits in the middle, including his awarding of the golden apple to Aphrodite and stealing away with Helen.**

Paris, best known for causing the Trojan War, was the son of Priam and Hecuba, and the brother of Hector and Cassandra. Priam was the ruler of Troy,[6] which was the capital of a kingdom in Asia Minor, situated near the Hellespont, and founded by Ilus, son of Tros.

Before the birth of Paris, her second son, Hecuba dreamt that she had given birth to a flaming brand, which was interpreted by Æsacus the seer (a son of Priam by a former marriage) to signify that she would bear a son who would cause the destruction of the city of Troy. Anxious to prevent the fulfillment of the prophecy, Hecuba caused her newborn babe to be exposed on Mount Ida to perish; but being found by some kind-hearted shepherds, the child was reared by them, and grew up unconscious of his noble birth.

Paris was remarkable not only for his wonderful beauty of form and feature, but also for his strength and courage, which he exercised in defending the flocks from the attacks of robbers and wild beasts; hence he was sometimes called Alexander, or helper of men. As we have already seen on page 32, Paris settled the famous dispute con-

6 Also called Ilion

cerning the golden apple amongst Hera, Aphrodite, and Athene. He gave his decision in favor of Aphrodite as the most beautiful goddess; thus creating for himself two implacable enemies, for Hera and Athene never forgave the slight.

Paris became united to a beautiful nymph named Œnone, with whom he lived happily in the seclusion and tranquility of a pastoral life; but to her deep grief this peaceful existence was not to be of a long duration, for Paris was fated to meet Helen and steal her away from her rightful husband.

PARIS REUNITES *with* HIS FAMILY

Hearing that some funereal games were about to be held in Troy in honor of a departed relative of the king, Paris resolved to visit the capital and take part in them himself. There he so greatly distinguished himself in a contest with his unknown brothers, Hector and Deiphobus, that the proud young princes, enraged that an obscure shepherd should snatch from them the prize of victory, were about to create a disturbance, when Cassandra, who had been a spectator of the proceedings, stepped forward, and announced to them that the humble peasant who had so signally defeated them was their own brother Paris. He was then conducted to the presence of his parents, who joyfully acknowledged him as their child; and amidst the festivities and rejoicings in honor of their newfound son the ominous prediction of the past was forgotten.

***The Abduction of Helen by Paris*, Giovanni Francesco Susini, 1627. Here Helen struggles and a maid-servant protests as Paris carries her off. Other versions of the myth portray Helen as a more willing accomplice.**

As a proof of his confidence, the king now entrusted Paris with a somewhat delicate mission. As we have already seen on page 233, after Heracles conquered Troy and killed its king, Laomedon, he carried away captive his beautiful daughter Hesione, whom he bestowed in marriage on his friend Telamon. But although she became princess of Salamis, and lived happily with her husband, her brother Priam never ceased to regret her loss, and the indignity that had been passed upon his house; and it was now proposed that Paris should be equipped with a numerous fleet, and proceed to Greece in order to demand the restoration of the king's sister. Under the command of Paris the fleet set sail, and arrived safely in Greece.

The ABDUCTION of HELEN

When Paris arrived at Sparta and sought hospitality at the royal palace, he was kindly received by King Menelaus and his fair wife Helen. At the banquet given in his honor, he charmed both host and hostess by his graceful manner and varied accomplishments, and specially ingratiated himself with Helen, to whom he presented some rare and chaste trinkets of Asiatic manufacture.

Whilst Paris was still a guest at the court of the king of Sparta, the latter received an invitation from his friend Idomeneus, king of Crete, to join him in a hunting expedition; and Menelaus, being of an unsuspicious and easy temperament, accepted the invitation, leaving to Helen the duty of entertaining the distinguished stranger. Captivated by her surpassing loveliness, the Trojan prince forgot every sense of honor and duty, and resolved to rob his absent host of his beautiful wife. He accordingly collected his followers, and with their assistance stormed the royal castle, possessed himself of the rich treasures it contained, and succeeded in carrying off its beautiful, and not altogether unwilling, mistress.

They at once set sail, but were driven by stress of weather to the island of Crania, where they cast anchor; and it was not until some years had elapsed, during which time home and country were forgotten, that Paris and Helen proceeded to Troy, where preparations for a war where already underway to defend Helen's honor.

The DEATH of PARIS

Paris was fated to die in the Trojan War, pierced by the fatal arrow of Philoctetes, who possessed the poison-dipped arrows of Heracles. However, death did not immediately ensue; and Paris, calling to mind the prediction of an oracle that his deserted wife Œnone could alone cure him if wounded, caused himself to be transported to her abode on Mount Ida, where he implored her by the memory of their past love to save his life. But mindful only of her wrongs, Œnone crushed out of her heart every womanly feeling of pity and compassion, and sternly bade him depart. Soon, however, all her former affection for her husband awoke within her. With frantic haste she followed him; but on her arrival in the city she found the dead body of Paris already laid on the lighted funeral pile, and, in her remorse and despair, Œnone threw herself on the lifeless form of her husband and perished in the flames.

ACHILLES

Achilles was the son of Peleus and the sea-goddess Thetis, who is said to have dipped her son, when a babe, in the river Styx, and thereby rendered him invulnerable, except in the right heel, by which she held him. Achilles became a distinguished hero in the Trojan War, and was a popular subject of artists, who depicted him as a towering solider with a broad shield in his beautiful suit of armor made by Hephæstus, leading armies into battle at the gates of Troy.

OVERLEAF: *Achilles Among the Daughters of Lycomedes*, Pietro Paolini, c. 1625–1630. Although he is wearing a dress and attempting to act ladylike, Achilles admires a sword and shield, which gives away his identity to Odysseus, who is disguised as a merchant.

ACHILLES AMONG the DAUGHTERS of LYCOMEDES

When Achilles was nine years old it was foretold to Thetis that he would either enjoy a long life of inglorious ease and inactivity, or that after a brief career of victory he would die the death of a hero. Naturally desir-

ous of prolonging the life of her son, the fond mother devoutly hoped that the former fate might be allotted to him. With this view she conveyed him to the island of Scyros, in the Ægean Sea, where, disguised as a girl, he was brought up among the daughters of Lycomedes, king of the country.

Now that the presence of Achilles was required by his fellow heroes, owing to an oracular prediction that the city of Troy could not be taken without him, Menelaus consulted Calchas the soothsayer, who revealed to him the place of his concealment. Odysseus was accordingly dispatched to Scyros, where, by means of a clever device, he soon discovered that among the maidens was the object of his search. Disguising himself as a merchant, Odysseus obtained an introduction to the royal palace, where he offered to the king's daughters various trinkets for sale. The girls, with one exception, all examined his wares with unfeigned interest. Observing this circumstance Odysseus shrewdly concluded that the one who held aloof must be none other than the young Achilles himself. But in order further to test the correctness of his deduction, he now exhibited a beautiful set of warlike accoutrements, whilst, at a given signal, stirring strains of martial music were heard outside; whereupon Achilles, fired with warlike ardor, seized the weapons, and thus revealed his identity.

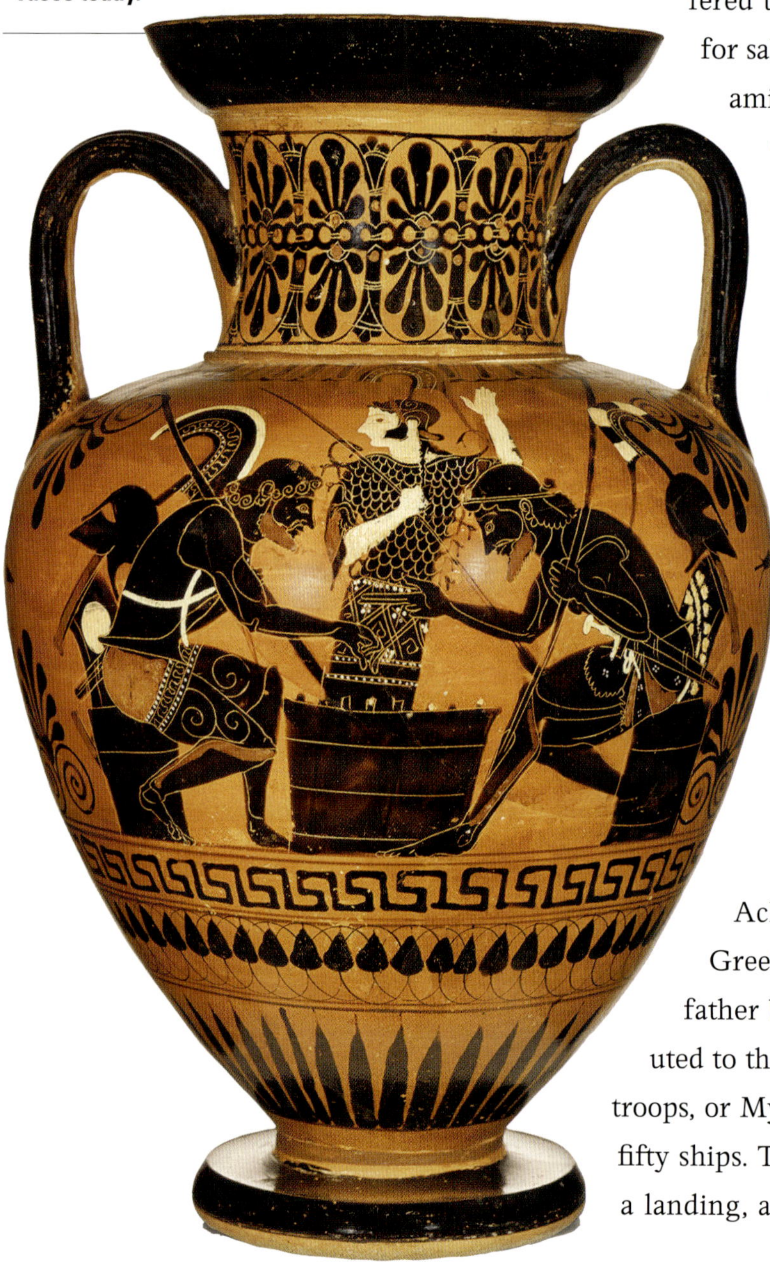

Attic black-figure neck amphora, attributed to Near Medea Group, c. 510 BCE. Achilles and his comrade Ajax plays a game during the protracted Trojan War. This scene, a popular one with artists during ancient times, survives on more than 150 vases today.

The BEGINNING *of the* TROJAN WAR

Achilles now joined the cause of the Greeks, accompanied at the request of his father by his kinsman Patroclus, and contributed to the expedition a large force of Thessalian troops, or Myrmidons, as they were called, and also fifty ships. The Greeks then succeeded in effecting a landing, and in the engagement that ensued the

Detail from ***Chronique de la Bouquechardière*, Master of the Echevinage de Rouen, c. 1475–1500. The forces of Achilles and Hector wage on in this depiction of the Trojan War, which is rare for showing King Priam (front left) and Helen (center, riding side-saddle) on the battlefield.**

Trojans were signally defeated, and driven to seek safety behind the walls of their city. With Achilles at their head, the Greeks now made a desperate attempt to take the city by storm, but were repulsed with terrible losses. After this defeat the invaders, foreseeing a long and wearisome campaign, drew up their ships on land, erected tents and huts, and formed an entrenched camp on the coast.

The impossibility of taking the city, which sat behind the powerful castle walls built by the gods themselves, was now recognized by the leaders of the Greek forces. The Trojans, meanwhile, on their side of the walls, being less numerous than the enemy, dared not venture into a great battle in the open field; hence the war dragged on for many weary years without any decisive engagement taking place.

The DEFECTION of ACHILLES

During the first year of the Trojan War, the Greeks ravaged the surrounding country and pillaged the neighboring villages. Upon one of these foraging expeditions the city of Pedasus was sacked, and Agamemnon, as commander-in-chief, received as his share of the spoils the beautiful Chryseïs, daughter of Chryses, the priest of Apollo; whilst to Achilles was allotted another captive, the fair Briseïs. The following day Chryses, anxious to ransom his daughter, repaired to the Greek camp; but Agamemnon refused to accede to his proposal, and with rude and insulting words drove the old man away. Full of grief at the loss of his child, Chryses called upon Apollo for vengeance on her captor. His prayer was heard, and the god sent a dreadful pestilence that raged for ten days in the camp of the Greeks. Achilles at length called together a council, and inquired of Calchas the soothsayer how to arrest this terrible visitation of the gods. The seer replied that Apollo, incensed at the insult offered to his priest, had sent the plague, and that only by the surrender of Chryseïs could his anger be appeased.

On hearing this Agamemnon agreed to resign the maiden; but being already embittered against Calchas for an earlier prediction that Agamemnon's own daughter Iphigenia should be sacrificed (as will be told on page 260), he now heaped insults upon the soothsayer and accused him of plotting against his interests. Achilles espoused the cause of Calchas, and a violent dispute arose, in which Achilles would have killed his chief but for

the timely interference of Athene, who suddenly appeared beside him, unseen by the rest, and recalled him to a sense of the duty he owed to his commander. Agamemnon revenged himself on Achilles by depriving him of his beautiful captive, the fair Brisëis, who had become so attached to her kind and noble captor that she wept bitterly upon being removed from his charge. Achilles, now fairly disgusted with the ungenerous conduct of his chief, withdrew himself to his tent, and obstinately declined to take further part in the war.

***Battle Before a Walled City*, 1450–1500. This massive painting, which once formed the front panel of a wedding chest, depicts the battle between Achilles and Hector in front of Troy. Achilles can be seen on the far left in his tent, nursing his wounds.**

Heart-sore and dejected, he repaired to the seashore, and there invoked the presence of his divine mother. In answer to his prayer Thetis emerged from beneath the waves, and comforted her gallant son with the assurance that she would entreat the mighty Zeus to avenge his wrongs by giving victory to the Trojans, so that the Greeks might learn to realize the great loss that they had sustained by his withdrawal from the army. The Trojans, being informed by one of their spies of the defection of Achilles, became emboldened by the absence of this brave and intrepid leader, whom they feared above all the other Greek heroes; they accordingly sallied forth, and made a bold and eminently successful attack upon the Greeks, who, although they most bravely and obstinately defended their position, were completely routed, and driven back to their entrenchments, Agamemnon and most of the other Greek leaders being wounded in the engagement.

Encouraged by this marked and signal success, the Trojans now commenced to besiege the Greeks in their own camp. At this juncture Agamemnon, seeing the danger that threatened the army, sunk for the moment all personal grievances, and dispatched an embassy to Achilles consisting of many noble and distinguished chiefs, urgently entreating him to come to the assistance of his countrymen in this, their hour of peril; promising that not only should the fair Brisëis be restored to him, but also that the hand of his own daughter should be bestowed on him in marriage, with seven towns as her dowry. But the obstinate determination of the proud hero was not to be moved; and though he listened courteously to the arguments and representations of the messengers of Agamemnon, his resolution to take no further part in the war remained unshaken.

ACHILLES AVENGES *the* DEATH *of* PATROCLUS

However, Achilles did entrust to his friend Patroclus the command of his brave band of warriors, and also lent him also his own suit of armor and war-chariot. Patroclus now made a desperate attack upon the enemy, which was led by Hector, son of Priam. Hector's forces, thinking that the invincible Achilles was himself in command of his battalions, became disheartened, and were put to flight. Patroclus followed up his victory and pursued the Trojans as far as the walls of their city, altogether forgetting in the excitement of battle the injunction of his friend Achilles to not advance too far into enemy territory. His temerity cost the young hero his life, for he now encountered the mighty Hector himself, and fell by his hands. Hector stripped the armor from his dead foe, and would have dragged the body into the city had not Menelaus and Ajax the Greater rushed forward, and after a long and fierce struggle succeeded in rescuing it from desecration.

Achilles wept bitterly over the dead body of his comrade, and solemnly vowed that the funereal rites should not be solemnized in his honor until he had slain Hector with his own hands, and captured twelve Trojans to be immolated on his funeral pyre. All other considerations vanished before the burning desire to avenge the death of his friend; and Achilles, now thoroughly aroused from his apathy, became reconciled to Agamemnon, and rejoined the Greek army. At the request of the goddess Thetis, Hephæstus forged for him a new suit of armor, which far surpassed in magnificence that of all the other heroes.

Thus gloriously arrayed, he was soon seen striding along, calling the Greeks to arms. He now led the troops against the enemy, who were defeated and put to flight until, near the gates of the city, Achilles and Hector encountered each other. But here, for the first time throughout his whole career, Hector's courage deserted him. At the near approach of his redoubtable antagonist he turned and fled for his life. Achilles pursued him; and thrice round the walls of the city was the terrible race run, in sight of the old king and queen,

who had mounted the walls to watch the battle. Hector endeavored, during each course, to reach the city gates, so that his comrades might open them to admit him or cover him with their missiles; but his adversary, seeing his design, forced him into the open plain, at the same time calling to his friends to hurl no spear upon his foe, but to leave to him the vengeance he had so long panted for. At length, wearied with the hot pursuit, Hector made a stand and challenged his foe to single combat. A desperate encounter took place, in which Hector succumbed to his powerful adversary at the Scæan gate; and with his last dying breath the Trojan hero foretold to his conqueror that he himself would soon perish on the same spot.

***Achilles and Patroclus*, Philippe-Auguste Hennequin, c. 1762–1833. Achilles, too disheartened to continue fighting in the Trojan War, rejoined his comrades after the death of his dear friend Patroclus.**

The infuriated victor bound the lifeless corpse of his fallen foe to his chariot, and dragged it three times round the city walls and thence to the Greek camp. Overwhelmed with horror at this terrible scene, the aged parents of Hector uttered such heart-rending cries of anguish that they reached the ears of Andromache, his faithful wife, who, rushing to the walls, beheld the dead body of her husband, bound to the conqueror's car.

The DEATH of ACHILLES

The triumph of Achilles was not of long duration. Intoxicated with success he attempted, at the head of the Greek army, to storm the city of Troy. But Paris, by the aid of Apollo,

Scarcophagus, c. 180–220 CE. This elaborate marble casket depicts the ultimate revenge of Achilles: dragging the dead body of Hector around the walls of Troy with his chariot.

aimed a well-directed dart at the hero, which pierced his vulnerable heel, and he fell to the ground fatally wounded before the Scæan gate. But though face to face with death, the intrepid hero, raising himself from the ground, still performed prodigies of valor, and it was not until his tottering limbs refused their office that the enemy was aware that the wound was mortal.

By the combined efforts of Ajax and Odysseus the body of Achilles was wrested from the enemy after a long and terrible fight, and conveyed to the Greek camp. Weeping sorrowfully over the untimely fate of her gallant son, Thetis came to embrace him for the last time, and mingled her regrets and lamentations with those of the whole Greek army. The funeral pyre was then lighted, and the voices of the Muses were heard chanting his funeral dirge. When, according to the custom of the ancients, the body had been burned on the pyre, the bones of the hero were collected, enclosed in a golden urn, and deposited beside the remains of his beloved friend Patroclus.

In the funereal games celebrated in honor of the fallen hero, the property of her son was offered by Thetis as the prize of victory. But it was unanimously agreed that the beautiful suit of armor made by Hephæstus should be awarded to him who had contributed the most to the rescue of the body from the hands of the enemy. Popular opinion unanimously decided in favor of Odysseus, which verdict was confirmed by the Trojan prisoners who were present at the engagement. Unable to endure the slight, the unfortunate Ajax lost his reason, and in this condition put an end to his own existence.

HELENUS

Helenus was the son of King Priam and Queen Hecuba. Like his sister Cassandra, Helenus possessed the gift of prophecy, and the unfortunate youth was coerced by Odysseus into using this gift against the welfare of his native city.

Once the Greeks were deprived of Achilles, their bravest and most powerful leader, operations were, for a time, at a standstill, until Odysseus at length contrived by means of a cleverly arranged ambush to capture Helenus, and force him to give them a prophecy on how to win the war.

The Greeks learned from the Trojan prince that three conditions were indispensable to the conquest of Troy: In the first place the son of Achilles must fight in their ranks; secondly, the arrows of Heracles must be used against the enemy; and thirdly, they must obtain possession of the wooden image of Athene, the famous Palladium of Troy.

The first condition was easily fulfilled by Neoptolemus, the son of Achilles, who not only enthusiastically resigned to Odysseus the magnificent armor of his father, but went with him to the Greek camp, where he immediately distinguished himself in combat.

To procure the poison-dipped arrows of Heracles was a matter of greater difficulty. They were still in the possession of the Philoctetes, Heracles's dear friend who had been abandoned by his comrades when he was bitten in the foot by a poisonous snake. Philoctetes had remained in the island of Lemnos, his wound still unhealed, suffering the most abject misery. But the judicious zeal of the indefatigable and ever-active Odysseus, who was accompanied in this undertaking by Diomedes, at length gained the day, and he induced Philoctetes to accompany him to the camp, where the skilful leech Machaon, the son of Asclepias, healed him of his wound. Philoctetes would soon use one such arrow to kill Paris (as recounted on page 245), turning the tide of the war.

As for the Palladium of Troy, it was once again up to the tricks of Odysseus, who, with the help of Helen, succeeded in stealing away that idol. The conditions of conquest being now fulfilled, a council was called to decide on final proceedings.

Detail from *L'Épître Othéa*, attributed to the Master of the Cité des Dames and workshop, c. 1410–1414. Helenus, son of Priam, advises Paris before he is forced to give prophecies to Odysseus and his men.

EPEIOS

The Trojan Horse, Louis-Joseph Le Lorrain, c. 1715–1759. The wooden horse that Epeios built was so large, a portion of the Trojan wall had to be removed to allow it inside the city limits.

Epeios was a Greek sculptor who had accompanied the expedition to Troy, and was called upon to construct a colossal wooden horse large enough to contain a number of able and distinguished heroes. On its completion, a band of warriors concealed themselves within, whereupon the Greek army broke up their camp, and then set fire to it, as though, wearied of the long and tedious ten years' siege, they had abandoned the enterprise as hopeless.

Accompanied by Agamemnon, the fleet set sail for the island of Tenedos, where they cast anchor, anxiously awaiting the torch signal to hasten back to the Trojan coast.

When the Trojans saw the enemy depart and the Greek camp disbanded, they believed themselves safe at last, and streamed in great numbers out of the town in order to view the site where the Greeks had so long encamped. Here they found the gigantic wooden horse, which they examined with wondering curiosity, various opinions being expressed with regard to its utility. Some supposed it to be an engine of war, and were in favor of destroying it, whilst others regarded it as a sacred idol, and proposed that it should be brought into the city.

LAOCOON

Laocoon was a priest of Apollo and a citizen of Troy who was famous for suspecting treachery in the gift of the Trojan horse. In company with his two young sons, Laocoon had issued forth from the city with the Trojans after the departure of the Greeks in order to offer a sacrifice to the gods. There, he saw the giant wooden horse, and heard of the debate of its designs.

With all the eloquence at his command, he urged his countrymen not to place confidence in any gift of the Greeks, and even went so far as to pierce the side of the horse with a spear that he took from a warrior beside him, whereupon the arms of the heroes were heard to rattle. The hearts of the brave men concealed inside the horse quailed within them, and they had already given themselves up for lost, when Athene, who ever watched over the cause of the Greeks, now came to their aid, and a miracle occurred in order to blind and deceive the devoted Trojans—for the fall of Troy had been decreed by the gods.

Whilst Laocoon with his two sons stood prepared to perform the sacrifice, two enormous serpents suddenly rose out of the sea, and made directly for the altar. They entwined themselves first round the tender limbs of the helpless youths, and then encircled their father who rushed to their assistance, and thus all three were destroyed in sight of the horrified multitude. The Trojans naturally interpreted the fate of Laocoon and his sons to be a punishment sent by Zeus for his sacrilege against the wooden horse, and were now fully convinced that it must be consecrated to the gods and brought inside the city walls.

Laocöon, **Giovanni Battista Foggini, c. 1720. When Laocoon voiced his misgivings that the Trojan horse should be brought inside the city, Athene sent serpents to destroy him and his sons. The Trojans misinterpreted this as a sign that Zeus was displeased and that Lacoon was wrong.**

SINON

Detail from *Aeneis*, c. 1483–1485. After Sinon convinces the Trojans that Athene will bless whomever owns the horse, it is brought inside the city walls.

Sinon was a trusty friend of Odysseus, who, along with the giant wooden horse, had been left behind by the Greeks with full instructions as to his course of action. Assuming the role assigned to him by his ingenious friend, he approached King Priam with fettered hands and piteous entreaties, alleging that the Greeks, in obedience to the command of an oracle, had attempted to kill him to offer as a sacrifice; but that he had contrived to escape from their hands, and now sought protection from the king.

The kind-hearted monarch, believing his story, released his bonds, assured him of his favor, and then begged him to explain the true meaning of the wooden horse. Sinon willingly complied. He informed the king that Athene, who had hitherto been the hope and stay of the Greeks throughout the war, was so deeply offended at the removal of her sacred image, the Palladium, from her temple in Troy that she had withdrawn her protection from the Greeks, and refused all further aid till it was restored to its rightful place. Hence the Greeks had returned home in order to seek fresh instructions from an oracle. But before leaving, Calchas the seer had advised their building this gigantic wooden horse as a tribute to the offended goddess, hoping thereby to appease her just anger. He further explained that it had been constructed of such colossal proportions in order to prevent its being brought into the city, so that the favor of Athene might not be transferred to the Trojans.

Hardly had the crafty Sinon ceased speaking when the Trojans, with one accord, urged that the wooden horse should be brought into their city without delay. The gates being too low to admit its entrance, a breach was made in the walls, and the horse was conveyed in triumph into the very heart of Troy; whereupon the Trojans, overjoyed at what they deemed the successful issue of the campaign, abandoned themselves to feasting and rioting.

When, after the day's excitement, the Trojans had retired to rest, and all was hushed and silent, Sinon, in the dead of night, released the heroes from their voluntary imprisonment. The signal was then given to the Greek fleet lying off Tenedos, and the whole army in unbroken silence once more landed on the Trojan coast.

To enter the city was now an easy matter, and a fearful slaughter ensued. Aroused from their slumbers, the Trojans, under the command of their bravest leaders, made a gallant defense, but were easily overcome. All their most valiant heroes fell in the fight, and soon the whole city was wrapt in flames. Æneas alone, the son of Aphrodite, the beloved of gods and men, escaped the universal carnage with his son and his old father Anchises, whom he carried on his shoulders out of the city.

The boundless treasures of the wealthy Trojan king fell into the hands of the Greek heroes, who, after having leveled the city of Troy to the ground, prepared for their homeward voyage.

***The Trojans Pull the Wooden Horse into the City*, Giulio di Antonio Bonasone, 1545. Obtaining the giant wooden horse was a cause of celebration for the Trojans, who didn't know the Greeks were hiding inside.**

AGAMEMNON

Plate from *Troy Book*, c. 1457–1460. Agamemnon gives council in his tent while a sickness rages in the background that was sent by Apollo, angry over his capture of the maiden Chryses.

Agamemnon was the commander-in-chief of the Greek army and the king of Argos, the most powerful of all the Greek princes. Against Troy, Agamemnon assembled the largest army every collected in the annals of Greece. Before the war began, a hundred thousand warriors convened at Aulis, where in the bay floated more than a thousand ships, ready to convey them to the Trojan coast.

ARTEMIS and IPHIGENIA

At the commencement of the Trojan war, as Agamemnon's fleet was about to set sail, he had the misfortune to kill accidentally a stag that was grazing in a grove sacred to Artemis. The offended goddess sent continuous calms that delayed the departure of the fleet, and Calchas the soothsayer declared that nothing less than the sacrifice of Agamemnon's favorite daughter, Iphigenia, would appease the wrath of the goddess.

At these words, the heroic heart of the brave leader sank within him, and he declared that rather than consent to so fearful an alternative, he would give up his share in the expedition and return to Argos. In this dilemma, Odysseus and other great generals called a council to discuss the matter, and, after much deliberation, it was decided that private feeling must yield to the welfare of the state. For a long time the unhappy Agamemnon turned a deaf ear to their arguments, but at last they succeeded in persuading him that it was his duty to make the sacrifice. He, accordingly, dispatched a messenger to his wife, Clytemnæstra, begging her to send Iphigenia to him, alleging as a pretext that the great hero Achilles desired to make her his wife. Rejoicing at the brilliant destiny that awaited her beautiful daughter, the fond mother at once obeyed the command, and sent her to Aulis.

When the maiden arrived at her destination, and discovered, to her horror, the dreadful fate that awaited her, she threw herself in an agony of grief at her father's feet, and with sobs and tears entreated him to have mercy on her, and to spare her young life. But alas, her doom was sealed, and her now repentant and heartbroken father was powerless to avert it. The unfortunate victim was bound to the altar, and already the fatal knife was raised to deal the death-blow, when suddenly Iphigenia disappeared from view, and in her place on the altar lay a beautiful deer ready to be sacrificed. It was Artemis herself, who, pitying the youth and beauty of her victim, caused her to be conveyed in a cloud to Taurica, where she became one of her priestesses, and entrusted with the charge of her temple; a dignity, however, which necessitated the offering of human sacrifices presented to Artemis.

His wife Clytemnæstra, in revenge for the offered sacrifice of her beloved daughter, formed a secret alliance during her husband's absence

The Funeral Procession of Agamemnon, Louis-Jean Desprez, 1787. In one version of the myth of Agamemnon's death, Clytemnæstra hosts a welcome-home party for her husband that is actually his funeral, and kills him upon arrival.

with Ægisthus, the son of Thyestes, and on the return of Agamemnon they both conspired to compass his destruction. Clytemnæstra feigned the greatest joy on beholding her husband, and in spite of the urgent warnings of Cassandra, who was now a captive in his train, he received her protestations of affection with the most trusting confidence. In her well-assumed anxiety for the comfort of the weary traveler, she prepared a warm bath for his refreshment, and at a given signal from the treacherous queen, Ægisthus, who was concealed in an adjoining chamber, rushed upon the defenseless hero and slew him.

ORESTES

OPPOSITE: **Bell Krater Depicting Orestes at the Altar of Apollo at Delphi, attributed to Hoppin Painter, c. 375 BCE. When Apollo directed Orestes to go to Taurica, Orestes didn't know that he would find his long-lost sister Iphigenia there.**

During the massacre of the retainers of Agamemnon that followed, his daughter Electra, with great presence of mind, contrived to save her young brother Orestes. He fled for refuge to his uncle Strophius, king of Phocis, who educated him with his own son Pylades, and an ardent friendship sprung up between the youths, that, from its constancy and selflessness, has become proverbial.

As Orestes grew up to manhood, his one great all-absorbing desire was to avenge the death of his father. Accompanied by his faithful friend Pylades, he repaired in disguise to Mycenæ, where Ægisthus and Clytemnæstra reigned conjointly over the kingdom of Argos. In order to disarm suspicion, he had taken the precaution to dispatch a messenger to Clytemnæstra, purporting to be sent by King Strophius to announce to her the untimely death of her son Orestes through an accident during a chariot-race at Delphi.

Arrived at Mycenæ, he found his sister Electra so overwhelmed with grief at the news of her brother's death that to her he revealed his identity. When he heard from her lips how cruelly she had been treated by their mother, and how joyfully the news of his demise had been received, his long pent-up passion completely overpowered him, and rushing into the presence of the king and queen, he first pierced Clytemnæstra in the heart, then her guilty partner.

But the crime of murdering his own mother was not long unavenged by the gods. Hardly was the fatal act committed when the Furies appeared and unceasingly pursued the unfortunate Orestes wherever he went. In this wretched plight he sought refuge in the temple of Delphi, where he earnestly besought Apollo to release him from his cruel tormentors. The god commanded him, in expiation of his crime, to repair to Taurica and convey the statue of Artemis from thence to the kingdom of Attica, an expedition fraught with extreme peril.

Accompanied by his faithful friend Pylades, who insisted on sharing the dangers of the undertaking, Orestes set out for Taurica. But the unfortunate youths had hardly stepped on shore before they were seized by the natives, who, as usual, conveyed them for sacrifice to the temple of Artemis.

The priestess of the sacrifice, however, was Iphigenia, who was still in exile from her native country, continuing to perform the terrible duties that her office involved. She had long given up all hopes of ever being restored to her homeland, when these strangers were brought to the temple. Discovering that they were Greeks, though unaware of their near relationship to herself, Iphigenia thought the opportunity a favorable one for sending tidings of her existence to her people, and, accordingly, requested one of the strangers to be the bearer of a letter from her to her family. A magnanimous dispute now arose between the friends, and each besought the other to accept the precious privilege of life and freedom. Pylades, at length overcome by the urgent entreaties of Orestes, agreed to be the bearer of the missive, but on looking more closely at the superscription, he observed, to his intense surprise, that it was addressed to Orestes. Hereupon an explanation followed; the brother and sister recognized each other, amid joyful tears and loving embraces, and assisted by her friends and kinsmen, they escaped together, and conveyed the statue of the goddess back to their native home.

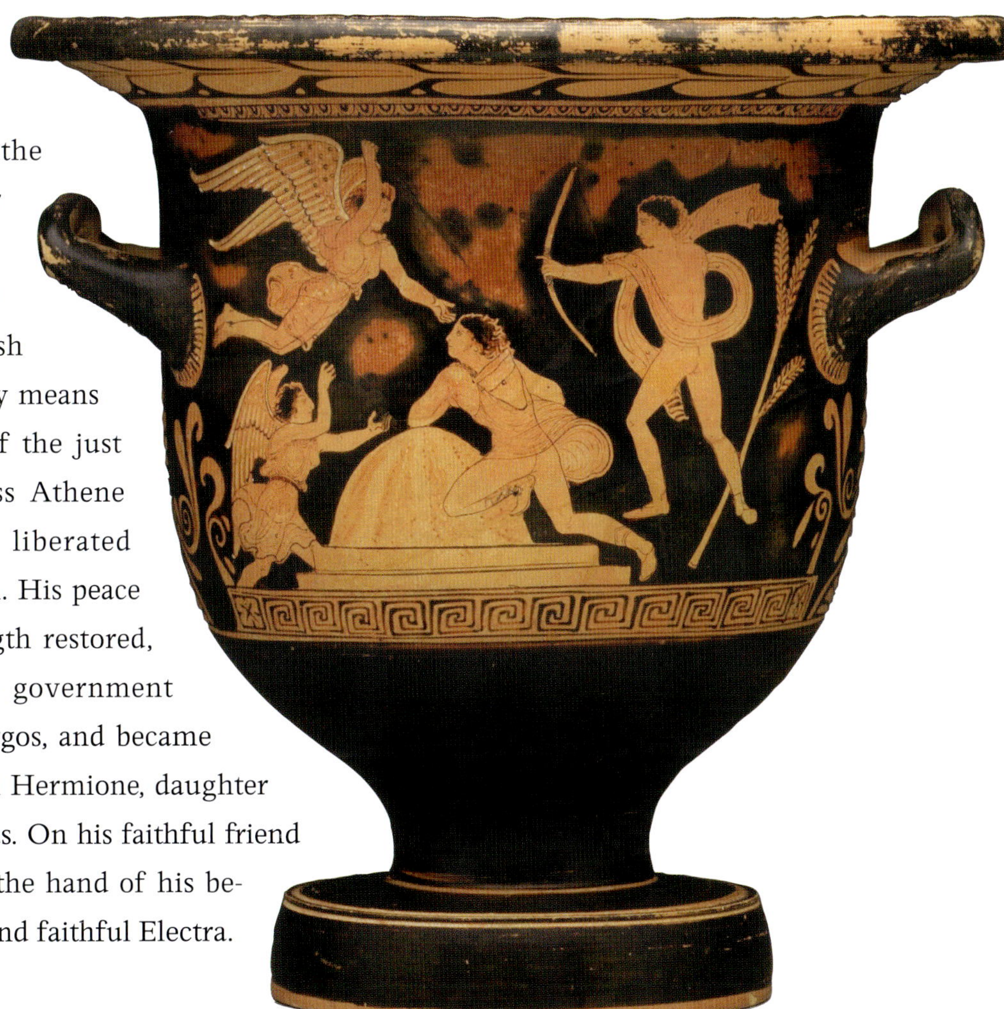

But the Furies did not so easily relinquish their prey, and only by means of the interposition of the just and powerful goddess Athene was Orestes finally liberated from their persecution. His peace of mind being at length restored, Orestes assumed the government of the kingdom of Argos, and became united to the beautiful Hermione, daughter of Helen and Menelaus. On his faithful friend Pylades he bestowed the hand of his beloved sister, the good and faithful Electra.

ODYSSEUS / ULYSSES

Odysseus was the king of Ithaca and a Greek hero, famed for his wisdom, strength, and skill. As we have seen, his gift for astute solutions in overcoming the obstacles of war—especially devising the plan of the Trojan horse—helped the Greeks defeat the Trojans.

Along with Achilles, who had to be retrieved from the custody of Lycomedes, Odysseus was the only Greek hero who did not immediately join of the cause of defending fair Helen's honor. Odysseus had been living happily in Ithaca with his young wife Penelope and his little son Telemachus, and was loath to leave his joyful home for a perilous foreign expedition of uncertain duration. Therefore, when his services as a soldier were solicited, he feigned madness; but the shrewd Palamedes, a distinguished hero in the suite of Menelaus, detected and exposed the ruse, and thus Odysseus was forced to join in the war.

Chalkidian black-figure neck amphora, attributed to the Inscription Painter, c. 540 BCE. Odysseus slits the throat of a enemy warrior on this ancient vase depicting the Trojan War.

The HOMEWARD VOYAGE of ODYSSEUS

After the fall of Troy, the happy hour had arrived that for ten long years Odysseus had so anxiously awaited. With his twelve ships laden with enormous treasures pillaged from the city, the hero set sail with a light heart for his rocky island home of Ithaca. But he had dreamt that ten more years must elapse before he would be permitted by the Fates to clasp to his heart his beloved wife and child. This prophecy came true, and the manifold adventures he had on the way home included outwitting the one-eyed Giant Polyphemus (page 106), surviving the Sirens' song (page 118), and rescuing his men, transformed into swine, from the goddess Circe (page 135).

Two-handled cup with relief decoration, c. 1–100 CE. Odysseus consults with Teiresias (seated on a rock) after sacrificing a ram in this scene from Odysseus's visit to the realm of the shades.

ODYSSEUS VISITS *the* REALM *of* SHADES

When Odysseus left the isle of Circe, she bade him go visit the blind old seer Tiresias in Hades, to learn of the future dangers he would face on his homeward journey. Though somewhat appalled at the prospect of seeking the weird and gloomy realms inhabited by the spirits of the dead, Odysseus nevertheless obeyed the command of the goddess, who gave him full directions with regard to his course, and also certain injunctions that it was important that he should follow them with strict attention to detail.

On arriving at the spot indicated by Circe, where the turbid waters of the rivers Acheron and Cocytus mingled at the entrance to the lower world, Odysseus landed, unattended by his companions. Having dug a trench to receive the blood of the sacrifices, he now offered a black ram and ewe to the powers of darkness, whereupon crowds of shades rose up from the yawning gulf, clustering round him, eager to quaff the blood of the sacrifice, which would restore to them for a time their mental vigor. But mindful of the injunction of Circe, Odysseus brandished his sword, and suffered none to approach until Tiresias had appeared. The great prophet now came slowly forward leaning on his golden staff, and after drinking of the sacrifice proceeded to impart to Odysseus the hidden secrets of his future fate. Tiresias warned him of the numerous perils that would assail him, not only during his homeward voyage but also on his return to Ithaca, and then instructed him how to avoid them.

Meanwhile, numbers of other shades had quaffed the sense-awakening draught of the sacrifice, among whom Odysseus recognized, to his dismay, his tenderly loved mother Anticlea. From her, he learned that she had died of grief at her son's protracted absence, and that his aged father Laertes was wearing his life away in vain and anxious longings for his return. He also conversed with the ill-fated Agamemnon, Patroclus, and Achilles. Achilles bemoaned his shadowy and unreal existence, and plaintively assured his former companion-in-arms that rather would he be the poorest day-laborer on Earth than reign supreme as king over the realm of shades. Ajax alone, who still brooded over his wrongs, held aloof, refusing to converse with Odysseus, and sullenly retired when the hero addressed him.

But at last so many shades came swarming round him that the courage of Odysseus failed him, and he fled in terror back to his ship. Having rejoined his companions they once more put to sea, and proceeded on their homeward voyage.

ODYSSEUS ARRIVES HOME

OPPOSITE: *Penelope Unraveling Her Web*, Joseph Wright of Derby, c. 1783–1784. Penelope told her suitors that she would choose one to marry after she completed the robe she was making for Odysseus's aged father. However, each night she unraveled all of the progress she had made.

After many more exploits and after being shipwrecked by the wrath of Poseidon, Odysseus finally arrived home with the help of King Alcinous of Phæaces, whose daughter was enamored with the commanding hero. When the vessel conveying Odysseus to his homeland arrived in the harbor of Ithaca, Odysseus had fallen into a deep sleep on top of the rich furs provided by the king. Concluding that so unusually profound a slumber must be sent by the gods, the Phæacian sailors guiding the ship brought him to the shore without disturbing him, where they gently placed him beneath the cool shade of an olive tree.

When Odysseus awoke he knew not where he was, for his ever-watchful protectress Athene had enveloped him in a thick cloud in order to conceal him from view. She now appeared to him in the disguise of a shepherd, and informed him that he was in his native land; that his father Laertes, bent with sorrow and old age, had withdrawn from the court; that his son Telemachus had grown to manhood, and was gone to seek information about his father; and that his wife Penelope was harassed by the importunities of numerous suitors, who had taken possession of his home and devoured his substance.

In order to gain time, Penelope had promised to marry one of her lovers as soon as she had finished weaving a robe for the aged Laertes; but by secretly undoing at night what

DAVID

she had done in the day, she effectually retarded the completion of the work, and thus deferred her final reply. Just as Odysseus had set foot in Ithaca, the angry suitors had discovered her stratagem, and had become in consequence more clamorous than ever. When the hero heard that this was indeed his native land, which, after an absence of twenty years, the gods had at length permitted him to behold once more, he threw himself on the ground, and kissed it in an ecstasy of joy.

The goddess, who had meanwhile revealed her identity to Odysseus, now assisted him in concealing in a neighboring cave the valuable gifts of the Phæacian king. Then, seating herself beside him, she consulted with him as to the best means of ridding his palace of its shameless occupants.

In order to prevent his being recognized, she caused him to assume the form of an aged beggar. His limbs became decrepit, his brown locks vanished, his eyes grew dim and bleared, and the regal robes given to him by King Alcinous were replaced by a tattered garb of dingy hue, which hung loosely around his shrunken form. Athene then desired him to seek shelter in the hut of Eumæus, his own swine-herder.

Eumæus received the old beggar hospitably, kindly ministered to his wants, and even confided to him his distress at the long continued absence of his beloved old master, and his regrets at being compelled by the unruly invaders of his house to slaughter for their use all the finest and fattest of the herd.

ODYSSEUS ENLISTS TELEMACHUS

It chanced that the following morning Telemachus returned from his long and fruitless search for his father, and going first to the hut of Eumæus, heard from him the story of the seeming beggar whom he promised to befriend. Athene now urged Odysseus to make himself known to his son; and at her touch his beggar's rags disappeared, and he stood before Telemachus arrayed in royal robes and in the full strength and vigor of his manhood. So imposing was the appearance of the hero that at first the young prince thought he must be a god; but when he was convinced that it was indeed his beloved father, whose prolonged absence had caused him so much grief, he fell upon his neck and embraced him with every expression of dutiful affection.

Odysseus charged Telemachus to keep his return a secret, and concerted with him a plan whereby they might rid themselves of the detested suitors. In order to carry it into effect Telemachus was to induce his mother to promise her hand to the one who could win in a contest of

OPPOSITE: *The Farewell of Telemachus and Eucharis*, Jacques-Louis David, 1818. The Greek myths inspired new tales of gods and heroes by writers and artists of every age that came after, including today. This painting is based on one such derivative, the French novel *Les Aventures de Télémaque*, which is about Odysseus's son Telemachus and his love, the nymph Eucharis.

shooting with the famous bow of Odysseus, which the hero had left behind when he went to Troy, deeming it too precious a treasure to be taken with him. Odysseus now resumed his beggar's dress and appearance and accompanied his son to the palace, before the door of which lay his faithful dog Argo, who, though worn and feeble with age and neglect, instantly recognized his master. In his delight the poor animal made a last effort to welcome him; but his strength was exhausted, and he expired at his feet.

When Odysseus entered his ancestral halls he was mocked and reviled by the riotous suitors, and Antinous, the most shameless of them all, ridiculed his abject appearance, and insolently bade him depart; but Penelope, hearing of their cruel conduct, was touched with compassion, and desired her maidens to bring the poor beggar into her presence. She spoke kindly to him, inquiring who he was and whence he came. He told her that he was the brother of the king of Crete, in whose palace he had seen Odysseus, who was about starting for Ithaca, and had declared his intention of arriving there before the year was out. The queen, overjoyed at the happy tidings, ordered her maidens to prepare a bed for the stranger, and to treat him as an honored guest. She then told the old nurse Euryclea to provide him with suitable raiment and to attend to all his wants.

As the old servant was bathing his feet her eyes fell upon a scar that Odysseus had received in his youth from the tusks of a wild boar; and instantly recognizing the beloved master whom she had nursed as a babe, she would have cried aloud in her joy, but the hero, placing his hand upon her mouth, implored her not to betray him.

ODYSSEUS REVEALED

OPPOSITE: ***Penelope Awakened by Eurycleia,*** **Angelica Kauffman, 1792. The maid Euryclea (Eurycleia) was the only person to recognize Odysseus in his form as a beggar.**

The next day was a festival of Apollo, and the suitors, in honor of the occasion, feasted with more than their accustomed revelry. After the banquet was over, Penelope, taking down the great bow of Odysseus from its place, entered the hall and declared that whosoever of her lovers could bend it and send an arrow through twelve rings (a feat that she had often seen Odysseus perform) should be chosen by her as her new husband.

All the suitors tried their skill, but in vain; not one possessed the strength required to draw the bow. Odysseus now stepped forward and asked permission to be allowed to try, but the haughty nobles mocked his audacity, and would not have permitted it had not Telemachus interfered. The pretended beggar took up the bow, and with the greatest ease sent an arrow whizzing through the rings; then turning to Antinous, who was just raising a goblet of wine to his lips, he pierced him to the heart. At this, the suitors sprang to their feet and looked round for

their arms; but in obedience to the instructions of Odysseus, Telemachus had previously removed them. He and his father now attacked the riotous revelers, and after a desperate encounter not one of the whole crew remained alive.

The joyful intelligence of the return of Odysseus being conveyed to Penelope she descended to the hall, but refused to recognize in the aged beggar her gallant husband; whereupon he retired to the bath, from which he emerged in all the vigor and beauty with which Athene had endowed him at the court of Alcinous. But Penelope, still incredulous, determined to put him to a sure test. She therefore commanded in his hearing that his own bed should be brought from his chamber. Now the foot of this bed had been fashioned by Odysseus himself out of the stem of an olive tree that was still rooted in the ground, and round it he had built the walls of the chamber. Knowing therefore that the bed could not be moved, he exclaimed that the errand was useless, for that no mortal could stir it from its place. Then Penelope knew that it must be Odysseus himself who stood before her, and a most touching and affectionate meeting took place between the long-separated husband and wife.

INDEX *of* NAMES

Page numbers in *italic* refer to images and captions. Page numbers in **bold** refer to main entries, which include images.

PHOTO CREDITS

British Library Catalogue of Illuminated Manuscripts
i, 20, 38, 74, 79, 92, 108, 135, 138, 159, 183, 203, 208, 209, 211, 228, 232, 249, 255, 258, 260.

Getty Museum Open Content Program
vi, 3, 5, 11, 13, 14, 19, 22, 23, 24, 26, 30, 32, 34, 39, 42, 44, 47, 48, 51, 55, 64, 66, 67, 69, 86–87, 91, 94, 97, 100, 106, 122, 130, 139, 143, 148, 152, 158, 161, 165, 170, 175, 177, 182, 190, 199, 202, 205, 220, 224, 234, 236, 237, 241, 242–243, 244, 246–247, 248, 250–251, 254, 257, 264, 265, 267, 268, back cover (Muse).

iStockphoto
©iStock.com/Svetlanka777: 133, ©iStock.com/timurka: 216.

Los Angeles County Museum of Art (www.lacma.org)
front cover, iv, 4, 7, 8, 16, 28, 35–36, 40, 41, 43, 46, 52, 53, 54, 58, 62, 83, 88, 105, 107, 109, 114, 116, 119, 120, 127, 136, 141, 149, 155, 157, 163, 166, 169, 174, © Michael and Linda Keston: 178, 180, 184, © Kate Ganz: 197, © The Ahmanson Foundation: 201, © Varya and Hans Cohn: 207, 212, © Estate of Howard de Forest: 231, 259, 261.

Library of Congress
15, 112, 142, 147, 150 (American Colony [Jerusalem] photo department), 168, 179, 188, 229, 239, back cover (Midas).

Courtesy National Gallery of Art, Washington
93, 101, 113, 115, 117, 118, 123, 134, 137, 145, 162, 171, 181, 186, 189, 191, 195, 200, 219, 252.

ShutterStock
Vitalii Masliukov/Shutterstock.com: 144, Only Fabrizio/Shutterstock.com: 206, Patricia Hofmeester/Shutterstock.com: 213.

Statens Museum for Kunst (National Gallery of Denmark)
56, 72, 80, 173.

Yale University Museum of Art
viii, x, 10, 18, 21, 29, 31, 33, 37, 68, 71, 77, 82, 84, 98, 103, 124, 129, 132, 151, 154, 160, 187, 192, 194, 215, 217, 221, 222, 227, 230, 256, 263, back cover (Herakles).

FRONT COVER: ***Bust of Neptune*, Adam Lambert-Sigisbert, c. 1725–1727.**
BACK COVER, LEFT: ***A Muse*, Rosalba Carriera, c. 1725.**
BACK COVER, MIDDLE: **Relief of Herakles, standing, c. 100–256 CE.**
BACK COVER, RIGHT: **Plate of Midas Bathing in the River Pactolus from *The Wonder Book for Girls & Boys*, Walter Crane, 1892.**

Ephemera

Plan of ancient Rome (1845): Originally engraved, this plan depicts the 14 regions into which Augustus divided the city. *Courtesy of Europeana.*

Perseus and the head of Medusa, Richard Rouse Bloxam and Sidney Hall (1824 or 1825): One of 32 printed and hand colored astronomical star chart cards known under the name "Urania's Mirror." *Courtesy of Library of Congress.*

Greek terracotta theatre mask (2nd or 1st century BCE): Used in ancient Greek theatre to represent characters and emotions. *Courtesy of National Museum of Scotland, Edinburgh.*

Belly Amphora with the Reclamation of Helen and Herakles and Kerberos, Circle of Exekias (540-530 BCE): A terracotta storage jar, depicting Herakles and Hermes as they return from the underworld with Kerberos. *Courtesy of The Walters Art Museum.*

Travel Photos Greece, Franz Grasser (1937/1939): A view of the Erechtheion, or Temple of Athena Polias, located on the north side of the Acropolis, Athens. *Courtesy of Europeana.*

Bust of Athena (2nd century CE): Bronze bust of the goddess Athena wearing the aegis and a Corinthian helmet. Original size. *Courtesy of Getty.*

Jason Returning with the Golden Fleece, Ugo da Carpi (about 1532): Chiaroscuro woodcut print of Jason returning to his ship with the golden fleece over his left arm. *Courtesy of Library of Congress.*

Engraved Gem with Apollo, Solon (30–20 BCE): The god of youth, music, and prophecy engraved into the surface of a large amethyst. Scaled 50%. *Courtesy of Getty.*

Tetradrachm with Antiochus I (about 281–261 BCE): A portrait of king Antiochus I decorates the front of this four-drachma coin. On the back, Apollo sits upon the omphalos, the symbolic navel of the earth located in Apollo's sanctuary in Delphi. Scaled 50%. *Courtesy of Getty.*

Theseus and Amphitrite, Euphronios and Onesimos (500-490 BCE): Interior of a red-figured clay kylix, or drinking cup, depicting Amphitrite placing a crown on the head of Theseus, a sign that he is the son of Poseidon. Between them stands the goddess Athena. *Courtesy of Louvre Museum.*

The Temple of Olympian Zeus, Greece, Edward Lear (about 1870): A watercolor painting showcasing the Temple of Zeus with the Acropolis in the background. Original size. *Courtesy of Getty.*

Arion on a Sea Horse, William Adolphe Bouguereau (1855): Painted oil on fabric, the ancient Greek poet Arion escapes death by fleeing on the back of a sea creature attracted to the poet by his song. *Courtesy of The Cleveland Museum of Art.*

Bellerophon Slaying the Chimera (2nd to 3rd century CE): A large medallion, originally a central part of a mosaic floor decoration, depicts the Greek hero Bellerophon riding Pegasus and slaying the chimera. *Courtesy of Musée Rolin Autun.*

Roundel with the Head of Medusa (150-235 CE): A silver roundel, or decorative medallion, depicting the gorgon Medusa. Original size. *Courtesy of Getty.*

Paris and Helen, Jacques-Louis David (1786): The subject of the drawing here is love, as expressed by the presence of Cupid, rather than Helen's abduction by Paris or the resulting Trojan War. Original size. *Courtesy of Getty.*

Pegasus, Johann Bayer and Alexander Mair (1603): A full-color example of the celestial chart of Pegasus from Bayer's "Uranometria," the first 'true' star-atlas. The Pegasus is composed of the Great Square, one of the most easily recognizable shapes in the sky. *Courtesy of Wikimedia Commons.*